WIRED *not* WEIRD

A handbook for living an
authentic, soulful life

MARION WEATHERBURN

Published by Marion Weatherburn

Copyright © 2025. All rights reserved. No portion of this publication may be used, reproduced or transmitted by any means, digital, electronic, mechanical, photocopy or recording without written permission of the publisher, except in the case of brief quotations within critical articles or reviews.

NO AI TRAINING: Without in any way limiting the author's [and publisher's] exclusive rights under copyright, any use of this publication to "train" generative artificial intelligence (AI) technologies to generate text is expressly prohibited. The author reserves all rights to license uses of this work for generative AI training and development of machine learning language models.

ISBN: 978-1-7640411-0-2 (paperback)
First edition, 2025

Edited by Words on Words Editing Services: wordsonwords.com.au
Book design by Hardshell Publishing: hardshellpublishing.com

For book orders or enquiries, please visit: www.marionweatherburn.com.au
Email: marionpw1962@gmail.com

 A catalogue record for this work is available from the National Library of Australia

Soul

I am Soul
My Me knows this
My I and my Me are separate to each other
They know this.

Marion 'Maz' Weatherburn

How would I like to be remembered?

In the future, when someone hears that
I have passed away,
I want them to know and be able to say …
I was Loved by that woman

REALLY Loved.

In Love, light and fair winds for sailing
I am
Marion Weatherburn
A Soul just like you
navigating this human incarnation.

Acknowledgements

Wired not Weird is dedicated to Mum and Dad, Opa D (Mum's dad), Opa B (Dad's dad), Joop (Mum's brother, my Guide and my son's Guide), Mark (my independent Guide) and Staven (my healer).

Mum's dad (Opa D) lived with us for the first five years of my life. Mum and Dad came to Australia from Holland for their honeymoon in 1960. Opa D joined them shortly after they arrived. Dutch is my first language, and it wasn't until my parents were getting me ready to start school that they realised that they needed to teach me English. Our Psychic and Spiritual Gifts come from Opa D and Mum's side of the family.

Most of this book has come to me from my Team. The information about the Readings and sessions I have held are my words, but the messages within the Readings and sessions themselves are all from them.

A few months ago, while meeting with Rommie, my publishing consultant, here in Airlie Beach in the Whitsundays, Queensland, Australia, Opa D showed me a vision of a mother handing this book down to her daughter, asking her to hand it down to her daughter. Opa told me that the information in this book is important and holds a key to your Spirituality, helping you to take a shortcut through your human life to truly live your beautiful and authentic Soul life in this incarnation.

In 2015, after immense personal trauma and loss that I don't share in my books, I felt like I had lost everyone, even myself. Fortunately, I found that not everyone had walked away. I still have very good friends from my youth. Sharon is always close by with hand and heart outstretched, as is Yvonne. Nairina is my best friend and light, and Jane H is my laughter. I've never known anyone to swear quite as beautifully and poetically as my dear friend Jane H – she's kept me alive.

Michelle T is my Archangel, and it's her two pieces of advice in 'What would love do?' and 'F*ck 'em' that have gotten me through my darkest times. Jay is a walking Angel but doesn't realise this, though I think she is starting to. Maxine is my rock too, a much tinier Angel in stature with the strength of a mighty mountain. Lori T blessed me by becoming my friend – I don't know when, but I cannot imagine my life without her or Lea B. In fact, I'm pretty sure we became friends many, many lifetimes ago. Lori says what I need to hear when I'm too scared to listen to my team, or in denial, and she tells me the same messages as my Team. Leonie L also hears my Team and gives me their words in human form exactly as I need to hear them so that I will take action. She is so Gifted. Amanda D, who tried to conceal the feathers on her collar from her wings (but I saw them) came to me at the lowest point in my working life in Victor Harbor. I will be forever grateful that my Team brought yet another Angel into my life in Amanda, who remains another of my dearest friends.

Rod is my Buddha in a caravan! He too knows me better than myself and he, along with Jane H, and with my two kids are the real reason I am alive today. Their Unconditional Love, compassion, understanding, patience and frigging awesomeness got me through both of my Dark Nights of the Soul and inspire me to be the best me I can be. They believed in me when I didn't. I owe them so much.

I would love to thank Rommie, my publishing consultant, who believed in me through each word. Rommie constantly inspired

ACKNOWLEDGEMENTS

me by applying and realising for herself the magic that this book entails and reminding me of it whenever I felt like giving up.

Writing a book is a tedious, laborious task. It takes hundreds of hours of solitude, concentration and exasperation, not to mention all the emotion that goes into recalling all of the Readings and the lessons. I've had to re-live each story again and again and again.

I've written this book for all of you because I would love to share not only the little bit of Spiritual knowledge, wisdom and experience that I have, but also to share my Team of Guides with you.

I hope to inspire you to believe, truly believe, in the beautiful, unique Soul that is you and to give you faith that there really IS more to that age-old question of whether there is 'life after death!' Trust me, there is, and this book, together with my first book *Caught between Two Worlds*, are my best way of sharing myself with you to help you build your hope and trust.

A huge thank you to Rebecca, my editor, for her patience and ability to see what I've been trying to achieve when I no longer could. This book would never have made it off the screen of my laptop if I didn't have her, so thank you Rebecca.

These beautiful humans have accepted me for all these years when I didn't accept myself, constantly reminding and showing me who I truly am. I genuinely do not know how I can thank them. I do know that they know how much I love them and how grateful I am.

My two kids, Ryan and Jess, have endured more trauma in their lives than anyone should. They know that I will ALWAYS be there for them, holding space and light for them in unconditional love. My two kids have inspired me to keep going when they couldn't, and now I want to inspire them to keep putting one foot in front of the other and be a shining example to show that Dreams really *DO* come true.

Thank you to all the very special members in our Soul Clinic Facebook group. Deb Clarke has been one of the most amazing earth angels I have ever met and helped establish our beautiful group.

Elyse Cahill is our 'Postie' and relentless in always finding exactly the right messages to post every day and night. I am so grateful to both these Earth Angels being in my life.

The Soul Clinic is a very special group, selected by my Team. A place where 6's can rest and find support within the group and share the funniest senses of humour and send support and healing throughout our community when requested. I feel so Blessed to have put Opa's vision into reality.

I would love to thank the beautiful Watson family who allowed me to live on their property for my two year duration in Airlie Beach. Without them this book probably would never have been finished.

To everyone else, way too many to name, always know how much better my life is for knowing you. I cannot imagine my life without you in it.

Thank you for believing in and loving me just as I do in you.

I have on two occasions in the past ten years attempted going 'home' prematurely. My Team of Guides just wouldn't let me come home though. I had endured so much trauma, heartache and depression, but throughout it all I have been able to remain positive and continue giving Readings in my usual way of Unconditional Love. I know that I am Wired into an unlimited source of this Love, and it is this Love that I want to share with my kids and you.

I write this book for all of you. It is the reason I was never allowed to go 'home' early.

Simple really.

Souls just want to Love and be Loved.

Contents

Acknowledgements .... *v*
Preface .... *xiii*

Introduction 1
The Awakening – post-Covid 7
My life since *Caught Between Two Worlds* 13
Introducing my Team of Guides 16
5s and 6s: understanding the human condition 22
Who's who in your zoo 25
    Soul Family vs Blood Family 45
    Gatekeepers 54
    Angels and Earth Angels 59
What it's like for me to be Wired not Weird 63
    Use your Wired GPS (Globally Positioned Spirit) 66
    Energy 67
    Teaching the teachers 69
    Manifesting – making things happen with just your thoughts 71
    Growing into being Psychic 74
What it's like to give people Readings and guidance 81
    Psychic Medium vs Soul Clinician 84
    Is it a bird? Is it a plane? No, it's Adrian 88

Uncle Herbie for Janice 92
   The 85/15 principle – how to embrace your fully Wired self.... 94
   Remembering all you've forgotten 96
   Bullshit meter – gotta love a sceptic! 98
   Accelerating your Soul Journey – a note from my Team 100

Soul Contracts 102
   The role of karma in Soul Contracts 104
   Recognising mirrors 105
   Spiritual development 108

Dark Night of the Soul 109
   The DNS for children 118
   The nervous breakdown vs DNS – your breakthrough to you!...119
   Soul levels and the role of the ego 128

Signs – how the universe is trying to get your attention! 135
   2023 – my Signs to leave Victor Harbor and travel again 139
   Do you know your confirmation sign? 149
   Animals as Signs 156
   Warning Signs 159
   My course in miracles 165
   Children as our Spiritual Teachers 173
   James' story 175
   Talea's story 177
   Jackson's story 179
   Levi's story 182
   So! You think you gave birth to a weirdo! 185

What happens when we die? 204
   How your Loved Ones may show themselves to you 212
   Will someone be there to meet me when I go Home? 214

The truth comes out in a Reading – are you ready? 222

Sharing Readings with you 233
    Phone line work 237
    How my Readings have changed over the years 243

Living with Spirit and the voice of your Soul 267
    Empathy explained 274
    Are you a worrier or a warrior? 277
    REGRETS and the role of the 'F' word 283
    The 'H' word – a lesson in Honesty! 285
    The importance of spending time on your couch! 286
    The role of detachment in your life 290

Tools for your spiritual toolbox 294
    We are not our human body 294
    Asking for a Gatekeeper 295
    Listening to and hearing your Guides 295
    Ouija boards 296
    Journalling – thoughts and knowing 299
    Pendulums 301
    Automatic writing 305
    Telepathy – the original form of social media 307
    Crystals 309
    Oracle or Angel Cards 310
    Meditation and mindfulness 314
    Manifesting 316
    Smudge sticks and incense 319
    Guides 320
    An interview with my Team 320
    Key messages 324

About the author *312*

Preface

A very warm welcome to you. My main reason for writing this book is to help stop you calling yourself 'weird'. You aren't weird just because you can see the truth in life that others can't or know things are going to happen before they happen. What you are is – W I R E D – connected to Source, to your You~niverse!

You can easily rearrange the letters in the word WEIRD to now read WIRED. When you do, you can start to understand yourself and your life better, along with those that you share it with. Just a simple reshuffle of the letters, and your understanding of life will change.

You are NOT Weird. You are Wired.

Me? I've always felt weird or like the odd one out: the black sheep, if you like. I've always been the way I am. You see, I've been waiting all my life for this time in history, right now, that people are calling the 'Awakening' or the 5th dimension.

During Covid, the universe hit the 'pause' button, and life as we knew it was put on hold. The world as we knew it was destroying itself. People were living to acquire material possessions, and Love was taking a back seat. People had lost touch with what was truly important in life. Their connection to all, seen and unseen, seemed lost forever.

So, when darkness set upon us, we became frightened and disillusioned. It was dark for so long. No one knew how it would all unfold. No one, that was, except the universe and the Earth Angels that had been placed here in the years prior in preparation for when the light would illuminate the earth and we would wake up to a brave new world.

I've been waiting for this time. I'm ready. Are you?

Have you felt the changes around you, in the people around you, or just simply in the energy around you? Life is very different post-Covid.

Prior to 2020, I felt out of place in our world, like no one understood me. I felt alone. Now, I have so much company it's extraordinary. People are waking up to realise that life is an illusion and that learning the lessons in our Soul Contract is the quickest way of moving forward in this incarnation. It is my calling to help you during this time.

Lifetimes ago, we would all 'wake up' to remember where we left off in our last incarnation at different times. This current Awakening, however, is causing many, many of you to all wake up at the same time to remember where you left off in your last incarnation.

The energy of the world has intensified. We now vibrate at a much higher level and, as such, now have access to more things we cannot see and touch than ever before. Touching the Spirit world is no longer only enjoyed by Psychics and Mediums – everyone can reach out and touch as the veil is at its thinnest ever.

We are now WIRED, and Wired means connected.

It is time for YOU to enjoy your very own connection and I/we hope that this book will help you make sense of your life in this brave new world.

You see, Psychic as I may be, I always thought everyone was like us. Our family Gift was such a normal part of our lives. We never discussed whether anyone else could, or rather could not, see or hear their Loved Ones or Guides or have access to universal wisdom like we did.

Living psychically and spiritually was as normal as breakfast, lunch and dinner. I have since discovered that no! *NOT* everyone can hear or see these things. Initially, that made me feel sad and disillusioned. However, following years of Spiritual teaching and lessons channelled from my Team, I now understand and find it comforting.

I wanted everyone to feel the incredibleness of being Wired – connected to Spirit and their Loved Ones. I still benefit every single day from the universal wisdom and guidance my Team share with me (when I listen!).

In my first book, *Caught Between Two Worlds*, it was my goal to share how normal I am and how normal you are. I also wanted to show that, if I can do it, then you can too. In this book, I share with you many ways that you may already be hearing and seeing Spirit, just not in the form that you are expecting, and that you too can be guided by universal wisdom and Love in this life. It's a handbook to include in your spiritual toolbox as I share the 'how to' by sharing the 'how it works for me!'

In *Wired not Weird*, we will look at the levels of Spirituality that my Opa D taught me that affect humans. This is to help you truly hear, see and understand how divine you really are, because you ARE!

So, hopefully, after reading this book you will see you are *not* Weird after all, but rather you are Wired in ... connected to the universe. There's a whole world out there full of connected ~~Weirdos~~ people, just like you.

*Notes to the Reader – Throughout Wired not Weird, you will see that I refer to I/We. The 'we' is my Team, and the I is me writing on behalf of my Team. I have also included conversations between my Opa/Team and me, so that you can understand how it is for me. Opa often refers to me as 'lieve meisje' which means 'my darling girl' in Dutch.

Why you should read this book

Want the truth?

Because I know how hard life has been for you these past few years.

Because I know how hard you have been searching and longing to be understood.

Because I know all of the S H I T you have been through, and that you feel like no one else is going through it. Let me reassure you that you are not alone … not in this world of 'humans' who are all experiencing these growing pains in the human world. You will be heartened to know that we all have our own Team of Guides. Use them! That's what they're for. If this book is in your hands, then you, my lovely reader, are Wired in. You are not a weirdo! Those days are gone.

How do I know? Because it's been exactly the same for everyone who has come to me for a Reading, especially since Covid.

Oh, and all those questions! If you can't seem to find the answers, my hope is that this book will answer a lot of your questions, fill any gaps and motivate you to get off the couch and live again! (Mind you, you can achieve a lot on the couch – I did!) This book will encourage you to be fully connected and Wired in to your life so that you can live with clarity and understanding of where you fit into our Spiritual post-Covid world.

In the recent past, I have also spent way too much time being a sloth on my couch when I should be … oh, I don't know, cleaning windows or doing something helpful! But the trauma kept coming to me, the sadness, the bad news, the hurt, the pain, the lessons to learn and teach! Argh! I just wanted out of this life. It was very hard to stay positive. Does this resonate with you?

The questions I kept asking were 'Why me?', 'Why my family?', 'Why so often?' – traumas had been occurring back to back for years. It was as if all the lessons I had ever ignored had finally come back, bigger and bolder than ever, together with all the lessons my Soul Family had chosen not to learn. I spent many, many days, when not working in my human job, lying on the couch just trying to breathe.

Were these lessons all karma related? Were they my Soul's journey? My Soul's purpose? Part of my Soul Contract? Did I inherit these from my ancestors who preferred to walk away when the going got tough? I just couldn't work it out … not on a human level, anyway.

I felt my pain, my children's (now adults) pain, my friends' pain, society's pain, a stranger's pain, the earth's pain and the world's pain! I felt it all ACUTELY.

But why?

That was when, during one of those sessions on my couch, I was shown that it's all interwoven with our Spiritual lessons for this lifetime. We all know that if we do not recognise or learn our lessons, they come back bigger each time with a higher price to pay! It seems that, at some point, I had reneged on learning or teaching lessons, and here they were, constantly bashing at me and those I loved.

Silly me!

I had to work out 'who was who in my zoo!' and whether I was their student, teacher or just their support person in this incarnation.

That was a huge wake-up call for me and had nothing to do with my being a human at all! That's when I was shown that we are merely a Soul taking a ride in a human body. Everything, it seemed, was an illusion. Life is an illusion.

Slowly, I continued working on the jigsaw puzzle that is my life.

I am still after the person who threw the box with the picture away. I mean, how on earth am I supposed to complete a puzzle without a picture, for goodness' sake?

So, I drew my own.

I didn't start at the edges – I started in the centre with ME! I then put together who was who in my zoo! It was a great place to start – a place to realise that I wasn't everything to everybody and that, as Opa put it, there were 5s and 6s in the world and everything in-between! And they weren't all my responsibility! Thank heavens for that, I say!

It is also vitally important and healing to step away from the illusion that is your life and to look at the traumas and situations from your Soul's perspective. This is the only way that this life makes sense to me! This is what I/we look at for you in our sessions together. We look at 5s and 6s, who is who in your zoo and what your Soul Contracts are, then we start piecing your puzzled life together so that it all starts to make sense (more on all of these later!).

As I explain later, I do not use my human self or brain for anything except working in my human life and ageing – both of which suck! I am giving myself permission to write this book purely from a Soul's perspective, and I give you permission to read it through your Soul. Use your inner eyes to *really* see the words through the way they feel to you and, 'feel the gaps between the words because that's where I put all my love for you, me, everyone!'

So, please give your human a break and look at life from your Soul's perspective. Read this book with the comfort of your Soul close by. It's Soul food. It's a necessary read. It's a handbook for this life.

I promise that if you read this book in the dark, metaphorically speaking, so many lightbulbs will go off for you, brightening your life with a luminescence that the stars will be jealous of! This book will light your way and your life.

You are WIRED, and Wired means connected … and you ARE!
Welcome home.
From my heart to your heart,

Marion 'Maz' Weatherburn

Introduction

Dear Wired one (formerly known as a Weirdo)! Who, me? Yes, YOU! I'm talking to you. After all, if you are reading this book, you must be weird, right? Welcome to my weird world. No! wait, it's W I R E D, no longer W E I R D! WIRED is the new normal. Welcome! You will feel right at home here.

We aren't born with a handbook to help us navigate this life, so I've created one. Feel free to add your own notes on every page. I believe books should be written in and added to as each piece of wisdom or lightbulb moment stimulates your own memories, experiences and wisdom. It's so important that you capture the part of you that is awakening.

As you read this book, you may also find that your own energy lifts and your Guides will be able to communicate their wisdom to you too. Write it down!

Oh, what joy it brings me to know that my book has again landed in exactly the right hands – yours.

Tell me, have you spent your whole life trying to understand yourself, only to conclude that you were WEIRD and not like anyone else?

Or have you wondered why everyone else thought you were WEIRD, but it was just your energy that was different, but they didn't know that. Nor did you, sadly.

Perhaps you found you felt happier on your own than in a crowd and always wondered why, then came to the conclusion that you were WEIRD.

Have you noticed that people always seem to come to you for advice, even when you are going through your own personal crises? Did those same people say things to you like, 'You always seem to know what to say and make me feel better/help me see things clearly'? That's why you could give them the advice they needed to hear – it came direct from Source. The information came right through you; you channelled it.

You were WIRED in to hear what they couldn't.

Perhaps, like me and many others on their Spiritual path, you have struggled with your mental health.

Or maybe you are starting to compare life before Covid and after Covid and can clearly see that nothing is the same as it was, and it's all WEIRD now.

STOP RIGHT NOW!

> *For way too long, you have been adapting to others*
> *to feel like you fit in by making them comfortable –*
> *now it's their turn to adapt to you so that you can be comfortable!*

All your life, you have been labelling yourself as WEIRD. I'm here to tell you that you have been spelling it wrong all this time.

Get it right …

<u>*You are W I R E D, not WEIRD*</u>

The dictionary definition of WIRED is 'connected to a source'.

INTRODUCTION

The dictionary definition of WEIRD is 'bizarre and unexplainable', among many other explanations, all of which you are NOT!

You have the You~niverse's approval to be Wired, and you are not alone. Look around, or should I speak in 'Wired' speak and instead say 'feel around'. Feel the connections – they are there, just waiting for you to plug in to them. Read the energies as a form of braille for you to feel. Just like braille, energy cannot be read by the seeing eye but is instead felt through your 6th sense. Braille does not lie, and neither does energy.

Get connected today.

It is clear to me, through countless hours alone with my Team and Soul searching, that I spent my last 40 years 'Wired' so that I could make sense of it all and share it with you. I can share what it means and help you feel the connection for yourselves so you can finally live your best life.

My Guides and I have just one request:

> Please don't call yourself ~~weird~~ anymore. Don't label anything as weird just because you don't understand it with your brain. Always remember that your Soul knows way more than your mind. When in doubt, consult your Soul. It will remind you that you are, in fact, beautifully and securely W I R E D to Source.

So much better than the internet!

So, what are you waiting for? Start reading ... the universe gives you permission to truly embrace who you are – who you have always been. It's only since Covid that you are now awake and ready to fully understand your life.

This incarnation is in preparation for all others, and those prior have prepared you for this one. All is well.

May the words from my Team and I jump off the pages and straight into your heart and Soul to begin their healing work.

How will this book help you?

When you are born, you are welcomed into the world and your new human experience. It's your 'birth-day!' Your birth parents are overjoyed to welcome you into their family. You, on the other hand, cry and scream as you realise the mistake you made by coming back.

Okay! So, you have woken up in this life and found yourself feeling claustrophobic in a bag of skin, blood and bones! What the?

You look around and see a bunch of faces you don't recognise, making a bunch of noises that you will, in time, learn are words.

You ask yourself, 'Am I dreaming?'

The answer you get back from yourself is 'No! You agreed to come here and experience this life as a human again. Soon, you will remember where you left off in your last lifetime and then you will feel more confused than ever! For the time being, just lay there, make the appropriate cooing noises and look cute! Oh! and just a word of warning, at points you will find yourself screaming to be put back where you came from, but it's all too late now! Enjoy the ride and see you when you get back Home!'

You may find yourself asking 'How long am I here for?' only to be met with silence.

And that is probably the last communication you will have with Home until you wake up in this incarnation. Then you will remember where you left off last lifetime and continue your Spiritual journey, learning the lessons you chose in your Soul Contract.

If you only read a few chapters in this book, make them these:
- 5s and 6s
- Who is who in your zoo
- The 85/15 principle

Your life will make so much sense after.

INTRODUCTION

Description of Wired

You are Wired, formerly considered weird,
if you tick any of these boxes:

- ☐ Feel 'connected' or 'wired' to everything and life itself at any point, anywhere.
- ☐ Love being outside with fresh air.
- ☐ Struggle to be with people or crowds.
- ☐ Believe in life after death.
- ☐ Question whether there is more to life.
- ☐ Feel easily overwhelmed by people.
- ☐ Frequently need your own space as you 'absorb' the negative energies of others.
- ☐ Love colour.
- ☐ Love the ocean and nature.
- ☐ Feel the moods and personal situations of others around you.
- ☐ Know of events or situations before they happen.
- ☐ Intuitively know the best advice to offer in almost any situation. Often, the advice that you bring through is actually 'channelled' advice.
- ☐ See and trust Signs for what they are and not as coincidences.
- ☐ Are empathic and capable of feeling and giving Unconditional Love.
- ☐ Are a non-judgemental person.
- ☐ Don't value material possessions (yes, we need them, but you place greater value on Spiritual values).
- ☐ Know that this life *is* an illusion and that 'dying' is merely 'going Home!'

You are Wired if you feel like you don't fit in with most people you work or socialise with, but you are finding more and more that you are meeting people you feel an instant connection with. This feeling can be described as 'I know I know you, but not from this lifetime'. This feeling of undeniable connection is exactly that: a connection. It feels just like 'Home'.

To me, if I don't have that connection or Wired-in feeling, then I don't pursue the relationship or conversation as I know they are not part of my Soul Contracts. This is not being judgemental or coming from a place of ego at all. It's merely a recognition of who is who in my zoo. It's a little bit like having the right connection plug to go into the right socket. It's awareness …

Awareness of where you fit and where you don't.

Awareness of where life makes sense to you and feels right and where it doesn't and why.

Awareness of being WIRED in … of being connected.

The Awakening – post-Covid

'Get out of your head and get back into your Soul to live your life and your Soul's purpose' was the cry from the universe in 2021 when Covid first hit.

Before Covid, the world was spinning out of control. What do I mean by that? Well, it seemed that almost everyone was busy … busy accumulating wealth, status and assets; buying things we wanted, not needed; and being busy, busy, busy on phones, computers and social media! We spent our lives being way too busy to make time for family and friends, unless it was on the phone or social media.

Please note that when I refer to people, I do so generally. It won't include everyone!

People had lost touch with their Souls.

The universe needed enlightened and awakened Souls to guide the rest of the population, and it had to get our attention somehow.

We die (or 'go Home' as I/we call it) and are born again many times until our Soul's lessons are all learnt. We do it this way because there are way too many lessons to learn in one lifetime, try as we might. Before Covid, many people were walking away from the lessons and situations that seemed just too confronting, hard or stressful. People weren't taking responsibility for themselves or their lives, and the repercussion was that we needed to die and be reborn into a new lifetime to try again!

However, people didn't understand. They talked about reincarnation but didn't necessarily believe it.

They were asleep.

You see, once we have completed all the lessons our Souls need to learn, practice and live throughout all our lifetimes, we go into our last lifetime. After we go Home for the last time, we become Guides. It is in a Guide's best interest to guide us and in our best interest to listen for our Soul's growth.

However, before Covid, our Guides were starting to feel redundant! No one wanted to be guided anymore. They would ask for help and not hang around for the answers, so Guides spent time working on other things instead. They worked together with Angels, helping those who went Home. They helped Souls go through their Life Review and helped them plan their next lesson and map out their next lifetime. This involved reviewing Soul Contracts with Soul Family about lessons to be taught or learnt. Then these Souls were sent on their way, back to the earthly world, to try again!

Some did.

Some didn't.

Things continued to spiral out of control spiritually. Even religion wasn't working! No one was listening, yet they thought they knew everything! On a human level, they thought they had it all covered! Spiritually, however, was another thing.

We have a body, and we also have a Soul. Part of the Awakening is for us to realise this. Our Soul has been with us for all of our incarnations. It knows the way and what we need.

Our Soul knows way more than our mind. It is your best friend in this lifetime, every lifetime, and it knows exactly what is best for you.

So the universe, in her wisdom, hit the 'pause' button, and the world suddenly stopped spinning.

Everything stopped.

Initially, we panicked.

We were forced to stay at home in isolation.

We were forced to be alone with our minds, hearts and Souls.

Some people were with people they wanted to spend time with and enjoyed the opportunity to sleep in and be at home. Quality time, they called it. Some, though, were forced to be with those they didn't want to be with and therefore hated this time of their lives. It scared them.

Lessons were learnt pretty quickly, or not! Then …

Offices, factories and workplaces closed!

Schools closed!

Airports and travel closed!

Shops closed!

Churches closed!

Sporting venues closed!

Hospitals were full of Covid patients, and doctors and nurses wore out-of-this-world, full-on protective hazmat suits.

Then Australian borders closed!

Countries closed!

Then … the world CLOSED!

We were scared and realised this Covid thing WAS serious.

As hours turned into days and days turned into weeks, our televisions remained switched on as we watched the death count rise around the world. We wanted to know how this BIG change would affect us.

What on earth were people supposed to do, they wondered?

What on earth were people supposed to do with all the toilet paper they had bought, I wondered!

How were people going to pay their bills and mortgages?

How were they going to buy things they didn't need but wanted?

Some panicked.

For some, mental health issues came to the forefront. Even drug addicts struggled to get supplies.

Some 'chose' to go Home early by taking their lives. The suicide rate was higher during Covid than during any other period of time. We wondered what life was really all about! What was the actual point of it?

The world as we knew it was in shock.

The world was in shock because it had been shut down, and no one knew for how long. People had to just 'be', and it felt impossible. A lot of people were alone with themselves during lockdown. Yikes! That was probably one of the hardest times anyone has had to go through.

Then the universe woke up.

There was a real sense of 'change' in the air. I had felt it coming for years. So had my mum. I had been waiting for a time like this all my life. While I had never 'seen' the virus coming, I always knew that there would come a time when I would no longer feel WEIRD and alone with my weirdness and that the world would catch up.

I trusted and had faith in the universe.

We turned our televisions off.

Then we breathed.

And we slept.

Some prayed.

Some meditated.

We started talking to each other again.

We learnt how to 'Love Unconditionally.' Loving Unconditionally means that we incorporate all our Spiritual learning into a big bubble of Love at all levels, without conditions. We started to learn how to love with our Soul.

Many started learning their Spiritual lessons of patience, tolerance, forgiveness, humility and how to live happily at a lower income level.

We found out that we didn't need to fill our lives with material possessions, toys and gadgets, but rather we could fill them with Love and joy.

We found the meaning of life because no one knew how much time they had left here on earth. Their ideas about how to live their lives and the meaning of life started to change.

Then Covid started to hit us personally. Our friends or family got it, and it started to spread around the country, our towns, our streets and neighbourhoods.

We made it through. However, our lives as we knew them would never be the same again.

They would be better.

We were starting to wake up, and the universe had our attention.

It was the ultimate wake-up call.

We slowly started to realise that there really was more to life. People started to seek out their reason for living and their truth. People woke with a renewed understanding of the role Love played in our lives. Their appetite for it was insatiable.

Toys and gadgets no longer fuelled their appetite, but meditation, healing and other Spiritual tools did.

They were starting to understand.

And now, four years later, where are we?

Well, there's a bit of a mixture going on, to be honest. Many have embraced their newly awoken Spirituality, and they are exploring what it means to them.

They are embracing their lessons and working out 'who is who in their zoo'. Many are now finding joy working with their own Team of Guides and realising that life as they knew it was an illusion. They are starting to see their own situations as lessons, and it has become very clear to them what they need to teach and/or learn.

For the first time in my life, I hear conversations of a Spiritual nature going on all around me. I finally have people in my life that are WIRED, not WEIRD, just like me.

Those who are WEIRD are now in the minority. Even social media is now full of Spiritual posts, and my heart and Soul literally sing! Why couldn't this have happened when I was at school?

Being Wired means coming from a place of universal Love, all the time, and helping ourselves be the best we can be in this life so that we're in a good place to help others. It's about being very conscious of being made of energy and how that energy is shared and/or interpreted by us and those around us. Our energy speaks much louder than words!

Those who are waking up are realising who they can and who they can't talk to about their awareness. Those who remain asleep have no interest whatsoever in knowing what it's like to be awake, because they prefer to hit the snooze button and stay asleep, and that's okay. More about that in my chapter about 5s and 6s.

It has been my/our recent observation, however, that those who remain 'asleep' are getting angrier and more selfish and entitled. This Awakening is also bringing everyone's lessons to the forefront and that's why life will feel toxic to you. My Team have explained that while they have no 6th sense at all and are what they refer to as a '5', they know that they don't like many of the changes in our world. These 5s are resentful and bitter about having had to isolate. They are hanging on by their fingernails and have taken the saying 'you need to look after yourself' to the nth degree, not giving a damn about the impact they have on anyone around them. As far as they are concerned, the world revolves around them. Their entitlement is poison, but they will remain like this for this entire lifetime and no Spiritual changes will occur for them.

This is the Great Divide. The differences between the awake and the asleep are obvious, and the battle between the light and the dark is greater now than ever before.

My life since *Caught Between Two Worlds*

I started writing my first book, *Caught Between Two Worlds* (CBTW), in 2000, back when people thought I was Weird. It was the start of the new millennium, the New Age. It was published in 2016. I wrote it to leave to my two children so that one day they might read it and perhaps better understand their mum, themselves and their own lives. It took me so long to write because I thought no one would read it.

I have honestly been amazed at the response to CBTW worldwide.

Since its launch, I nursed my parents through ill health till they passed away very close together: Dad on 19 August 2017 and Mum on 6 December 2017 – my birthday.

I have been through extremely traumatic times with my family that will not be shared out of respect for their privacy.

It was after all this stress that I was guided by Mum and Dad after they had passed to buy a caravan. I had always hoped to travel Australia in a caravan with my husband, and for years I had a recurring dream about the caravan I would do it in. I will share my story about all the Signs that lined up for the caravan journey and how it came together later in this book.

I found that caravan in February 2018 and left South Australia on 4 July 2018. This journey was not a holiday. My caravan was the cocoon for my Dark Night of the Soul. I headed for Port Stephens not knowing when or if I would be back, how long I would be away or, more importantly, how a caravan worked!

After 12 months away, I received a phone call in June 2019, completely out of the blue, from a businessman back in Victor Harbor who offered me a full-time job. So, I went home.

During this time, I worked for a skydiving company in addition to my full-time job as I love the fear factor and watching/helping people overcome their fears. I worked with a fantastic team who faced their fear every jump and lived loud and proud with a real sense of authenticity, passion and love for life.

My life was full-on between 2019 and 2023 with stress, Stress and STRESS! It was relentless, and I came very close to giving up completely again. Come on, universe! How much stress can one woman bear? Turns out that the stressful situations were tied to my Soul Contract as a teacher and a support person.

I drew on my Team of Guides and best friends (my earth team) for strength many times. I know for a fact that, without them, I would not be here today.

In September 2023, I again left South Australia towing my 22-foot caravan solo. This time, my goal was to fulfil my lifelong dream of sailing the Whitsunday Islands and to finish writing my second book. It's now February 2024, and I write with so much to share. I again struggle to think that anyone will be interested in what I have to share; however, I will continue to dedicate hours and hours writing with the hope that my words will help even one person embrace their own 'weirdness'.

It is my dream to share this craft with as many people as possible so that they too can learn to trust in the unseen, yet very tangible, Spirit world.

Dreams really DO come true! Yes! I had to go through a lot of trauma, way too much trauma if I'm honest, to achieve this dream. But I see those times as lessons now – lessons I had to learn and/or teach. I never gave up.

Pay attention to your daydreams – they are your night dreams visiting while you are awake. They are showing you glimpses of your future so that you don't give up! They are showing you what's coming up so that, when you go through your Dark Night of the Soul, you know there really IS something beautiful on the other side for you = your life. Your authentic life! Your YOU! Your You~niverse!

I am now living my dream, sailing weekly in the Whitsunday Islands and writing this book on behalf of my Team for you, the reader, the Gifted Soul. The stress and dark clouds are way beyond the horizon now for you, me, us! They have made me who I am today, and I am proud of the genuine, authentic person I have become. She was always there; I just didn't like her … now I love her! I wake up every day with a smile on my face, excited at the prospect of what my Team will show me or bring to me. I live in pure Unconditional Love every second of every minute and hope to inspire you to do the same.

Introducing my Team of Guides

I will introduce my Team using the names they were known by in their last lifetime. Remember that your Loved Ones have been known by many different names. Souls become Guides after returning Home after their last lifetime and no longer need to reincarnate into another human form.

After my parents emigrated from Holland, Mum's dad, Opa D, came to Australia to visit. He ended up staying for the first five years of my life, and we talk several times a day. I would be lost without him.

My dad's dad – Opa B – is my rock and Gatekeeper. Opa B gives me such strength, helping me to keep moving forward every time life knocks me down, which it has done more times than I care to recall. He sometimes does this so quickly that my head spins, and other times it takes all my energy to put one foot in front of the other or even just to breathe.

I met Staven, my healing Guide, through a ouija board session with Mum and Dad years ago. Without him, my Team and my belief in my Gift, I know for a fact that I would *not* be here today.

Dear Mark, bless him, is my personal Guide and not a family member. He is also not Dutch, which makes him laugh at our quirky, traditionalist ways at times. Mark is always just there: my soft place to fall. My 'There, there, you will get through this, now get up … one foot in front of the other, GROW UP!' person. He is also matter of fact – 'Why on earth did you make that human decision? Now you've got a $496 speeding fine because you went against my repeated suggestions to take Marion Road to the airport. No! You thought you knew better and decided to take the Sturt/Diagonal Road! Maybe next time you WILL listen!' It's funny how I feel at times they would love to use all the swear words under the sun to make me listen, yet they don't … it's always gentle. They don't mind if I swear, but I never swear during Readings out of respect for them, and those coming for a Reading or similar.

Mum's brother Joop joined a few years later. This was all confirmed when my parents made what they called 'long-distance calls' to them via the ouija board that my dad had made years earlier. It was a brilliant system. We never thought anything of it … I never even thought to ask other people what their life was like. After all, we don't ask each other things like what we saw today with our eyes or heard with our ears, so why should we ask about this 'stuff'?

They are always there to support me, and their energy is aMAZing to experience. Their Love is endless, and I feel like I've tapped into a never-ending source of it. Right when I think I can't take any more trauma, they fill me with Love again, and I can face anything.

I'd like to add that it's not a one-way street having this Gift, let me tell you! They MAKE me work for their guidance. If lessons are shared with me and I don't learn them, they patiently bring me another way to learn the same lesson. I also don't take this connection for granted. It's like any relationship in my life, which are all based on LOVE. Sometimes I actually look around for my Guides in the physical world … that's how real they feel. Then I smile, knowing they *are* in my physical world *and* Spiritual world – in fact, they are everywhere!

When I need to make a life decision, I do so with my Team. My head/brain, you see, only belongs to the body in this incarnation and, to be honest, it's always gotten me into trouble! My brain thinks it knows all, but we know what it really knows, right? Nothing!

If I need to make an important life decision that doesn't involve what to eat or what to wear, I always chat with my Team.

You see, Guides have been with us for all of our incarnations, and they know exactly what we need and what is good for us, even when the lessons are particularly … no, make that *extremely* … hard and include a lot of heartache and trauma! (Who the hell chose these lessons for me, and why did I agree to this Soul Contract anyway! Argh! *Opa interjected here and said, 'YOU did!'*) But I'm pretty sure that I am not alone in thinking that way … our Soul only knows honesty!

Don't waste time using your brain. Just like the computer in your car is only good for what it has been programmed to do, your brain is only good for your current lifetime.

Let me put it to you like this. If you rented out a room in your house to a psychologist or counsellor, you would look for every opportunity to gain some insight or guidance about your life, wouldn't you? Cripes, you would even resort to washing the dishes just so that they would dry them and you could pick their brain! I would. You would be very tempted to say 'Can I just ask you a question?' or 'Can I ask your opinion on something that's bothering me?' or 'I have to make a decision and I am really struggling … would you please help me?'

Well, seeing as you don't have a counsellor living in your house, ask your Team of Guides instead. After all, as I said earlier, it's in their best interest to help us and in our best interest to listen!

I can help you learn to hear, feel, see or get to know your Guides too. Please send me a message through my website marionweatherburn.com.au – I have some very simple techniques to help you tell thoughts from messages, and I personally answer all questions sent to me.

Through my Dark Night of the Soul, there were literally days when all I could focus on was breathing. Mostly because I wanted it to stop! I wanted to breathe my last breath so I could collapse on all levels back into the arms of my gentle Team and leave this world for good.

But the next breath always came.

Taking my own life was obviously a lesson I had to feel and learn through its entirety.

I cringe as I write this part. However, I feel that you need to read it … or perhaps I need to write it as part of my healing. Maybe you will feel that finally you have found, in me, someone that understands you.

What is coming next IS written with their permission. You see, I used to hope and pray that I didn't actually have the Gift of hearing people after they had passed away. I once expressed this to my dearest friend, saying I couldn't bear the thought of my dad coming through to me after he passed – our relationship was so toxic, or rather the Soul Contracts that we had agreed to in this lifetime were so heavy.

I had a very tumultuous upbringing. Yes, I own my part in reacting to Dad the way I did. I saw it as defending myself. I didn't see our relationship through my Spiritual 'eyes' at that time, now I cannot see it any other way. Maybe you understand.

I only became truly aware of my Psychic sense in high school. It was then I first started using it for my benefit. We lived just down the road from my high school. I had two ways of getting there: the short way and the long way. I often found myself standing at the school gate at home time, wondering what mood Dad would be in when I got home. I would 'look' from where I stood. If I 'saw' he was in one of his dark moods, I would walk home the long way. Often, I would stop at my friend's house just to make it take longer. Of course, I would end up getting home late, and this would just infuriate him even more.

I/We see now that it was clearly part of our Soul Contract and lessons to learn from and teach to each other. Argh! Last lifetimes are so frigging hard.

On the other hand, if I saw it was safe to go home, I always went home. I was happy to do that as the short way took less than 10 minutes and the long way took up to 40!

Being Psychic back then was my saving grace: a forewarning.

In 2014, after seven years estranged from my parents, my beautiful son encouraged me to reunite with my parents as he felt it was very important. He was right. We arranged for him to fly down from Sydney where he was working on the harbour, and I flew across to Adelaide from Perth. That reunion was so hard, but nothing worth doing is ever easy. The lessons of Forgiveness and Unconditional Love are two of the hardest to learn.

But learn them, Dad, Mum and I did.

Dad and I finally made peace with each other in 2015, after I returned to Adelaide to live after the breakup of my 25-year marriage. From mid-2015 to the end of 2017, not only did I have to help myself get over my divorce and move back to Adelaide from Perth, leaving my adult kids, friends and my life of 20 years behind, I also cared for Mum and Dad when they were very sick. They both passed at the end of 2017, which is when my Dark Night of the Soul truly began.

I am so very grateful to my son, because it was at his insistence that Mum, Dad and I reunited three years before they went Home. Such wisdom at the age of 23. He has always been a 6, an Old Soul, and it tortures him most of the time. This was him playing out his role in his Soul Contract with me. He was my teacher, and I am so grateful, even though the emotional price has taken a massive toll on him. I am grateful to now be able to welcome Mum and Dad into my life every single day and night as part of my Spiritual Team.

At times, they share their 'Home' with me, and it's truly incredible. Truly. I find it aMAZing. So do they.

If you want to find out how spiritually evolved you are, then spend time living with your parents under their roof! You will soon find out what lessons you are yet to learn and/or teach. They are our hardest teachers.

5s and 6s: understanding the human condition

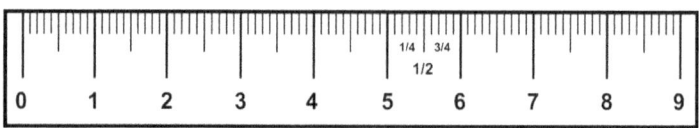

Do people call you Weird because you know about things before they happen and you can't explain how you know?

Do people call you Weird because you believe in life after death, past lives, Angels, crystals, and anything Spiritual that you can lay your hands on or get involved in?

Do you ever have times when your life doesn't make any sense whatsoever? Yet it does!

Me too!

So, 5s and 6s! What on earth do I mean by these two numbers?

Well ... this is a scale Opa taught me to help me understand the curious behaviour of 'humans' and to help me cope with living as an enlightened Soul in this human life. It's my hope that you being aware of this principle will bring you great freedom as the illusion that is our life is stripped away.

5s AND 6s: UNDERSTANDING THE HUMAN CONDITION

Look at the ruler at the start of this chapter. You can see that between 5 cm and 6 cm are 10 x 1 mm increments. I will ask you to use your imagination as I prefer to explain pictures. A 5 is a brand-new Soul in its first incarnation, and a 6 is a very Old Soul in its last. Each millimetre represents different incarnations (metaphorically speaking). Please keep this in mind as you read this chapter – it will help you picture what I/we are describing.

5s have been described to me in a non-judgemental way to be a person or Soul that has lived only one or a few lifetimes and learnt very few spiritual Soul lessons. They are what we call 'asleep' – spiritually immature.

They only have 5 active senses in this lifetime: sight, smell, hearing, taste and touch. On a Spiritual scale, they are a young Soul with a big ego.

5s do not grow spiritually in this incarnation, so don't wait for them to change or wake up! They are unaware of the presence of their Soul and basically only exist as a human.

Note: A good way to remember what 5 stands for is that the word 'human' has 5 letters.

6s have been described to me in a non-judgemental way to be a person or Soul who has lived many, if not all, their lifetimes and learnt many, if not all, their spiritual Soul lessons. They are what we call 'awake' – spiritually mature.

They have all 6 senses intact and are completely intuitive – their Psychic Gifts are fully evident, even if they don't realise or recognise them. Having lived close to all their lifetimes, they have accepted their Spirituality and that there is more to life than life itself. They have most likely been through the Dark Night of the Soul (more on this later) and their egos have been shattered, probably more than once. They are love itself. On a Spiritual scale, they are a true Old Soul and very capable of Unconditional Love without ego.

6s are generally in their last incarnation – the hardest! 6s are training to be Guides in the afterlife and are completing their apprenticeship or work experience here in this lifetime.

Note: A good way to remember what 6 stands for is that the word 'spirit' has 6 letters.

My two worlds have finally become one.
I too am 'Home' while inhabiting life in this human body.

As a 5 ½ / 6, you will have already learnt Spiritual lessons in your previous incarnations to help you understand 5's in this incarnation. Apply what you've learned into practice... You don't need to learn them again.

Who's who in your zoo

Many people come to me for a session after reaching a crisis point in their lives.

When life makes no sense on a human level, I/we recommend that you look at it through the eyes of your Soul. This will help you see 'who is who in your zoo' and see people for the role they are playing in your life, and vice versa. You will hopefully be able to recognise repeating patterns where they present Soul lessons to you. By learning these Soul lessons, you will understand their role in your life.

Life as we know it is an illusion. I look at it as a zoo.

There are the nocturnal animals that sleep all day and only come out at night to play and only then, if it suits them.

We all know people like this who are still 'asleep.' They prefer to play when no one else is around to nag them to wake up during the day and become more active in their lives.

We call them young Souls, or 5s on Opa's scale.

Then there are the sloths, lazy and slow in their lives, or tigers and lions that love to fight, sometimes for no reason.

We all know people like this too, who are lazy and slow to learn or those who prefer to fight and then play the victim in their lives. They tend to ignore signs and lessons, preferring to blame others for anything bad that happens to them rather than owning their part in it.

We call them 'immature Souls' or 5 ¼s on Opa's scale.

Then there are the polar bears, chimpanzees, meerkats and elephants. They are the sweet animals in the zoo just going about their day, making adults and children alike smile.

We all know people like this too. They are the sweet Souls that love to please others, make them happy and make them smile. They are good natured and believe that there is more to life than what we can see.

We call them 'middle aged' Souls or 5 ½s on Opa's scale.

Then there are the giraffes and monkeys, always reaching higher for the ultimate prize.

We all know people like this too. They are Souls that like to reach for a better view of life and attain higher learning. They go about their daily business not hurting anyone and just looking after themselves.

We call them 'mature' Souls or 5 ¾s on Opa's scale.

Then there are the dolphins. Who doesn't love to watch dolphins? Oh, how we envy them … they certainly know how to enjoy a carefree, simple life. They trust that everything they need will be provided for them. They duck and weave through their lives, often jumping for joy for no real reason.

We all know people like this too. They've lived many, many, if not all, incarnations. They developed their faith and trust in the universe lifetimes ago and now it guides them in all that they do. They know that the universe has their back. They Love Unconditionally, just like the dolphin, and love to play with life and not take it too seriously.

They are Old Souls or 6s on Opa's scale.

It is always good not to take life too seriously. When I do not understand my life from my human point of view, I step outside of it and look through the eyes of my Soul. I very quickly see the roles people play in the zoo that is my life. Sometimes, I've had to say 'not my zoo, not my animals' and realise that, no matter what I do, I cannot change the animal they are. However, I can influence their Soul by reminding their Soul of their contracts and the people around them.

Take a look at your life as a zoo. Do you see the roles people have chosen to play in your life? Can you see where you fit in. Do you understand their behaviour more now we've explained it this way? We love to help you help yourself.

Advice for 6s about 5s:
If you find yourself feeling humanly frustrated with someone in your life, this may be a sign of incompatable Spiritual levels or a Soul Contract. You may like to try telepathically talking to their Higher Self. It will listen.

5s are very young Souls

5s are the equivalent of a kindergarten and/or lower primary school student – fully asleep spiritually. They will always be 5s in this incarnation.

5s can be cold, matter of fact and self-centred. They have no empathy and very little, if any, compassion. People may describe them as having anger issues or as narcissistic. They may be standoffish, preferring not to give anything of themselves to you – they prefer to take. Their world revolves around them. 5s will always blame others for anything that goes wrong and will always play the role of the victim.

5s have lived very few lifetimes. Many are on their first or second incarnation and are only aware of having 5 senses: sight, hearing, smell, taste and touch. They do not believe in life after death, and anything weird is considered complete nonsense! To 5s, this life, right here and now, is all there is. To them, 'connection' means their phone or the internet! Full stop! And please don't mention the words meditation, Spirit, Psychic, Soul, Angels, crystals or pendulums. Some 5s believe in religion, but don't mention Spirituality to them or they'll mention the time that witches were burnt at the stake in Salem!

Incidentally, I loved Salem when I visited there on Halloween in 2014. It's where I purchased my beautiful crystal ball that travels with me everywhere. Photos through the crystal ball are amazing. You can see them on my Facebook page 'Crystal Ball Reflections' by Marion Weatherburn. Check them out!

5s are the new 'weird' ones in this book!

5s are complete EGO – however, they can still be very good people. They tend to collect material possessions instead of Spiritual lessons. They can be highly intellectual, and some of them run our businesses and governments.

5s can be very judgemental people. They do have pity and sympathy, but they won't learn traits like empathy, compassion, tolerance, patience and Unconditional Love in this incarnation.

Lessons for 5s

5s will always be 5s in this lifetime, and that's because they present opportunities for the more evolved to learn from. Their time to learn will come in later incarnations!

Example of a 5 = They don't even see the feather on the ground!

5 ¼ are young Souls

5 ¼s are the equivalent of a middle primary school student – starting to awaken spiritually, but still preferring to hit the snooze button and avoid lessons for the Soul and life's harsh realities.

5 ¼s are very curious about life. They have lived and died a few more times than 5s, and life is starting to get somewhat 'Wired in' for them.

5 ¼s still only use their 5 senses – however, their curiosity about the meaning of life is growing. 5 ¼s may have childhood memories of seeing a spirit form, and they may be exploring the Psychic realms and start a crystal collection, but they don't really believe in the power of crystals ... yet!

They work for the good of their families and are really good people, as far as humans are concerned, and accumulate wealth and material possessions. Status in life is important to them – is there anything else?

Death is a curiosity to them, nothing more.

Lessons for 5 ¼s

5 ¼s have started to participate in Soul Contracts (more on these later). They agree to learn lessons in compromise, trust and faith.

Example of a 5 ¼ – They may see a feather on the ground and assumes it belongs to a bird – or they may not even see it!

5 ½s are medium-aged Souls

5 ½s are the equivalent of an upper primary/lower high school student and are starting to become Wired! They are moving back and forth between wanting to be awake and wanting to be asleep on a Spiritual level.

They may start to become restless and impatient as they try to understand the changes they are feeling. 5 ½s have lived and died quite a few times already and are curious about life itself. They are starting to ask questions like 'What is my purpose?' and 'Why am I here?'

There is very little balance at this Soul age. They don't want life to be too serious and they may hop from job to job and even relationship to relationship, always trying to find one better. They will astound you by always landing on their feet. 5 ½s are fun to be around – they live life big, with high 'highs' and low 'lows'.

5 ½s still only have 5 senses. Their awareness is starting to grow further, however, they are still happy to hit the proverbial 'snooze' button and not explore what is changing, as it may lead to things they don't want to know about or are not yet ready to hear!

When stress hits them, they often prefer to walk away from a lesson rather than learn it.

5 ½s like to 'believe' in life after death, but only if they get evidence or proof. They may get this through seeing a Spirit in the room or hearing a voice in their ear, or they may start to question coincidences. However, they can also just as quickly rationalise and explain things away. Sometimes, when they do 'see' or 'experience' something that their brain can't quite comprehend, it falls into the 'weird' category rather than being seen for what it truly is – a 'connection.'

As a 5 ½, you will start to dream in colour. Take note as to whether people talk in your dreams. If they do, do you see their lips move, or is their communication telepathic?

You may experience dreams of flying or astral travelling to places you have never been or seen. It is now very important to keep a dream journal. Write down all your dreams, even your daydreams, as you will be able to track their importance and any messages they contain. Spirit communicates through our dreams at night and 'thoughts' during the day, which are really dreams as well (more on this later!).

5 ½s start 'window shopping' – trying to find where they fit into this ever-changing life they are experiencing, yearning to fill an emptiness inside them, waiting to be acknowledged. They often don't even realise they feel this way, turning to meditation, tarot, oracle cards, candles, walks in nature, massages, music, Reiki and yoga for answers. They may seek a psychic reading and will read books on Spirituality, hungry for knowledge, understanding and information about life like never before. They are starting to wake up.

Their intuition and awareness of energy sharpens. They become empathic and find that they are good judges of people and situations in their life, but they aren't sure how to interpret or understand this, or what to do with what they are feeling, seeing, hearing or even just knowing … not yet!

A 5 ½'s ego is constantly tested. Anxiety levels will increase as they unknowingly absorb the energies of others around them. When they walk into a room, they will pretty much 'know' what is going on for most people in that room. They may get home at the end of a day feeling like they have been hit by a bus and will postmortem their day and wonder why they feel the way they do. Once they realise that they have absorbed the energies from the people they have been around during the day, it will become very important for them to protect themselves from being drained by what we commonly call 'energy vampires'! This realisation will help them feel much better and lighter as the feelings/issues do not belong to them, so they can let them go.

5 ½s are halfway through their Soul journey.

You can easily recognise 5 ½s by their people-pleasing traits, their endless kindness, compassion and their tendency to not cause conflict – they are the peacekeepers in our world. They are learning not to judge or gossip, but invariably get involved in it as it makes them feel better about themselves. 5 ½s are being prepared and trained, if you like, to learn how to work with, feel and know the energies of their Guides and Loved Ones that have returned Home. This happens by seeing Spirit or Loved Ones more often so that they become comfortable in their presence. This will build their faith. Around this time, they will also find that they magnetically attract likeminded Souls. This is great, as experiences can be shared and great comfort taken from these relationships.

Mental health can be quite challenging for this group. This is because sometimes they see and know things about people and situations before they happen. They wonder whether this is a Sign or just a coincidence. Or they question whether they actually saw anything at all. They may feel like they are losing their minds! They may feel self conscious, like its obvious to others that they are 'weird' and try really hard to not be 'too obvious' when in social situations, leading to paranoia, over thinking and hyper vigilance. On the other hand, colors, smells and sounds are more vibrant than ever before as is your intuition. This is all normal. They sit on the proverbial fence, swaying between believing that there is more and believing that there really isn't anything. But they just don't understand. No one has ever talked to them about these types of events.

Why do they need to know, you may ask? Great question!

Ultimately, we are here as Souls to remember LOVE.

LOVE without condition.

LOVE for love's sake.

Not physical, not emotional, not sexual, not psychological, not heart-based love, but pure Unconditional LOVE.

Spiritual LOVE.

The LOVE that we feel when we go 'HOME', when we pass away. The LOVE that we feel in-between each incarnation.

It's that love that the universe wants us to remember in our physical lives and to share.

Lessons for 5 ½s

5 ½s are very emotional people and have many highs and lows. Some may even be labelled as having bipolar or borderline personality disorder by therapists. They are usually given this label by 5s who do not have the patience or insight to understand them. 6s just love them and support them, as is their way.

5 ½s fluctuate between having all 5 senses and their 6th sense is starting to heighten. They are starting to 'know' things about people, places and things before they are obvious to anyone else. This is the universe's way of training you to be a 6: to hear, feel, see and know Spirit in its entirety. This period may take a few incarnations to master, as some people become so overwhelmed by their 6th sense opening up that they turn their back on it, whereas others will embrace it and it will all feel quite natural to them, mostly because they are ready!

The main change they will feel is an increase in empathy and compassion. This is a responsibility in itself and can be overwhelming. Most people are used to being and doing for themselves – to now be aware of others' needs can be all too much (note that this is not the same as being a people pleaser!).

During Readings, people have said things like, 'Oh Maz, I'm an Empath! I'm exhausted. So many people are drawn to me and all they do is dump on me, or whinge to me. It's so tiring. They don't listen to me when I have a problem, yet I have to listen to them and help them solve their lives. And, when I don't or I make myself unavailable, they cut me out of their lives and block me on social media. What the hell is going on?'

Ah ha! Spirit has your attention!

I tell them then that they are doing it all wrong! Being an Empath merely means to OBSERVE what's going on around you.

It is NOT your job to fix anyone. Not even monks will do that! They'll stay comfortably seated with their legs crossed and eyes closed while others around them are stressing out. Everyone needs to be working on their own shit and learning their own lessons, not avoiding them by helping others. If everyone would own their own shit, the world would be a much lovelier place to live!

You see, the universe is very clever. It provides training to you so that when you eventually incarnate as a 6 after learning your Soul lessons, you will be tested through the Dark Night of the Soul. Only then can you work with, hear and see Spirit personally: your Loved Ones and potentially the Loved Ones of others. Your Spiritual Gift and Soul's purpose will become evident. However, this will not happen if you get stuck in the 'I don't want to be an Empath' rut. If you can't tolerate 'feeling people' around you in the physical world, then there is no way you will progress to feel the energy of Spirit or your Guides and Loved Ones at Home. You just won't be able to cope with Spirits energy, which is very different to ours.

There's a huge responsibility with being Spiritual and receiving messages for people, which I'll talk about later. If you are going through this, know that you are halfway through your incarnations!

Example of a 5 ½ – They see a feather and pick it up to take home to put in with their feather collection as they love the colours and textures.

5 ¾s are a more mature Soul

5 ¾s are the equivalent of an upper high school student in the physical world. They are seen as 'weird' by others and still hit their snooze button most days, but they have started to engage further in the magic and wonder of life itself.

5 ¾s have reincarnated quite a few times. Things are definitely getting harder for them, but also more interesting and amazing.

5 ¾s are warm, loving people who would do anything for anyone. They are beautifully selfless. They would give you the shirt off their back and put you before themselves, but only if it doesn't hurt them. They know to put themselves first and will not engage if it is to their detriment. This is very appropriate self-care!

Lessons they ignored lifetimes ago will come back to haunt them. Lessons always keep coming back, whether in this lifetime or the next. Sometimes we are the teacher, and sometimes we are the student, even to ourselves.

5 ¾s may be living what could be seen as alternative lifestyles, choosing to live as naturally as possible so that they feel connected to source and their You~niverse. Life is getting very interesting now for 5 ¾s.

Ooh, you are loving the weird, I mean WIRED-in, stuff now, right?

The veil is being lifted, and you may start to have many unexplained happenings or knowings. It's so important to keep a journal now. An exercise book is fine. Write down the things you experience and/or see. Use the 85/15 principle that I/we share later in this book when you are journalling – it will help BIG TIME.

Everything will feel like it's changing very quickly. Coincidences are no longer coincidences, they will have become signposts/Signs for you to follow. You may see an increase in repetitive numbers or names. Pay attention – your lessons have begun in earnest, and you will be tested regularly. You are ready to truly step into your Wiredness. You are starting to recognise where you left off in your Spiritual journey in your previous lifetimes. You are seeing through the illusion that is human life. You begin to clearly see the roles and levels of other people in your life. This new understanding and awareness brings with it clarity, excitement and impatience as it becomes more obvious to you that you are sharing this incarnation with people of many different Spiritual levels, all wearing human bodies.

This was our choice. We signed up to and agreed to this, and this is where Soul Contracts and the role of people in our life as teachers and students become profoundly clear. Lessons for 5 ¾s include patience, tolerance, non-judgement, acceptance, charity, selflessness, honesty, integrity, compassion, empathy and understanding.

These lessons may take a few incarnations and many Soul Contracts.

You chose to learn these lessons in your Soul Contract prior to incarnating. You chose the lessons that you wanted to learn, the type of scenario you wanted to learn in, the approximate point in your life when you felt you would be ready to wake up and the circumstances around that situation. You also chose who you wanted to learn it with and what role they needed to play in your life.

We make these agreements with members of our Soul Family, who are with us in every incarnation in one form or another. We recognise our Soul Family easily by the instant connection, whether beautiful or completely terrible, that we have with them.

We may instantly love or instantly loathe them. Either way, they are your signal that you have reconnected as planned.

Our blood family, however, are the people in our lives that support the Soul Contract. More on the difference later.

> *Example of a 5 ¾ – They are excited to see a feather on the ground and interpret the finding as an answer, sign or confirmation to a question they posed to their Guides. That feather will hold pride of place in their special sanctuary at home filled with candles, statues, plants and books. Experiences like these support that the feather is indeed a sign, and it spurs them on and builds faith in the unseen.*

6s are Old Souls

6s are the equivalent of university/college students in human form and are generally in their last incarnation/lifetime, and usually the most intense.

6s will always look within first and own their role in their Soul Contract or any interaction in their human experience

6s are 'sense'-itive! They read energy; they listen to Souls. They know … they just 'know!'

6s are intensely passionate, loving and insightful. To be in the company of a 6 is to be in the company of Angels. Their Souls are wise and whole. Their hearts are full of the Unconditional Love they learnt through incarnations. They know that any other kind of love is painful to give and receive. 6s are empathic and sensitive to everyone and everything, including animals and nature.

6s just *know* when and where they need to be. They also know when they are in the presence of another 6. They have all 6 senses: sight, hearing, smell, taste, touch and now their 6th Psychic sense. At this level of awareness, words are no longer necessary as all communication is made through energy, the eyes or telepathy.

When you are with a 6, you *will* feel surrounded by the purest of unconditional, almost angelic love. They just know how to 'be'. 6s are connected to the unlimited supply and source of Unconditional Love in the universe, and this is how they can keep going in our 'human world!'

6s can, if they're not careful, feel very drained and used by 5s; however, they are aware of this drawing of energy by Psychic vampires. They transmit Unconditional Love and acceptance towards the higher selves of others, often repelling the lower energy, which is a good thing, believe me!

6s are often referred to as Old Souls and are definitely seen as the weirdest most Wired ones. This can include children and babies – you may have heard people exclaim, 'Oh they are such an

Old Soul' as they peer into a pram at the shopping centre, as the Old Soul peers out thinking 'Oh! are you still here?'

Children are our Spiritual Teachers. I have spoken about this many times in groups, on my 'lives', on my website, in my first book and in a video on my YouTube channel. Check them out!

Being a 6 is also *the* hardest lifetime of all. Remember all those times that you chose not to learn lessons? Well, all those lessons you reneged on in your Soul Contract will be waiting for you in your last lifetime.

For a 6, their Psychic senses and ability to communicate with those back 'Home' as well as with their Guides are clearly understood. Spirituality can come naturally to a 6, but not always. They have learnt over many lifetimes to have faith in and trust their sense. They've learnt the lessons and are now benefitting from them. (Oh, if only we'd recognised them sooner, our physical lives would have been a lot easier! Everything is in divine order and divine timing!)

6s see the beauty in everything *and* feel the pain in everything. You will never hear them complain, mind you! They are grateful for their existence.

6s experience seeing Signs everywhere and allow them to guide the way Home. That is their job.

You trust.

You know.

You will be able to manifest easily and also experience how these manifestations can be taken away from you if you revert to gossiping, judging others and being negative.

You learn the power of you and will understand and live by the Spiritual Laws.

6s may now see, know and/or talk to and be guided by their Guides. They may work in any one of a myriad of healing modalities as guided by their calling and Soul purpose. We are shown visions and/or hear messages for you. We have agreed to take on the responsibility of this role and must be respectful of all we see and hear when delivering Spirit messages and healings.

Please remember that Guides are just us 'dead!' and deserve our utmost respect. They too are going through their own Soul journey and have agreed to help in this way for the benefit of their Soul's growth. It is important for them that they deliver their visions and messages in a way that can be interpreted correctly by us to receive their message.

You can recognise a 6 just by their light and energy alone. They always seem to know just what to say, what to do when, and where to be. This ability to 'read' everyone comes with responsibilities and choices. As a 6, you can choose to just 'observe' the Soul in front of you, or you can, if chosen by Spirit and also by your/their human self, 'choose' to help guide them with the issues you see for them.

It's imperative and a priority that you only intervene with their permission or if you play a role in their Soul Contract. You may not interfere with another's Soul Contract or Soul Journey. You may think that you are helping … believe me, you are not. If you are part of their lessons, journey and/or healing, you will know. You will also accept the responsibility of identifying the level that person is at, that is engaging with a 5, a 5 ½ or another 6, as communication will need to be tailored to be understood. Just like in our human school, we all speak a different language at different stages of life. The way you would explain something to a 6 is not how you would explain it to a 5 or 5 ½, as they just wouldn't 'get it'.

During their last lifetime, 6s will experience a Dark Night of the Soul. This period may last months or even years. It's a time when everything they thought they knew gets blasted out of the water. They will lose Loved Ones to illness, divorce, grief and death. On top of that, they may lose their homes, cars, jobs and bank balances.

Many will turn to addiction for comfort.

Many will turn to suicide for escape.

Personally, I tried both after losing my husband through divorce after 25 years together, losing both my parents and almost losing my kids! More about my Dark Night of the Soul later.

6s know that dying is just going Home, where Soul Contracts are designed, written and agreed upon with Soul Family.

We 6s were once 5s

and

5s will one day be 6s.

Human life is a complete illusion or lie to a 6. Part of our lesson in human form is to see this life for what it is. Take the letter 'f' out of the word 'LIFE' and you get the word 'LIE!'

6s have no judgement. You no longer see flesh and blood, material possessions, egoic possessions and attitudes and behaviours – you see Soul.

Their 6yness!

6s see through everything. They understand that incarnating into a human body is how we get to learn Soul lessons. Our brain is only as old as our body is in this lifetime; that's why I don't trust it to make any of my decisions. If I need to make an important decision, I consult my Soul and my Team. After all, they have been with me in all my past lifetimes/incarnations and know what is best for me. They've never been wrong, but my mind has! Yours too! So many times, my mind made a bad decision until finally I learnt the lesson. Jeepers, I hope I have now! There's absolutely no way that I'm coming back!

Our Soul knows way more than our mind – trust it!

6s will definitely experience bouts of 'Home' sickness in this lifetime. They are tired and ready to go Home and not come back. Their traumas and lessons of have been full-on and, at times, way too hard to live with as a human. This was me when I published

Caught Between Two Worlds in 2016. Through Annie's story, in this book, suicide was explained to me. Years ago, I tried to end my own life, and I carry the scars to this day. Obviously, I am still here for a reason. Maybe that is the reason for the sharing of the information by Opa and my Team through my/our books. I hope so! Many 6s don't cope in this incarnation and take their own life. If only I'd been able to reach them sooner! They're probably nodding their head in agreement right now!

One of the main reasons people seek out a Reading with me is because of relationship troubles. When I look at who is who in their zoo and their Soul Contracts, everything begins to make sense.

> *Example of a 6 – They are overjoyed to see the bird feather right when they pose their question to the universe or their Guides. They just know to accept the bird/feather as their sign and take great comfort in the experience. Experiences like these are totally accepted by a 6 and not questioned. These experiences confirm to a 6 that they are on the right track!*

The responsibility of being a 6

So, you think it should be easy when you incarnate as a 6? Ha! Your Guides, Spirit and the universe have saved the best lessons till the end.

It's tempting to want to go back to being a 5, as you think their life is far easier. However, you have earned your Soul's maturity. After all, if you were to go back to being a 5, that would mean that you are not 'awake' or enlightened and that you don't believe that there is more to life (which, of course, there is). That would be the same as completing your final year of school then wanting to start all over again in first year. No thanks!

Remember:

- You and I also started our Soul journey as young Souls.
- Previous 6s thought the same of us when we were 5s.
- 5s give 100% over a week = approximately 15% per day (if you are lucky!).
- 6s give 100% every second of every minute of every hour of every day and they do it easily and soulfully.

Preferring to be alone is all part of being a 6. That feeling of 'not fitting in' is a very relevant and significant feeling. This is your key to knowing that you are *not* a 5. 5s love being the centre of attention, all the time! Being a true 6 and walking your talk as a true spiritual being is a solo journey. One becomes very comfortable being alone.

It's so hard seeing everyone's contract and who is who in their zoo during a session. So many people just aren't aware. Believe me, I see it every time I do a Reading/consultation. In fact, if I choose to, I can see 'it' anytime, anywhere. I'm literally switched on 24 hours a day.

You can compare yourself to another, but not as a Soul, only as a person. Even then, I wouldn't recommend it.

6s tend to be the ones who work in the Spiritual modalities of Readings and healings. We are shown visions and/or hear messages for you. We have agreed to take on the responsibility of this role and must be respectful of all we see and hear when delivering Spirit's messages and healings to you.

I was always called 'too emotional' growing up. I never saw that as a bad thing, as I was always able to pre-empt what Mum, Dad, partners or bosses needed before they even asked. Friends too. It was like they thought something because they couldn't be bothered talking … and I heard it then acted on it!

In some ways, it was extremely tough growing up, because I was surrounded by minds that thought things I didn't want or need to see but saw anyway. I still do, so be very careful what you think around me – or make it really juicy, so I enjoy it too! I have always tried to come from a place of honesty and asked this of friends and work colleagues too. It was always hard when they would 'say' one thing verbally, but their energy yelled 'lies, lies all lies!'

Never lie to a Psychic, as you're the one who looks like a fool.

If you would like further clarity and insight into your Soul Contracts and who is who in your zoo, my readings can provide you with direction and guidance. I work on a Soul Level for you, right here, right now in this life.

What can I expect next?

Honestly? If you are reading this, then your life must be starting to feel aMAZing! It will have already been unfolding in all sorts of beautiful ways. Signs are in abundance, and Spiritual guidance is clear, as is your Soul Purpose.

No? Oh, okay! Perhaps your world feels like it's falling apart? You are losing friendships and family members? Maybe your life doesn't make any sense at all ... you may have even lost a lot. That's good – you are still right on track.

Welcome to the rest of us here in the same place, waiting to be W I R E D up to Source and truly connected to your life.

We've all been there ... that's how we got here!

It's a good thing, spiritually, anyway. Humanly, it feels like shit though, right?

Wait and see. Your 'You~niverse' is making room for all the good things still to come into your life. These endings are the beginnings of the rest of your life. Finally, it's your turn to experience true, pure joy. From here on, you will be able to make decisions attuned to what's best for you and your Soul for the rest of your life.

If you feel this for yourself and would like to truly live it, please reach out to me through my website and book a session. I can help you learn how to hear the guidance for your Soul and You~niverse for yourself. I can also help identify and teach you exactly who is who in your zoo. You will see that your zoo needs to accommodate only 5 ½s and above – 5s just don't fit anymore!

We will establish who needs to stay in your life to fulfill Soul Contracts. Anyone outside of this is not required, especially if you aren't getting on. Spiritually awakened people and those still asleep can't cohabitate peacefully – it just doesn't work. We can work through your Soul Contracts so you can move through your lessons with ease and honesty. Life will soon become easier, I promise.

You *are* starting to see this now, aren't you? You see that by having given and given and letting others take and take, you have been sucked dry, leaving you confused and disillusioned. Energy vampires are those Souls that are too lazy to take on their own growth, and they don't want you to benefit from yours. They ask you for solutions to their questions and life issues. They want you to listen to their problems non-stop and never show interest in your life. Is this resonating with you right now? You are merely a show-and-tell, or rather a tell-and-show, tool that they can use. Urgh!

Let me reiterate that cutting people out of your life has nothing to do with judgement and everything to do with awareness of what is right for you. No more saying 'yes' when you mean 'no' and 'no' when you mean 'yes'! The freedom of it all! Life was not meant to be this hard!

You will learn to Love your time alone rather than needing to fill it with people who use you. Once you become spiritually awake, you will no longer fear your own company, like I used to. You will look forward to it – crave it, even.

I promise.

Trust the process – your Guides are VERY experienced. It's in their best interest to help you and in your best interest to listen to them.

Soul Family vs Blood Family

Look at yourself as a beautiful old oak tree. See your Soul Family as the branches of this beautiful tree. See the roots firmly in the ground being nourished by Mother Nature. These roots are also the people who will be with us throughout our entire lives, their love is never questioned it just is. The leaves are the people that come and go, just like the seasons! These 'leaves' look fresh and new at the beginning, then provide shade and security at times before falling away in the autumn. The smaller branches are the people in your life that come and go. They stay for a reason or a season. The main branches stay for your lifetime. Our lives follow the same cycle.

As an exercise, draw yourself as a tree. Name your branches, your twigs and your leaves. This will put the 'who is who' in your life into perspective!

As you become more aware of your 6th sense and Spirituality, you will become very aware of the energy of others. You may not resonate or connect with them, but never cut anyone off from your friend group or just dump them because you are 'sick and tired' of them – they may in fact be the *VERY* teacher (or student!) you need. This was agreed to in your mutual Soul Contract. By dumping people, like so many people do these days, you are shirking your Soul Contract and their lessons – we all know what happens when we do that!

Blood Family refers to members of the family who gave birth to our Souls into this lifetime. They do not take a role in other incarnations. This is why sometimes, within families, we feel like we don't fit. This is why it's so important to know 'who is who in your zoo!' Understanding these roles will help you see and understand your Soul Contracts. It will help you understand the roles people play in our lives, and to understand when and why things get ugly, bad and sad.

Soul Family are the family that are with us in every incarnation. Our Soul Contracts are made with Soul Family members before we reincarnate. Between each lifetime, we spend time with them, reflecting on the lessons we/they wish to learn, teach or share. We discuss the scenarios we will play out together during our incarnation. We discuss all aspects of the experiences we need for us to learn a lesson.

For example:

Soul #1 has finally agreed to learn the lessons of forgiveness, self-acceptance and Unconditional Love. These lessons have been 'postponed' during various lifetimes – I'm sure you can relate, as they are pretty much the biggest of all lessons to learn.

In the past, Soul #1 has struggled with self-esteem and confidence issues. These come down to a deep self-loathing, a lack of self-love and self-acceptance, and the belief that if they feel that way about themselves, then everyone else must too. This has put enormous pressure on all relationships in past incarnations and broken many of them beyond repair.

This time, Soul #1 has agreed to work with Soul #2 and Soul #3 to work through these lessons once and for all.

Lifetime lesson scenario

So, let's set the scene. Soul #1 incarnates into this lifetime as a human body called Janet. Janet has suffered from severe self-loathing and a lack of self-acceptance in all her time as a Soul. Every time something goes wrong, Janet blames herself for what's happened. Regardless of whether the so-called event happened to her or someone around her, she still feels it was her fault.

Janet has a life pattern of overthinking, ruminating and worrying, along with singing the song 'nobody loves me, everybody hates me, think I'll go eat worms!' Due to this severe lack of self-awareness and Unconditional Love, Janet has projected this belief into the life of her partner Soul #2, Anthony.

Janet and Anthony fell in love. Janet fell in love with Anthony because he loved her, and she felt loved. Janet was grateful to Anthony for loving her. She agreed to marry him because she felt deep down that, if he loved her, then maybe she really *was* an okay person. She didn't really believe she was, and she believed she didn't deserve to be loved, but she was grateful not to have been 'left on the shelf'.

During their marriage, Anthony tried to show Janet how lovable she was. He always pointed out her good points and picked her up when she beat herself up. She was, in fact, in an abusive relationship with HERSELF! Ouch!

Janet had zero self-love or self-acceptance. Because she had lived with herself all her life and had lots of experience to go by, she believed she was flawed. Let us interject here that there was nothing wrong with Janet at all, just the fact that she had stubbornly refused to learn her Spiritual lessons along the way. Now she had to.

Janet believed that she knew herself better than Anthony did and was determined to prove that she was right. Although Anthony loved her unconditionally, despite his best efforts all he could do was dry her tears and hold her tight. She continued to push him away to prove she was right, when all she really wanted to do was believe everything he told her.

Maybe you can relate to this scenario yourself or someone you know or love.

Janet persisted in unknowingly sabotaging the relationship, continually pushing Anthony away so that when he finally saw that she was right (even though she wasn't right!), he would leave her and she would then have the proof of everything she believed about herself.

Then he met someone else and fell in Love. Soul #3, who shall remain nameless, agreed to play the part of a love affair in this Soul Contract. Anthony's relationship with Soul #3 grew, and his relationship with Janet became distant.

Soul #3 was a safe place for Anthony's Soul during this Soul Contract. There was no infidelity. Anthony confided in Soul #3. He expressed his deep love of Janet. They discussed how he had tried to help Janet throughout their marriage. Soul #3 and Anthony agreed that this was Janet's lesson to learn.

Soul #3 and Anthony agreed that Anthony would tell Janet how he felt she had pushed him away and how, because of this, he had met Soul #3. Anthony believed it was his role in Janet's Soul Contract to give her the opportunity to learn the lessons of forgiveness and self-acceptance.

So, he did.

Anthony opened up by asking Janet to listen, then telling her how much he loved and believed in her, and that he wanted to grow old with her (aww!). He asked Janet to be honest with him for the first time in her life, for both their sakes, as he did not want to break up.

Anthony asked Janet to trust him.

Do you recognise this as a lesson for you?

Anthony continued to explain how he felt that Janet was trying to talk him out of loving her, all because she felt she wasn't good enough for anyone. Janet had previously expressed wanting to take her own life as she believed the people who knew her would be better off without her in their lives.

Janet broke down and told Anthony that after what he had told her about meeting Soul #3, she again felt like she wanted to take her own life. She felt completely broken that Anthony was rejecting her!

Little did she realise that all along she had been rejecting herself before anyone else could. Janet lived in constant fear of people finding out what she was 'really' like. She believed that people just pretended to be her friend or were her friend out of pity – who could Love her? She didn't, so why would anyone else? She felt like a fraud!

Can you relate to Janet? I can!

Anthony was at his wits' end. He had always been considered by people and friends that knew him as an 'Old Soul'– he seemed to attract people who had problems and needed help. Anthony had unlimited patience and tolerance due to his Soul's age.

Anthony was a 6. Anthony had learnt the lessons of self-love/acceptance and forgiveness in previous incarnations. This was why he agreed to play this role in Janet's life.

Janet was a 5 ¼ and about to learn these lessons of self-love/acceptance and forgiveness.

Thank goodness for Anthony!

Janet broke down and sobbed for almost an hour. She couldn't speak and was retreating into her Dark Night of the Soul, all while Anthony was reassuring her that he would help her through this and that he was not going to leave her side.

Over the following months, Anthony helped Janet rebuild herself entirely from scratch (that's what happens when Humpty Dumpty falls off the wall!) Anthony's wisdom allowed him to tell Janet exactly what she needed to hear. Janet had never realised that Anthony was so Spiritual – she thought that she was the enlightened one! She was very wrong.

All she could do was listen. Her Soul made her listen.

Anthony patiently described Janet to her through his eyes, the eyes of her friends and the eyes of her children. He patiently outlined various scenarios he had witnessed and wanted to remind her about … times where the real Janet shone through, mostly when she thought no one was watching.

Anthony also pointed out how others saw her. How they respected and loved her. Anthony gently pointed out that the very fear she had of no one loving her or being accepted by others was unfounded and that she didn't have to spend her whole life trying to talk others into believing her beliefs.

Janet felt very confronted.

Anthony asked her to trust him.

And she did.

They started working on Janet accepting herself. They worked together journalling the positives and negatives through Janet's eyes. Anthony then countered every one of the false beliefs with his own truths.

Slowly, Janet's ego began to subside; her need to prove to others that she was right, that she was unlovable, was her ego trying to keep its control.

I see you nodding your head in understanding!

Anthony had seen this all along. He had been shown the entire sequence before they had agreed to the Soul Contract. He had been excited to play this part in their lives.

Over the weeks, Janet tried counselling. However, she told Anthony that she would rather talk to him as she felt he went right into her Soul where the work needed to be done, and standard counsellors don't work this way.

May I interject here and say that, as a Soul Clinician, I work on the Soul level with you. After all, this is the level that counts in this lifetime and where you can truly make sense of YOU, your life and where you fit in. This is why I don't work on past lives – it's this life, right here and now, that is the culmination of all your past lives. This is the one that counts.

In life, we have heart specialists, lung specialists and eye specialists, but we don't have Soul specialists. I am a Soul Specialist. When you go to see a health specialist, you will visit their consulting rooms. With me, I will meet you anywhere, anytime to help you navigate your Soul path. It usually only takes one or two sessions at most.

Anyway, back to Janet, Anthony and Soul #3.

Anthony explained to Janet that he didn't want to break up with her and that he had not crossed any boundaries with Soul #3. He told Janet that he felt she had been pushing him away, even though she really didn't want to.

Janet admitted that she had been and also that she truly loved Anthony.

Anthony asked Janet to forgive herself and to treat herself like her best friend would.

Janet felt something 'shift' inside of her. There was a light shining at the end of her tunnel, and that light was her Soul.

Janet said that she had no idea how to forgive herself, or to live with what she had done to herself and how she had let herself and others down. Anthony explained that there were many others in the Soul Contract who had chosen to support them both through her lesson. Such is the power of Unconditional Love.

Anthony explained it like this (this is also how Opa explained forgiveness to me):

> Janet, thank yourself FOR-GIVING yourself the opportunity to learn the lesson of self-acceptance and Unconditional Love. Thank yourself FOR-GIVING yourself the opportunity to learn about SELF-LOVE and ACCEPTANCE through the dark side of self-loathing. Accept that you have just been through a Spiritual lesson as opposed to a human experience.

Soul #3 then disappeared out of the scene as she was no longer needed. Soul #1 thanked her for playing her role so beautifully.

Janet took baby steps towards her new 'normal'. She and Anthony now live a spiritually enlightened life filled with Love.

Unconditional Love. Tick! Lesson learnt.

She could have walked away. Anthony could have as well. But neither did.

Janet and Anthony were both Soul Family. Soul #3 was not.

Twin Flames

There's so much information on the internet or what I call 'Dr Spirit not Dr Google' about Twin Flames, so I asked Opa and my Team for their wisdom. The conversation went like this:

Me: Hey guys, this whole Twin Flame thing does my head in. Would you please help me understand?

Opa: A Twin Flame relationship is a contract between two Souls to help one or the other during an incarnation with the undertaking of difficult lessons. The best way that we can show you is through a Reading. This afternoon, you have Leslie coming to see you for a session. Leslie is in a Twin Flame relationship and coming to see you about it.

Me: Thank you.

Leslie has given me permission to share her story with you in this book. Below is part of our session together:

Me: Leslie, I have Greg here with us this afternoon. He is still with you in this life and hasn't gone Home yet, don't panic! Do you know Greg?

Leslie: Yes, he is the main reason that I have come to see you today. I am so confused about my feelings for him. I love him, then I hate him, then I love him again, then I hate him again. I can't get him out of my head, heart or life, and I don't think I even want to. It's just so confusing!

Leslie began crying at this point. Greg's Soul had come to visit with us that afternoon. Greg goes pretty much everywhere with

Leslie, even when he is not with her physically. It was certainly a relationship I had not seen before, and I asked Greg for insight and clarity. The following is my conversation, telepathically of course, with Greg's Soul.

Me: Greg, please help me understand what is happening between the two of you.

Greg: It's simple, really. Leslie has struggled with learning lessons during her past incarnations. She keeps avoiding them and putting them off. They are painful lessons for her and include personal integrity and trust. Prior to incarnation, I was asked if I would help Leslie work through them in this incarnation. Her other lessons were building up and her Soul was becoming overwhelmed. So, I agreed to take half of it. I carry half of her Soul and Leslie carries the other half. I agreed to put my learning on hold in this particular incarnation and undertake some of her lessons for her on her behalf. I do this when I am not with her. When we get back together, my half of her Soul reconnects with the other half and, for lack of a better word, 'uploads' the learning. It's during the reconnecting that our energy is so passionate. She does not know that I have agreed to this role – she wouldn't understand, she's just not at that level of understanding. I am. Our union is very passionate and complete. Leslie says things like, 'Every time you come back to me, it feels like I am home again, and every time you go away, I feel ripped in half! I cannot cope with our on-again, off-again relationship.' I am giving her a Gift … the Gift of herself. Would you please explain it to Leslie as I'm sure it would help!

I asked Opa to help me find the words that would reach Leslie. First, I told Leslie what Greg had shared with me. I was completely amazed that this kind of thing was even possible. In a nutshell, I said to Leslie:

Me: Greg loves you enough to have offered to take on and learn half of your Spiritual lessons for you. Greg has taken on half of your Soul in this incarnation, and this is why you feel like you have come 'Home' when you are together, because you have been reconnected with the other half of your Soul. The Unconditional Love that Greg has for you is very special. Greg knows what he signed up for in this incarnation. As humans, it's nigh-on impossible to understand what is going on here for you two on a Soul level. You feel the intensity and the build-up when Greg needs to leave again to undertake the next lesson. You hate him for leaving you, and you feel ripped in two because he literally is taking half of your Soul with him to fill it with the next lesson. Once that lesson is learnt, he comes back to you, and you are both overjoyed at being together and filled with incredible love. It truly is a love/hate relationship. However, please see it for the Gift that it is. His Love for you is without bounds or conditions.

Leslie: I just don't know what to say. I know to trust you because it feels right!

Me: There you go, you are on your way to learning your lesson of trust! Please thank Greg for his Gift now.

And she did. Witnessing this was extraordinary. I did not even know that this was possible. Opa had shown me firsthand through a Reading session what a true Twin Flame relationship was all about, and I thanked him.

Gatekeepers

Gatekeepers are extremely important when you choose to start working with your Gift as a 6. Gatekeepers are there to protect you from invasive or nuisance entities or earthbound Spirits.

Most invasive and earthbound Spirits have never been shown nor heard of 'the light.' Going to the 'light' is not automatic when you leave your body.

Working with Spirit IS real. I spend more time in their world learning from and helping them than I do in my own. As weird as this may sound to the sceptic, I know that I'm just 'Wired' to Source and Spirit and it's my role to be the go-between!

That's what we are! The go-between! Or as I referred to myself in my first book, 'the Psychic postie!' It's very important to have a Gatekeeper protect you from the unseen in the Spirit world.

Please remember that I can help you navigate the trip of a lifetime – *your* life!

Energy vampires

Have you ever come home from socialising, the supermarket or being out with friends and felt completely drained and exasperated? You make yourself a cup of tea, or pour yourself a wine, and flop onto the lounge questioning why you feel this way.

Firstly, STOP! It's got nothing to do with you. Well, it does have something to do with you, and that's because you were unaware that energy vampires exist.

When you realise that life *is* an illusion and that you are sharing it with other 'Souls', not just humans around you, your eyes will be opened to the way they function. Let's go back to the 5s and 6s in your life. Now would be a good time to find out who the 5s are!

Have you ever visited a zoo? Once you enter through the front gates, you are free to 'view' animals in all shapes, sizes and ferocity from the safe distance and restraints of the boundary fencing. There are also Signs warning you not to enter the enclosures dedicated to keeping both you and the animals safe.

Our human existence is exactly the same, yet many ignore the warning Signs, travelling among others without boundaries to keep them safe from energy vampires and low-level entities.

People want to believe in the Spirit world (many say they do but only do 'in case' it is real, which it is!) and I get that, but please don't be naïve in thinking it's a safe place to venture all the while ignoring the warning Signs. You wouldn't ignore the warnings signs placed around the lion's den, would you?

My Team have a totally different example that might 'shock' you into understanding.

We all know that electricity is energy. We also understand this is energy that we cannot see. We know it's there, and we also know that if we jump into the bath with a plugged-in hairdryer that we will get a 'shocking' experience and probably not make it out of the bath alive.

Human existence is exactly the same.

As humans, we are dealing with energy all day, every day. We are energy, all of us, regardless of Soul level. It's what makes us 'us'. I read people's energy before they even introduce themselves to me. It tells me so much about a person – I like to 'read' someone to see if I feel a 'connection' to them.

This is why people who are 5 ½s and above are best suited to mixing with other 5 ½s and above. Energetically, they are on the same wavelength and Soul journey.

Many people that come for a session with me complain about not being able to understand their partners, family and/or friends. They experience personality clashes and arguments. When I/we delve deeper, we uncover that they, potentially a 5 ¾, are clashing with a 5 or 5 ¼. This would be the equivalent of a university student hanging out with a grade 2 student at lunch time. It just doesn't work. On a Soul level, it shouldn't happen either, unless of course you are involved in a Soul Contract with that person.

The older Soul in this scenario would normally be sensitive to energy, but they may also be a people pleaser and thus ignore the energy. The young Soul in this equation would be completely oblivious to energy and only be interested in what they could get out of the relationship. The only time they won't clash is when the older Soul sacrifices themselves to please the young Soul. Again, this would be like the university student answering every beck and call of a primary school student.

If the older Soul trusted their energy detection and heeded the warning Signs and red flags, they may have avoided a relationship with this young Soul altogether. However, human life doesn't work this way.

That's why I always say that I struggle to human as humaning makes no sense to me at all. Why would I walk into a lion's den only to be mauled?

Be aware of your surroundings at all times! Who are you with? Read them. Read their energy. Are you seeing green flags or red flags? Trust your own intuition and sensitivity. Keep judgement out of the situation and don't be a people pleaser.

Get to know your own energy boundaries

Here's an experiment you can do:

Sit quietly with a pen and paper and rule it up similar to below. First, write a list of all your friends, colleagues and the people you know and mix with.

Then read their energy and identify where you feel they fit in with your life.

POSITIVE ENERGY	NEGATIVE ENERGY
Name	*Name*
Name	*Name*
Name	*Name*

Once you have identified where these people fit into your world energetically, you may then like to experiment with them in person. Many people have a lot of people in their lives and thus a lot of differing energies – not all good, and not all bad. Consider what type of energy you want in your life. If there are negative energies that do not bring out the best in you, consider first whether there is a Soul Contract in place between the two of you. If there is, identify it, work through it then reassess where they sit in your life.

My Team call this 'weeding your garden'! They say to 'pull out the weeds to make way for new growth'.

There's no need to feel bad for doing this. In the Spiritual realm, it is perfectly normal. If you don't do it, there's a good chance that your Guides will do it for you and sometimes that can be the hard way. Your Guides will remove anyone that hinders your Spiritual growth. My experience says don't overanalyse or overthink this, because a 'thank you' is all that is needed.

This is why it's so important to know who's who in your zoo. Once you have done this, it's time to sit with your Guides and ask for protection in the form of a Gatekeeper. A Gatekeeper will work on only allowing those who are for your highest good or in your Soul Contract to get through to you. This is both on a human level and a Soul/Spirit level. I hear you ask how you can do that – my Team says:

> Remember that while you cannot see your Guides yet, they can see you. You may, over time, as you practice, be able to feel their presence. In the meantime, you can still talk to them like you would any friend. They can hear you. Sit quietly and ask them to provide you with protection from all that is not for your highest good, whether Spiritual or in human form, and to bring you those who are meant to be in your life for your highest good. Ask them to help you become more sensitive energetically so that you can make the right choices for yourself and your life too.
>
> Then consider it done.

To start with, you can do this every time you meditate or socialise. Energy vampires are low-level Souls that thrive on negativity. They loathe people who are happy and positive, because they are jealous of them. They feel that positive people show up their negativity, and this infuriates and intimidates them. Basically, they don't want to see anyone happy and will suck the life force out of you, if you're not careful. We've all experienced people like this. As humans, we call them users, narcissists and sociopaths. On a Soul level, I/we call them 5s or young Souls.

So, if you have come home from being out and feel completely shattered, stop and take a look at who may have stolen your energy during that time. Ask your Guides to shower them in love and light, then let them go. You do not have a Soul Contract with them and therefore have no obligation on any level to either help or change them. They will find their own way, on their own path, with their own teachers showing them the way.

Angels and Earth Angels

Angels

Angels believe in YOU, even if you don't believe in them! Angels are Celestial Beings that offer Unconditional Love, guidance, protection, strength and, at times, healing for our physical bodies and comfort for our Souls. They epitomise and symbolise pure Unconditional Love, compassion and wisdom.

Guides have Angels too. So do all of us. We do not need to believe in them for them to be real – they already are!

Angels often appear when they are least expected, sometimes right when our faith is at its lowest. Many stories and photos have been shared by people who have seen Angels. They share their experiences in a variety of ways, and all their stories are similar. They are beautiful to read.

Earth Angels

Earth Angels work in cafés, hairdressers or similar places as teachers. Later on, you will read Marie's story. She is a true Earth Angel.

Doctors have their own clients regardless of location – Earth Angels also draw Souls to them that need their attention, care and messages.

Q: How do I know if I'm an Earth Angel?

A: Do people seem to gravitate to you and tell you their problems? Not just that, but do you find that you always seem to give them exactly what they needed to hear, and they tell you so too? Have you ever wondered where the 'words and/or messages' came from or questioned why you were in exactly the right place at the right time? It's because you are an Earth Angel. The universe will also put you exactly where you are needed to help other Souls on their journeys. Yours is a very important job. You are a representative of the universe, and your Soul knows its work. Thank you for stepping up!

Q: How do I recognise an Earth Angel?

A: In addition to the above, Earth Angels have a certain 'feel or energy' about them. They feel like Home. Earth Angels are the oldest Souls walking on our earth today. They are in their last incarnation, and they share their Angel energy and wisdom with you/us. There are no words that can describe the feeling they bring. You will 'feel' an Earth Angel is with you before they've even spoken. Trust them. They come in Love. If you have been blessed with the presence of an Earth Angel coming into your life, please accept their help. Lean on them … they know what they are doing when we don't and are here to help.

Some people see Celestial Angels. I've only ever seen one, and it was at my friend Maxine's. I will never forget the Angel that came to visit that night. Our lives were changed forever in the proof of their existence.

The Angel at Maxine's

Back in early 2018, my beautiful Earth Angel friend Maxine asked me to come over and have dinner with her and her dad, Morrie (in Spirit). Prior to dinner, we chatted for ages, as we do. Maxine shared stories about her dad while showing me some very special photos of her life before I knew her. As we were looking through the photos, a song came on that Maxine said was very poignant combined with the photos.

We both became quite still as the light and atmosphere changed in the room. Maxine said she could feel her dad was with her – she always knew when he was. They'd had a beautiful relationship when he was alive, and Morrie still came through to her today from Home.

As Maxine cried softly, we were both completely filled with the most amazing feeling of Unconditional Love that goes hand in hand with a visit from Spirit. I'm not sure how much time passed, but I remember being reluctant to 'come back' once Maxine announced that we better have Morrie's lamb roast 'before it goes cold'!

Dinner was exceptional, and we ate mostly in a very comfortable silence. Maxine was sitting opposite me with her head down, putting food on her fork, when I noticed something peculiar. It was like someone had sprayed hairspray, only it wasn't hairspray. It was a very fine mist, but this mist had a shape and was moving from right to left behind Maxine. It felt incredible and looked amazing. I realised that I was witnessing my first Angel. I was completely mesmerised. I watched it for a full ten seconds, easily. I was scared to blink in case it disappeared, but I did and it didn't. It rocked like a sea horse behind her about shoulder height. The feeling was extraordinary. I couldn't bring myself to look at Maxine. Funny how the music had stopped right at that point too!

I found tears slowly rolling down my face. I felt like I had just visited Heaven. The Angel had moved away from us through the wall. The music came back on. Maxine looked up at me. Tears glistened in her eyes too. She asked, 'That was weird … did you feel that? It felt like an Angel to me!' Yay, she had felt it too! I responded, 'Oh Maxine, I felt it and saw it!' I then described her visitor, and we sat in awe at the power of Love that had come to visit us that evening. 'You are so blessed,' I told her. 'No,' she said, 'we are!'

And she was right. We believe that her dad Morrie had sent the real-life Angel to us to confirm that all we had talked about *was* real. Thank you from the bottom of my heart, Morrie.

I had never experienced anything like that before and haven't since. I would love to hear if you have!

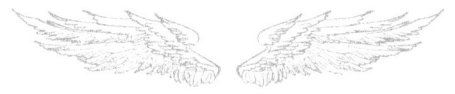

What it's like for me to be Wired *not* Weird

One of the hardest times for me being Wired is when my Team choose to give me messages that are important. These messages can come through so distinctly that I have no chance of forgetting them, or they come through in automatic writing and can be quite lengthy. Normally, they show me when I don't have a pen and paper on me, usually because I'm …

… driving

… on the loo

… in the shower

… trying to sleep.

Yes, they are available to me anytime, but I have learnt to manage them and teach them that I need 'alone' time, just like they do.

I've even mastered writing on my hand or in one of the many notebooks I carry when I'm driving or working. Sometimes, I even put them on my phone. Normally they involve names that I have to give to someone who is coming in for a Reading! These names can be from people who have passed or who are still alive. It doesn't make a difference, because ultimately our Soul is an energy, and it is their energy that comes through.

If you have read my first book *Caught Between Two Worlds*, you will remember the amazing Reading for Sophie and Peter! Peter shared the most amazing explanation that I have ever heard as to why living 'Souls' come through to me for sessions complete with their names and the reasons why they came.

You see, the messages can come thick and fast, usually as visions. A picture can speak a thousand words, and each vision replaces the previous one. If I haven't caught the message in the first picture, the whole message can be affected, so it's important that I immediately jot down the key words. Soul Readings require a lot of responsibility and experience to interpret the visions, much like the old fashioned slide show.

I am very sensitive to energy, and energy speaks louder than any words, as I am sure you know all too well. I can be anywhere in the world and know when someone's energy has changed, because I feel it. When I give of myself to anything or anyone, I give 100%. I have made many, many mistakes in my life and learnt from them. I have learnt to live with them through forgiveness of myself and others and have put them into perspective. I have boundaries in place to protect my energy and that of my Team.

I thought everyone could 'see' what was going on in other people's lives. When I 'saw' something of interest, most of the time I would discreetly raise the topic in conversation. This always gave me feedback as to whether I was getting it through my brain or whether it was through my 6th sense. It helped me tune my antenna, so to speak! Perhaps you also 'see' things for other people but, because these visions are interpreted by our human brain, you may dismiss them as just a thought or even a judgement. I offer my techniques to those who wish to learn how to differentiate between a thought and a 'knowing'. I explain this in my chapter, 'The 85/15 principle.'

I have a deep respect for people's privacy and do not go looking into their lives out of curiosity. While I am naturally a nosey person, I decided to draw the line when walking through the shopping centre one day ... there was a man walking towards me and I could very vividly see the kind of sex he'd had the night before – alone! That's when I said that these were not the types of visions I wanted to be shown. I only want to work at higher frequency levels and for the good of a person's Soul Journey.

These days, I only use my 'visions' to help people for their greater good. I feel it's a huge responsibility to be able to see what people are up to in their lives and how their choices and decisions play out for them, particularly when they want the opposite to happen! That's when my Team offer the guidance the person sitting in front of me needs. I never offer what I see or know without my Team's permission. Unless I am part of their Soul Contract, I stay away, knowing in full faith that the right teacher will come along for them when the time is right.

I have developed strength and resilience as a result of immense personal trauma over many, many years. I believe I have a direct link to download and connect to abundant Unconditional Love. It's this Love and connection that gets me through all the S H I T that I have had to endure. Everyone has access to this loving support from the universe.

None of this S H I T has made any sense to me as a human. I simply cannot understand why these situations happen to anyone, let alone my family. Even my counsellor and friends have asked me how I got through everything I've been through, and I say, 'It's because I don't use my human brain to understand. I use my Soul instead!'

You see, our human brain is only to assist us in this lifetime while we inhabit this human body. Our human brain functions just like the computer in a car. It's not smart at all and is only as good as what we put into it. It's just way too frustrating. I tend not to use my brain unless it's work related.

Our Soul, on the other hand, has been with us during all our lifetimes/incarnations and has access to everything we need for our higher good. It understands that some of these difficulties stem from a previous lifetime because it has brought that knowing with it. It knows US. It IS US! It is the only thing I trust about me, and it's the only thing that makes sense about being me!

I find my life to be staggeringly fascinating. Every day I wake up wondering what and who will come my way. What beautiful Signs will I be shown to guide me that I'm either on the right track or off it? I get excited about life these days. The worst parts are behind me now, and I know am in the right place at the right time.

Many old Souls are going through incredible trauma in this lifetime. This is because all the lessons we walked away from, in this lifetime and previous ones, have come back for us to learn – finally. It's time to learn those lessons and be rewarded with an elevation in our frequency and connection to our Guides and our Loved Ones who went 'Home' before us.

Use your Wired GPS (Globally Positioned Spirit)

Just like you have a GPS in your car that you rely on to keep you going in the right direction, your Soul will guide you on your Spiritual Journey navigating your Soul Contracts. If you have been reading this book and nodding at certain points, then you are at least a 5 ½ or above. That's good news. You have matured through your incarnations to see where you now fit into in your life and in your 'zoo!' Please allow this book to confirm who you are and allow it to provide you with insight, direction, clarification and even validation of your own journey.

If you look at recent events and find that a lot of people have left your life, cut you off or just fallen away, don't take this personally. It's their gift to you. The universe is making room for the people who DO count in your life – people who will complement your life and love you for you, without needing justification or adding complication.

You may find yourself withdrawing from the world altogether. This is a good thing as now you can concentrate on really learning your lessons and growing your Soul and Spiritual self.

Once you are awake, there is no need to rush into relationships or friendships anymore, or even jobs. Your GPS is active and ready to take you in exactly the right direction for your Soul's benefit and growth. You will magnetically gravitate to others on your level, and this is where the magic happens.

It's time to find your own Wired-in clan. Before you rush into any new situation, friendship or relationship, ask yourself where this new person fits on the scale between 5s and 6s. Remember: this is <u>NOT</u> a judgement. It's just seeing clearly through your Soul's internal vision.

Knowing who the people around you are is crucial to understand why you're experiencing crisis or confusion!

Energy

Years ago, people used to greet each other with a smile, their words, an outstretched hand or a pat on the back. We were able to interpret the gestures straight away to determine whether someone was kind, genuine or false.

These days, many of us, predominantly 6s, greet each other first by connecting through our energies. We have always done it this way, but we are more aware now. We are all energy, and it radiates out from us, introducing us before we even speak or arrive. This energy is tangible to many people, even 5s, although they couldn't acknowledge it or put into words what they're feeling. It would come out as judgement. We are surrounded by and bumping into other people's energies all the time. For those very sensitive to it, you must protect and put boundaries around yourself, or you may become a victim of negative energy by absorbing it.

We all vibrate at different energy levels or frequencies, like how radio stations transmit at different frequencies. Spiritually evolved beings have an energy that is tangible to others, who may react to the energy without realising it. They can't put their finger on it though and the energy may make them feel uncomfortable, yet they can't see it and they don't understand it.

The Soul *is* energy. We ARE energy, and it's the most reliable radar known to the Soul. In fact, it's the language of the Soul.

Have you noticed 'energy' yourself? If this is a new concept to you, I would be more than happy to share my experiences and knowledge with you. Energy is key to having peace in our lives and using it for our highest good. After all, that's why we have it.

When the propeller on a plane begins turning, you can see it initially, but the propeller rotates faster and faster, so fast, in fact, that it looks like it's not turning at all. However, when the plane lifts off the ground, you know the propellor is spinning really fast. The wheels on a car do the same when you watch them drive past you. They look like they are not doing anything, yet they are doing something very powerful indeed, just like we do energetically.

It's a wonder we can walk half the time because of the negative and positive energy fields all around us. If you could actually see everyone's energies, along with all the text messages, social media messages, emails and internet searches, which are also an energy or frequency, as real and very tangible objects in the air, we would be ducking and weaving all the time. There would barely be any oxygen left for us to breathe.

These days, spiritually awakened people prefer to stay home. Is this why Covid came – to sort the frequencies out? Covid was the great universal pause.

The universe has been trying to get everyone's attention for a very long time, wanting everyone to realise what IS truly important, outside of the illusion that *was* our lives as we knew them. Humans who don't like being alone with themselves will experience anxiety and depression and their own Dark Night of the Soul until they wake up. Potentially. Hopefully. Ultimately, it comes down to where you are in your Soul's lifecycle.

For now, however, many continue to hit the snooze button and avoid going through their lessons while living, choosing instead to just exist while feeling that they can't cope.

Hey, don't get me wrong. I have family that live overseas in Holland, Canada, Belgium and Chile. Covid is real. It is a virus. It is a potential killer of bodies and minds through suicide.

But NOT of Souls.

Spirituality is our vaccine against sadness, emptiness and loneliness. Spirituality has a long history, and its main ingredient is LOVE!

Teaching the teachers

I have chatted to many school teachers who have come to me for Readings. I remember one in particular. She asked me to meet with her in the city, which I did. She was telling me that she had been trying to leave her school for almost 12 months. She was also hoping to find a job in another state, but nothing ever came up. She said that she was continually facing hurdles being put in front of her and was starting to get really frustrated.

My Team and I 'read' her situation. My Team showed me a young boy in her grade two class who sat at the back of the classroom. He was constantly overlooked by her. I described him to her and told her he really needed her help. I explained that he was having a lot of trouble with his hearing and needed hearing aids. I asked her to put this child in the front row so that he could lipread. I also told her I was being shown that once she had helped him, her job opportunity would come up.

Later in the year, I received a short message of thanks from her. She told me that she had followed everything I had said in our session and that, a month later, she received the opportunity to transfer to a school in Queensland from South Australia and that everything was working out well.

I was so pleased to hear from her and thanked her for the feedback.

It's always wonderful to hear about the accuracy of the Readings and the information and/or visions shown to me by my Team of Guides. It stops me from thinking I'm going insane and yes! I do think that at times!

The lesson behind the story is this: if something in your life isn't going the way YOU want it to go, broaden your vision. Take a look around you. Maybe the holdup isn't about you at all. Maybe obstacles are being put in your way on purpose. Maybe you need to teach someone something, or they need to teach you something.

Many people make the mistake of thinking that everything happening in their lives is about them, but it's not. Each one of us is merely a link in a chain. What happens to us will then cause something and/or affect someone else. Nothing happens to us alone. We are a beautiful ripple effect.

We are one – as soon as you realise it, you will also be shown the bigger picture and where you fit in. If something isn't happening for you right now, maybe it's because a 'something' hasn't happened for someone else. I hope this makes sense to you, because it truly is the key to understanding your human life as a Spiritual being.

In summary, never give up … always remember to expand your thinking and 'think' with your Soul, not your mind.

In school we learn lessons and then get tested.
In life, we get tested and then learn lessons.

Manifesting – making things happen with just your thoughts

Ooh, the power of the mind! Have you discovered it yet?

Many years ago, after the relationship breakdown with my first fiancé (you may remember him from my first book), my dad said to me, 'What do you want to do with your life now, Marion? Because you can make anything happen just by thinking about it!' I was 21 then. I accepted this advice as gospel and started writing what could then have been called my 'bucket list'.

Except it wasn't.

It was my life's to-do list.

First on my list was wanting to travel and to get paid to do it. Shortly after writing that list, I was successful in getting a job as a waitress and living aboard paddle-steamers on the Murray River in South Australia. Passengers would embark every Sunday afternoon, and on Monday mornings we would leave Goolwa and travel right past Clayton Bay where my parents lived. Mum and Dad would always stand on the cliff's edge waving to me onboard the boat. We would cruise back again five days later, where we would wave hello to each other again.

They were proud, as was I. I had made this happen just by thinking it real. Many call this 'manifesting'.

Then the travel bug got me, and I wanted to go further, wider AND get paid to travel.

After an interview with my new boss as we were walking on Henley Beach, I walked right into a job as safari cook/hostess with a national bus company that conducted 25-day barramundi fishing tours through the Northern Territory and the top of Queensland! I had never cooked for more than two people in my life! Now that WAS exciting!

My life was blessed even then. I found this to-do list thing really worked for me! That was 40 years ago, and manifesting has never let me down!

The second thing on my list was to learn to skydive – gosh, how I envied birds! I remember vividly on my second jump that, shortly after my parachute had opened, a seagull flew next to me. He looked at me, and I said to him, 'You are SO lucky!' I'm sure he winked at me!

The third thing on my list was wanting to meet the man that I had seen in my dreams. He wore athletic sandshoes and drove a sports car. Two years later, through skydiving, I met my husband in Canberra who was indeed wearing the same style sandshoes and later decided that we should buy a left-hand drive sports car.

Years later, when I was back in South Australia, I was blessed enough to walk straight into a part-time job as a ground control officer for a skydiving company near where I lived. It was one of the best jobs I've ever had.

I knew without a doubt that anything I wrote on my list would come true; they weren't just words on a page. I looked at the list often, adding many things to it and crossing off many things after they came true.

I now see that I had been manifesting right from an early age.

Have you ever written a wish list for yourself? For me, way too many fantastic things were written on that list, too many to write about here – I don't want to bore you! What I would like to do though is really, REALLY influence you to watch everything you think and say. If you want something to happen in your life, particularly something positive, then think it, say it … live it as if it was already real and true. Your request will be granted. The same is true for the opposite. If you don't want something to happen, then don't think about or mention it. To this day, I am VERY mindful of everything I think and say. If I don't want something to come true, I don't say it, and if I do want it to come true, I share it with the universe, then I wait.

I'm writing this in December 2023, and I have exactly the caravan I wrote about on my list, and the white beach house I saw in my dreams. Even my kids' personality traits and features were included on my list and granted by the universe. In fact, if I'm honest, everything on my list has come to fruition. I've always felt them to be instructions to an invisible, omniscient source that loves granting wishes. For me, writing my to-do list was better than writing a letter to Santa, as it actually came true. I share this information not to boast but to inspire you and tell you firsthand how very real manifesting is.

I KNOW manifesting works. I would feel I was dishonouring my Gift if I didn't share this beautiful wisdom so that you can enjoy how wonderful it is when you realise you have the power to live the life you want.

I want to inspire you to write your own lists and truly believe that they will come true. Write them, believe in them then watch the magic happen.

Focus, really focus, on what IS right for you in this life, what you feel is truly meant to be for you. Write it down. Show it to your Guides. Focus on it like it will happen, like it has already happened. There is no question. Write a timeline for it to happen by or in, then wait and TRUST.

Now, as positive as the power of positive thinking is, so is the power of negativity and doubt. My advice is to stay away from negativity. Every time doubt comes into your mind, you undo all your good work. Your Guides are literal and will take your instruction as gospel – after all, they want to please you.

Trust is the biggest key here. I had NO doubt at all and, as the years rolled past, I added more to my list because I'd achieved the goals on it. My faith grew. I can only hope to inspire you a little bit ... no, a lot!

Growing into being Psychic

I've always felt normal! Weirdly normal! After all, I had no thoughts about the 6th sense I'd always had. Mum always used her 'magic eye' and told us kids growing up that her dad and his mum in Holland had one too. We accepted it as normal.

As I got older, that gap widened for me. So, when I was first called 'weird' for saying, doing or having something happen that was normal for me but not normal for others – like knowing things that would happen before they did or seeing Loved Ones who had passed over – I felt judged and misunderstood and took their jibes very personally. Maybe you have experienced the same and that's what has drawn you to read this book.

Sadly, this developed into huge anxiety for me, because I became aware that I had never had these kinds of conversations with other people. No one ever gave me messages or told me about things that were going to happen for me in the future or gave me names of Loved Ones that had passed over. I did feel weird. These are now my best assets, funnily enough. My sensitivities make me ME, and I wouldn't change them for the world.

Growing up, it was easier to be alone because I didn't feel lonely like I did when I was with other people.

I soon learnt that, as long as I didn't talk about things I knew or that were going to happen, I could feel like I fitted in. Unless what I saw was life-threateningly important, I kept it to myself.

I no longer apologise, hide or justify the air I breathe. Nor should you!

I realise I have been blessed with a Gift and now, finally, through this beautiful Spiritual Awakening, as hard as it might have been, I am finally surrounded by other beautiful 6s and we are all connected by energy and Love. We are all just walking each other Home.

Being Wired has always been a struggle for me in my human life because I saw it was a struggle for those living around me.

Deep inside of me, in my Soul, I always knew that I was okay. My Gift itself has never been a struggle for me, but sometimes the things I've known, seen or experienced on a Psychic level have hurt me.

It wasn't just being called weird that upset me – it was that people chose to avoid me or not hang out with me. I assume that they felt something different about me and didn't like it. I'll never know, but I took those rejections personally. Thing is though, I could see right through them anyway and still liked them for who they were, even if I could see their 'reality'.

Being Psychic can lead to feelings of paranoia in your human life. It's disconcerting. People would say one thing to my face, nice enough, yet their energy and words told me otherwise – that's how I would know people were lying. At times, I tested it. I knew I wasn't a judgemental person – it was more about the feeling I got when I was with people.

It was always about energy, and I always trusted it.

All these years – 10, 20, 30, 35 years – I thought there was something wrong with me when it was really that people didn't understand what being Psychic was. I guess it was my energy they were reacting to. I've been told that I give off an aura of being able to see straight through people, which I can. But hey, I'm a human first and I do try to encourage, develop, love and cherish the relationships I have in my life. I try very hard to be a good friend. If I choose you as a friend, it's because I trust and love you and that you trust and love me too.

I have many people that I feel this way about, and they feel this way about me. We accept each other for who we are and how we feel with each other. We trust our friendships and we do not take them for granted – that's what 6s do.

I have thanked my connection many, many times for showing me insight into another's behaviours and lies that, at the time, I couldn't understand with my mind. My Wiredness has given me many timely warnings about roads not to drive down, people not to trust, and places to hide my savings safely because the house would be broken into. But best of all is knowing where I'm needed, when and by whom. As I look back over my life, I can very clearly see it has been a series of what I call 'Angel Assignments.'

It's this part of my 6th sense that I love the most. Whenever I am needed by the universe and my Team to be in a certain place at a certain time, I am given the most amazing resources of energy, Unconditional Love, insight, time, patience, understanding and messages. It's at these times that I truly feel I vacate my body and an Angel moves in.

I accept that it is my Soul's purpose to be here in this lifetime to help people through this period of Awakening. I went through something similar in the '80s and '90s and have been taught and shown so much by my Team in the years since. I now stretch out my hand and pull you close to help you feel safe and understood.

A funny thing in recent years is that those who once kept their distance from me are now reaching out to have sessions with me. I find that to be aMAZing.

To me, it's like so many have been climbing to the top of the highest mountain on their hands and knees and now feel completely lost and don't know which way to go. In extreme conditions, metaphorically speaking, I've helped them over the last few obstacles, showing them the way, so they too can stand triumphantly at the top, seeing the 360-degree view with an awestruck, humble clarity, and an overwhelming feeling of abundant Unconditional Love. To watch the Love, realisation, awareness and understanding unfold is for me just like a parent watching their child walk for the first time.

Each of us learns to walk for the first time with just a hand to guide us. Awakening spiritually can be like that too.

One day, you will look back and realise that you can't remember not being awake. If you do remember the time before Awakening, there's a good chance you will experience tinges of grief, remorse and sadness at having hurt people, including yourself.

Please forgive yourself for not knowing the difference until now. Be kind to yourself always. Your Soul is VERY forgiving. Trust me, my Soul has had to be too!

But hey, wasn't that the idea all along? To learn and grow? As I always say, we keep growing until all our fingers are the same length. Go on, check! You know you want to!

However, one thing is certain – you will never, ever forget your own Spiritual Awakening, the actual time when you first felt, saw, heard and experienced this connection for yourself. It was also when you saw and accepted yourself for who you truly are and were suddenly no longer Weird.

It's like graduating from university – you've worked very hard for years, studying, learning lessons and being tested. In life, we get tested and learn lessons. You don't give yourself a hard time for graduating university … in fact, you feel relieved! Awakening spiritually is the same. Your life just magically clicks into place … not without hard work though, mind you! Nothing for nothing.

For the first time, I now find my life filled with more friends of a compatible energy level than I've ever had before. I am no longer alone because of Opa's lesson to me about 5s and 6s all those years ago! We Wired ones are now in the majority, and the sceptics and naysayers are in the minority.

'Woo hoo' is all I can say!

I hope you are still with me! You may need to put this book down and pick it up at a later stage if the information is hard to take in, as you might not be ready to absorb it yet. Just let yourself be guided by your Soul. It will know what it wants to read and gravitate towards it.

Opa just gave me a funny thought that I'd like to share, 'The information in this book was actually written many lifetimes ago. Only now does it need to be shared.' Thanks, Opa.

I am WIRED and I am proud. Wired is the new normal. It's now okay to be me! It's also okay to be you. In fact, it's preferred. I am a wayshower, showing you the way. You will then show someone else the way, and that's how the ripple effect works. We all get to take a turn at some point in our incarnations.

I am proud of myself, and I am proud of you too! More than likely, if you are reading this book, you have come through your own Dark Night of the Soul, loved and lost and survived. You are a warrior.

Only those who embrace their 6yness will understand what it's like to crawl up that proverbial (feel free to add a stronger word here!) mountain called Life, on our hands and knees in all types of weather, to now stand at the top, triumphant in our relentless pursuit of a feeling … the knowing that we are WIRED not WEIRD! Weird is the new normal! As Souls, we are hard WIRED to wake up to realise and finally embrace who we truly are and our Soul's purpose.

I have also *had* to go through horrible trauma so that I can help you through your journey. I'm sure you can relate to this sentence! You are not alone – you never were.

Your Awakening and Dark Night of the Soul help you cross your own barriers to understand and carefully unwrap and discover your Gifts and Soul purpose in this life and embrace the associated responsibilities.

I have to tell you this funny story. When I returned to Victor Harbor after my 14 month period of travelling in my caravan and sailing in the beautiful Port Stephens area to help me overcome my grief, I found a new supermarket had opened. One evening, I went to check it out. The local busybody pushed her trolley over to me and said, 'Are you new around here? I haven't seen you before.' I politely replied that I had just returned from a 14 month caravan journey and was building a house here. Her reply was, 'Oh you won't get a job here. What will you do?' I had actually been headhunted to return to SA with a job offer, but I didn't tell her that … why should I? I replied, 'I'm a professional Psychic and author.' In response, she crossed her arms across her face and her legs and seriously said, 'No! Don't read me!' I laughed and said, 'Don't worry, I've already read you and you are not that interesting. Bye!'

As I pushed my trolley away to get more groceries, I heard her calling after me, 'What do you mean, I'm not that interesting? I AM interesting!'

See ya later, lady! Another 5! They're everywhere!

I have no idea what people think I see, or why they think I would be remotely interested in randomly reading them. Most of the time they are as boring as TV commercials that I use my remote control to avoid. I don't watch shit on TV ... I won't watch it in real life either.

I thank my Team every day for their teaching around 5s and 6s. I hope it helps you too.

By the way – if I ask 'How are you?', it's because I care ... not because I see something that you can't!

I love dogs more than people!

'I love dogs more than people,' my dear dad announced one day. I was shocked!

'You can't say that, Dad. We are Spiritual people, and that's such a judgemental comment!'

Dad stuck by his comment and told me that dogs have never let him down.

Now I understand what he meant. Mum always said Dad and I were more alike than I knew. But he was the last person I wanted to be like when I was growing up, and I took it as an insult every time she said it.

I think this may have been my dad's way of referring to people as 5s and 6s! Dad saw dogs and animals as 6s.

Dad, I hate to admit it, but you were right, and I understand now. I really do.

Dogs Love Unconditionally and fill all the places in your heart that people can't. If Dad's coming back, I'm sure he will be a dog.

Me too, actually! I've always wanted a tail – that way people will know exactly where they stand with me!

A Christmas Angel says hi

It was the day after my dear mum's funeral. I was in Strathalbyn to undertake further volunteer firefighter training. My friend and I had decided to spend the night there and walk to the training centre the next afternoon. Unfortunately, we had timed it badly as the local Christmas parade was streaming down the streets exactly where we wanted to cross!

It was a very long parade!

Suddenly, a little 'cherub' broke away from the main group. She was probably six years old, and a 6 by nature.

As soon as she saw me, we locked eyes. She kept walking in the parade, all the while looking over at me. She then broke away and ran up to me, giving me the biggest, warmest hug I have ever received from a stranger! I'll never forget it. 'Thank you for seeing me!' she said and ran back to the parade.

My friend said to me, 'If I hadn't seen that for myself, I wouldn't have believed it. You really do have something special, Marion, don't you?'

I just smiled with tears in my eyes and hugged myself. Was my mum behind this? Quite possibly – she had always loved the Christmas parade as it brought out the child in her. Maybe this was her first reconnection with me to let me know she had made it 'Home' safely. I'd like to think so.

I looked back at the parade, wanting to wave to the little Angel again, but I couldn't see her anywhere.

Was she even real?

What it's like to give people Readings and guidance

The first thing I would like to say is that I wish I could just download the visions I receive in your Readings onto a USB stick or my computer so that I could email it to you. It would save us both so much time and worrying about how to interpret the images shown to me during your session.

I'll explain it this way – if I asked you about your favourite movie, you may get a picture in your mind, or maybe even the movie itself! I would then ask you to tell me about it, and you would go ahead and narrate it as you saw the pictures opening in your mind.

That's what a Reading is like for me

When I look at you, I do not see you as a human body. Well, I do, but not for reading purposes. I see the whole movie that is You. I see the 'characters' in your movie – I see the script, the highs and the lows. I also see the Soul Contracts. Before you arrive, I connect with my Team and ask them for permission to read for you. I also ask them to bring forward any characters from your 'movie', your Soul Contracts and your Soul Family. I am then able to 'see' your life in full Technicolor vision. This is all then shown to me as a slideshow. I will also give you the names of anyone who comes through for you. I always take notes of each vision as I see it.

Often, I will mention something to you, and you will either embrace it or dismiss it. If you embrace it, we then chat about it. If you dismiss it, my Team and I move on. Nonetheless, we will give you everything we see, and I'll give you a copy of any notes at the end.

When you book in for a session, I will know straight away whether I am the right person for your Reading or not. If I am, I set up a time. I will also ask you to consider any questions you would like to ask and any issues you would like to chat about. I explain it like this:

> Let's say you are driving down the road and you drive past a supermarket. You quickly pull over because you know you need milk. You park the car, rush in and come out with chips, chocolate and ice cream but alas no milk! Milk was your priority. If you had written yourself a shopping list with milk on it, you would have come out with milk too! Right?

By bringing your questions, issues and anything else to your session, it means you have taken responsibility for them and are prepared for any guidance that comes through for you. Time goes very quickly during Readings and if we address your priorities first, then everything else will just follow. Sessions offer insight, clarification, direction, confirmation and guidance on both a Psychic and a Spiritual level.

If you are hoping for contact with a Loved One, please 'talk' to them before our session and invite them to come through. My Team and I work on this before you arrive, but we have no idea who will come through for you! Opa B is my Gatekeeper, and he ensures that the riffraff are kept away! If someone comes through for you, they must present with the name you knew them by in their lifetime with you.

We won't say anything like, 'I have a male here; he has grey hair and smells like cigarette smoke' or 'I have a grandmother figure here, and she loved roses!' To us, that is way too general and could apply to pretty much anyone. It may not even be real.

With a name, the connection is unmistakable and real. It will move you to tears ... me too, most of the time. You may not get what you expect, but you will get what you need. Connections like these are incredibly important and, most of the time, part of their Soul Contract with you. Honesty is the Spiritual language spoken so that healing can take place on both sides of the veil.

When someone comes for a session, I ask them to leave their human self at the door while we communicate Soul to Soul in Soul language. It's a beautiful energy to work with, and you will feel it too. My Team is happy to work on a Psychic level, however they are happiest when sharing their Spiritual teachings and wisdom. This is because, by helping us, they are helping themselves grow too.

To be honest, I prefer working on the Spiritual or Soul level. After all, if you look at life through the eyes of your Soul, recognising your Soul Contracts and who is who in your zoo, your life will unfold beautifully in front of you, thus negating the need to even have a Psychic Reading.

Opa would like me to share a few things here. He is sharing because there are more awakened Souls at this point in time than ever before. This makes it vitally important that, if your Loved One is getting ready to 'go Home' or pass away, you make an agreement about what Sign they will show you when they reach out to you. This will mean you have no doubt it is them when they show themselves to you.

Because of this agreement, your Loved Ones will be more comfortable coming to you as you will welcome them with knowing Love and they won't need a Medium to bring you through. This way, there is no doubt for you at all.

Note: Many Loved Ones prefer to come through directly to you rather than me as a stranger. This book has been written to help you keep in contact with your Loved Ones yourself. I also offer personal one-on-one sessions to help you 'hear' and 'know' when your Loved Ones reach out to you.

Opa also shares that if you are going to ask for Signs from your Guides, please specify a timeframe and what you would like to see as your Sign from them, then make sure that you look for it. Opa said that Guides get really frustrated when people ask for Signs and then don't look for them. This is why seeing a number sequence, such as 11:11, 2:22 or 4:44, is significant, because if you see these numbers, you know that you have just missed a personal message from your Loved Ones or Guides. So, if you are going to ask, specify a timeframe so that you do not miss their efforts.

Our Soul is energy regardless of whether we are in human form or in Soul form. Remember always that we have died many times and have been born again many times as well. This energy is the essence of who we are. This energy knows no limitations or boundaries.

It IS us.

It IS REAL! Nothing is *more* real.

We cannot kill our Soul; however, we can choose not to listen to it, and many do. But why would you?

Psychic Medium vs Soul Clinician

In high school, I read the book *Voices in my Ear* by Doris Stokes from cover to cover many times. It was the only book of its type in the library at that time. Doris was a renowned Psychic Medium in England in the 1980s. When I first started doing public Readings in 1997 in Perth, the TV shows *Touched by an Angel* and *Highway to Heaven* were my visual Soul food, and suddenly my life made sense. In *Touched by an Angel*, the apprentice Earth Angel, Monica, was constantly being tested and placed exactly where she was needed at exactly the right time. Monica made my life feel normal, and it began to make sense as to why I would see visions of the circumstances around people who came for a session. I would often 'test' myself and describe these circumstances to people, and they confirmed them as accurate. Interesting! In this way, I discovered the difference between a 'thought' and a 'knowing', and this is a practice that I share today to help people 'see and hear' for themselves.

Now, I've never considered myself a Doris or a Monica; however, after thousands of Readings (small, medium and large), I know there IS more to life, and my Team have proved that to me time and again. I never believed in my Gift as a Gift and certainly never charged anyone for it during the first 20 years I shared it. Now I charge for my time only, and it's been the same price for over 10 years.

I say 'I never believed in my Gift as a Gift' because I never had to prove it to anyone, it was just one of my 6 senses. I trusted it without question just as I trusted my eyes to see, ears to hear, nose to smell, mouth to talk and hands to heal and touch. As we all had eyes, ears, noses, mouths and hands, I figured we were all the same.

Doubt only filled my mind once others heard about what I did and wanted to 'test' me out or didn't believe me. Them asking that felt weird as I never asked them to prove themselves to me. Now, I no longer feel the need to prove myself to people. My Team and the universe know what I do, just as your Team and your universe know what you do too!

The other thing for me is that I am fully aware of being watched by my Team. However, particularly when doing sessions, you will see me talk to them. They sit up to my right. We communicate telepathically during your session; the whole time I am with you, I am also talking to them. They often give me the answers to your questions before you have even asked them. You may sit there thinking that I am not 'doing or saying' much, but that's because I'm listening and interpreting their visions, working out the messages and what you really need to hear or not hear at that point in time.

During your session, I am either shown a movie or slideshow of your life and my Team narrate it to me. As a picture tells a thousand words, I need to interpret each 'vision' quickly and note down the essential messages within that vision.

They will communicate messages to me to help you on your Spiritual path here in your human incarnation. These messages may or may not include timeframes. Of course, your life is your own and you have your own free will. However, you will 'know' when a message is true for you because you will undeniably 'feel' it. It's moving and beautiful for me to watch and for you to feel.

In these 'visions,' I may be 'shown' Loved Ones that have either gone Home or are still significant in your life now. Loved Ones that have gone Home sometimes only get one or two chances to come through. When they do, their messages are always with their name (from their last incarnation with you) and with Love. There is generally healing felt on both sides. It is a miracle to witness, to be honest. I will be forever in awe of the power of Spirit.

If they 'show' me visions of significant 'Loved Ones' who are still alive, it will be because there are lessons involved. They always give me the 'names' of these Loved Ones, and I/we will guide you through these lessons that many of you have postponed. I/we will hold your hand and your heart, because honestly there is nothing more REAL than a session like this.

Sessions also offer insight, direction, clarity, confirmation and guidance on a Psychic or 'seeing into the future' level. Once again, there is still free will and, just like if you were to drive to Darwin, there would be many routes that you could travel – but they all take you to the same place!

Often, we will show you what is planned for you in this lifetime. It is still up to you how you choose to get there, but you will end up in your pre-determined and pre-destined place in the end. Guidance will be given as to your best route of travel, but remember that we are all free to practice free will.

At times, sessions may also feel like a counselling session, except we don't counsel your mind and brain, we counsel your Soul. After all, that's where life IS real. I/we work on a Soul level.

I've never liked the title of Psychic/Medium. Personally, I prefer 'Soul Coach or Psychic postie.' I just deliver messages long distance, and I am good at delivering them, not 'medium' at it!

If the visions are too fast, I ask my Team to slow them down so that I can instead write the messages through automatic writing. This way, you get to read and re-read them. During Covid, my Team shared so much with me. I'm really not sure how many A4 notebooks I filled. I spent hours talking to them about the new world coming and the hopes and dreams for all of you held by the universe.

My Team shared my Soul Contract with me during Covid. They asked me to embrace this, my last lifetime, as all those lessons I had put off learning, finally need to be learnt (which explains why it's been so disastrous and hard to endure as a human!).

They told me that my Gift of bringing through Loved Ones will go to the background now as others are waking up and are ready to talk to their own Loved Ones themselves. They said this was best for everyone. They explained that many people 'go Home' with Spiritual awareness that life does continue, and that this lifetime is an illusion. It is just our classroom.

More than ever before, Earth Angels walk amongst us. They are always in the right place at the right time. They say and do exactly what you need at the right point in time. Some are never seen again. They float among us weaving their magic, encouraging you to do the same. You see, that's because the universe knows exactly what is needed at this point for humanity, and its magic, nurturing and Unconditional Love that changes lives.

Any Loved Ones that come through during Readings to provide confirmation and Love are always an unexpected surprise, one that fills the room with light and incredible warm, Unconditional Love.

I Love my Gift, and I love sharing it with you.

Is it a bird? Is it a plane? No, it's Adrian

This story happened a few years ago while I was travelling. I had been asked by Vanessa to do a Reading for her. Vanessa's husband, Adrian, had died very young of cancer. She missed him terribly. Here's how our scenario played out:

Me: Vanessa, thank you for our session today. May I ask where you would like me to start looking for you?

Vanessa: Oh Maz, I'm so sad. My husband, Adrian, died just over a year ago of cancer, and I miss him so much. I've had no Signs from him. I want to know how the boys and I are going to get through this time. I have so many decisions to make, and he was the one I used to talk to. We had so many plans too. Why did this happen to us?

Ah! So many questions and very few answers this time from above the clouds!

Me: Opa, is Vanessa's husband Adrian there with you wanting to reconnect to Vanessa?

Opa: No!

Me: Opa, is there anyone there with you that would like to connect to Vanessa today?

Opa: No!

I told Vanessa what I had been given – however, me being me, I couldn't just accept 'no' as an answer. So, I got on the telepathy phone to Opa! I asked, 'May I ask if Adrian just isn't around, or if he just doesn't want to be in contact with Vanessa?' Opa responded:

Opa: Lieve meisje, please give Vanessa this message. Adrian does not want to come through someone he doesn't know. He said he would prefer and will try to make contact with Vanessa directly. Adrian said that she will know to look for willy wagtail birds because they talked about it before he died. She will understand.

Me: Vanessa, I have a message for you. It's come through my Opa. I'm not sure if it's actually from Adrian himself or one of his Guides. Apparently, you will understand the message.

I then relayed what Opa had said to me.

Vanessa: Thank you so much, Maz. That makes perfect sense to me. You would not have known that willy wagtails were our agreed Sign. I will keep a look out.

It only took a couple of weeks for Vanessa to give me a call again.

Vanessa: Maz, I'm at the beach and I'm being followed by a willy wagtail! Can you believe it? I've tried calling him to me, but he won't come near me. What should I do?

Me: Just keep trying.

A few more days went past, then she rang again.

Vanessa: Maz, I'm at the beach again! This time the willy wagtail is swooping me, but it flies away every time someone comes near me. What shall I do?

Me: Opa, what shall I do?

Opa: Go down there, it's not far!

Me: Vanessa, I'm on my way. Just keep walking. I will hide myself and watch what's going on and see if I can talk to 'him'. I'll give you any messages that come through, okay?

Vanessa: Yes please, that would be great!

When I got to the beach, I spotted Vanessa walking and could see the bird flying around her. I chatted telepathically with the bird. I asked it if it could tell me who it was and what it wanted. I got this message:

Bird: It's me, Simon. Vanessa knows who I am! Tell her it's me!

Me: Vanessa, I'm talking to the bird (I hope no one heard me)! He told me to tell you that his name is Simon, and you know him.

Vanessa: I don't know any Simon!

I spoke to Simon.

Me: She said she doesn't know anyone called Simon!

Simon: Oh, she knows me alright! Ask her to sit on the sand and stretch out her arm, and I will walk up it and nibble her ear. She likes that!

Me: Vanessa, Simon has asked me to ask you to sit on the ground and put your arm out so that he can walk up it and nibble your ear. He said you like that!

Vanessa: You are kidding me, right?

Me: Nope, that's what he said. What have you got to lose? Please try it.

So, Vanessa sat on the sand and stretched out her arm. I wouldn't have believed it if I didn't see it myself, but this black-and-white willy wagtail climbed up her arm!

Simon: Please tell her it's me, Simon. I won't hurt her – she can trust me. Tell her not to jump when I nibble her ear.

I told Vanessa everything Simon had said.

Vanessa: I still don't know any Simon!

Then something amazing happened! When the bird nibbled at Vanessa's ear, she shivered and suddenly said:

Vanessa: Oh Marion, it's Simon! Of course I know who he is! Simon is Adrian's middle name! I had told you his name was Adrian ... I'd never told you that his middle name was Simon. Why would I? When he nibbled my ear, I shivered and it reminded me of exactly how I used to shiver when he nibbled at my ear when we were being intimate ... I would cry out his middle name in ecstasy. Only I could know that.

Vanessa said she felt his 'energy' flow into her. The energy was what connected them immediately.

Vanessa: How amazing, Maz. He feels exactly the same.

Vanessa was crying now! Amazing it was indeed!

Me: Vanessa, I'll just take a couple of photos of you two together so that you can always remember this special time. He's very happy to be with you and happy that you have acknowledged him. He told me to tell you that he will come back a few more times, then he needs to get on with the rest of his Soul Journey. Enjoy this special time together. It IS real, and it IS beautiful.

Vanessa: Thank you so much, Maz! This feels so beautiful to me! I'll talk to him too. See you soon!

I took a few photos then left the two 'lovebirds' together on the beach, alone again, this time forever.

Later, when I sent the photos, Vanessa told me that they sat that way together for nearly an hour! She said it felt 'healing' for both of them!

I'm glad.

I never saw Vanessa again, and that's okay. People come into your lives for a reason, a season or a lifetime – or a visit from a tiny little bird named Simon!

Uncle Herbie for Janice

I met Janice late in 2023 in a caravan park I was staying at. Janice had asked me for a Reading a few times, and she was also reading my book *Caught Between Two Worlds*. I kept telling her that I didn't get anything around her. This happens sometimes.

I really liked Janice. She was such a warm, caring, genuine Soul and getting pretty close to being a 6. Her husband was a 6 already.

A few of us had gathered outside someone's caravan late one afternoon for a few drinks and banter. It was a lot of fun. Uncle Herbie had been in my ear several times that afternoon, and he was with us again.

Me: Hey Janice, your Uncle Herbie wants to say hi!

Janice: What the? Uncle Herbie does? I haven't thought about him for years!

Me: Well, it seems he would like to talk to you, so how about we have 'that' chat you keep asking for?

Janice got up straight away and said, 'Let's go!' So, we went to my van and had a chat. Uncle Herbie wanted her to know that he was her Guide. He also showed me that she lives with a monk – her husband! She laughed as she told me that he even wore an orange shirt to work!

Our conversation that afternoon was very enlightening and healing for Janice. She was not only a beautiful Soul, but also a beautiful person. One day, I came home to my caravan and some very wild winds. My awning had collapsed and almost gone over the roof. I ran around looking for the local guys to come and help. Janice said to me, 'Don't worry about them, I'll help. We can do this,' and off she marched. Janice took control. I felt very embarrassed that I had gone looking for a guy to help me when Janice was more than capable. I needed an extra hand, and Janice was there right when I needed her, no problems at all.

My notes to Janice's session

While the person that Janice wanted to come through in a session for her didn't, she was really pleased about her favourite uncle, Uncle Herbie! What a character he was ... I can see why she liked him! Later that evening, I asked my Team why people we don't expect come through, and those we want, don't! This was Opa's reply:

Opa: Lieve meisje, there's so much to learn, isn't there? Don't make it complicated, keep it simple! Once people come back 'Home', they review their life's lessons. They are also given the option of starting to learn to 'guide,' if they are an older Soul. They don't have to incarnate straight away – they can spend time up here with us learning the ropes, so to speak. No one in Janice's Soul Family chose to spend time guiding Janice, mostly because they are still very young Souls and are not in a position to guide. Just because a 'person' is dead or has come 'Home' doesn't mean they know how to, or want to, make contact.

Making contact could be part of a Soul Contract as well. It's also a skill they need to learn. In this case, Uncle Herbie wanted to let Janice know that just like she had been able to count on him in life, she can now too. Most of those who do make contact are members of our Soul Family. Blood family tend not to as they have their own Soul Family to reach out to if necessary.

Me: Thanks Opa. It's all so fascinating – I love learning about everything!

The 85/15 principle
– how to embrace your fully
Wired self

Here's another one of Opa's profound teachings that he has asked me to share with you. Trust me when I say that it would be far easier for me if you could hear your own Team of Guides and Loved Ones! This chapter will help you do exactly that.

A lot of our Loved Ones, bless 'em, are going Home at the end of their Soul Contracts with a great deal of Spiritual wisdom. Many have discussed what Signs they will show to their families when the time comes to make contact. Both parties agree that yes! When you see XYZ, you will know it's me and I will know it's you! Just like Adrian's willy wagtail. It's fabulous, bring it on!

The truth is, most people will still have trouble recognising and interpreting Signs and messages on their own without awareness and practice of the 85/15 principle. Why? Because your human brain is where Spiritual messages from Loved Ones and Guides lands. You are simply not used to differentiating between thoughts and messages yet. Your brain receives messages and guidance from your Guides and Loved Ones, often daily. However, your stupid brain doesn't know how to interpret these messages, so it turns them into a thought, and your very important messages go out the window.

What we now have to do is train your brain to learn the difference between a thought and a message. This is where Opa's teaching about what he calls the 85% / 15% principle comes in very handy. This is how Opa explained it to me:

> Lieve meisje, I have something to teach you that you will share with many. You may not understand, as you never had to be taught this as you always understood how to interpret our messages. When the time comes after much darkness, the world will reawaken and many will want to make contact with their Loved Ones, mostly to ask for forgiveness and share expressions of love. They won't know how to hear or make contact with them once they've gone Home because they are all stuck in their heads.
>
> What we would like to teach you, and it *will* be your Soul's purpose to share with many people, is this ...
>
> Let's use this breakdown: say 85% of what goes into your brain is a thought created by the brain, and the remaining 15% is often taken up with messages coming through from your Loved Ones that have gone Home or messages and guidance from your Guides.
>
> But because humans only have one brain and it acts like a computer for the vehicle that is your body in this incarnation, messages are often left unread. Your brain

thinks that everything that goes into it is of it. We would like you to share the difference between what a thought and a message or Spiritual guidance feels like, so that others can benefit from knowing the difference.

Approximately 85% of what goes into our brain is a thought and approximately 15% is a message from a Guide or Loved One. For some people, it may be more of a 50% split.

Opa then went on to teach me how, through telepathy, we can easily decipher the difference. The best way to start is by journalling and getting 'used' to what your Guides and/or Loved Ones' voices and/or energies feel like. This way, you will know what belongs to you and what doesn't.

Using telepathy, together, we work through exercises using colours, shapes and numbers. The actual exercise needs to be experienced through a session together rather than explained. However, once you have touched this world for yourself, you will most likely exclaim, 'Oh I've been doing and getting it all along and not realising!'

Once you realise, you will never forget it, and it will become a method of daily communication and contact with your Guides and Loved Ones.

Remembering all you've forgotten

At some point in this lifetime, you will wake up to remember where you left off in your last lifetime. Your Soul knows this. Regardless of the level that you reincarnate at, you will continue your earthly ride in this human body until your alarm goes off and you have the option to hit the snooze button again or wake up and continue your ride.

I've said it before … we are Spirits having a human experience in the material world. Therefore, most of our experience will be the

WHAT IT'S LIKE TO GIVE PEOPLE READINGS AND GUIDANCE

human kind. Think of it this way: during a year, we experience one birthday, one Easter and one Christmas. Our Spiritual experiences are much the same in that they are often incredibly special and significant but may be greatly spaced apart in time.

You may only get one significant experience a year or less – a series of Signs or serendipitous moments to guide you right when you are not looking for one. Mind you, if you are on your path, you may not experience any Spiritual moments until you stray from it. These moments will seem insignificant to you as a human, but huge as a Spiritual person. For instance:

- the sunrise that brings a wow factor to your morning
- the sunset that brings tears to your eyes as you remember a lost Loved One
- the dragonfly or butterfly (right when you needed it!)
- the phone call from the person you were just thinking about
- the new opportunity to change jobs that you had been hoping for
- the random act of kindness that leads you to meet a new significant friend in your life
- finding a $50 note in your jeans pocket right when you needed petrol in your car.

Being Spiritual is about living your best life for you, without ego or expectation, and with Unconditional Love, trust and faith that the universe really *does* have your back, regardless of where your human body is parked.

You see, it's right when you are on track that you will take your Spirituality for granted, forget about it or even become complacent. This is exactly when the universe will throw you a test, just to be sure that you are still awake and paying attention.

This is why the only response to tests is gratitude.

6s understand 5s
But 5s don't understand 6s
... and that's okay!
We all start off as young Souls
And gradually mature through each incarnation

Bullshit meter – gotta love a sceptic!

Mary was a sceptic with the biggest bullshit meter around (according to her)! A group of Adelaide Hills women had invited me to spend a day with them on their farm so I could read each of them individually in the most beautiful of surroundings. When Mary and I started our session, she began by telling me that she has the most accurate bullshit meter around Psychics. This is an excerpt of our session:

Me: Hi Mary, thank you for wanting to have a session together today.

Mary: I've got a bullshit meter that can smell bullshit a mile away, just so you know!

Mary didn't faze me at all as I already knew that Opa had some information that she would not be able to deny! I've dealt with sceptics before and I have nothing to hide, so I gave it to her straight up!

Me: That's fine with me, I'll give you what I get and see how the meter reads it ... Ben's been missing for nearly four weeks now, and you are really worried about your grandson. He had been living with you with no obvious problems at all until he went missing!

WHAT IT'S LIKE TO GIVE PEOPLE READINGS AND GUIDANCE

By the time I looked at Mary, she was sobbing.

Mary: I feel so guilty! I promised his parents that I would look after him. He's gone, and I've had no word for four weeks! Do you know where he is?

Me: No, we don't know where he is right now, but we can tell you that he is safe. He didn't want to upset you. He's just working himself out and needs to do this alone!

Mary: Can you see him? Can you describe to me what you see so that we can be sure that we are talking about the same kid?

Mary agreed that it was undeniably Ben that I saw in the visions I had been shown. Mark from my Team told me, 'Ben felt overcrowded at home and at his grandma's. While everyone wants the best for him, he just wants to be alone right now. We know where he is, and rest assured he is safe. Tell Grandma he will make contact when he is ready.' So I did. I then asked, 'How's that bullshit meter going, Mary?' She laughed.

Mary: Marion, it's off the scale, but in a really good way! You're the real deal – there's no way anyone could have told you that apart from your Team. I haven't told a Soul. The burden has been almost too much for me to bear. However, what you've told me has given me so much comfort. It will be hard for me to wait, but I also know that's the right thing for me to do. I trust you and your Team. Thank you.

Mary and I finished our session looking at other very 'bullshit free', factual information. The hug that Mary gave me at the end of our session was one of the biggest I've ever received.

Notes to Mary's Reading

Readings are *not* always about the person coming to me for a Reading. And sometimes a Soul's secrets are kept by the universe. This is for the highest good of all concerned. In this case, Mary received reassurance that her grandson was safe and also respected that he did not want to be in contact as he wanted to show his family he could work through his shit by himself! They had been telling him for ages that he needed to grow up, and he was doing it, albeit his way!

I respect that as a Reader.

Accelerating your Soul Journey – a note from my Team

My Team told me:

> During Covid, the universe was put on pause while you all took an honest, good, hard and long look at how far off your path you were. No more hitting the snooze button, you slackers, which means no more blaming others for everything that was going wrong in your life. Accept your responsibility to yourself and the universe.

> Before Covid, Soul Contracts were made that were to last one incarnation with death and rebirth in-between. Well, that's all been taking way too long, so the universe decided things needed to be sped up. Anyone alive in this lifetime has been given the opportunity to live multiple Soul Contracts rather than 'go Home' or die in-between. This is why many of you are going through such intense crises and back-to-back despair … or, rather, back-to-back opportunities to finalise lessons in your Soul Contract, both to teach and to learn.

Many of our ancestors were not strong enough emotionally and mentally during their incarnation and consequently avoided or did not complete their lessons, preferring to just go 'Home' instead. Due to the sheer strength of a 6, we have agreed, through our Soul Contracts, to take on their learning for them, clearing our Soul Family of karmic debt in this incarnation.

For many, this lifetime will be their last. All their lessons will need to be completed as they will not be returning. Instead, you will be able to choose what type of Guide you would like to be. Many of your lessons during your incarnations have prepared you for this choice.

You will know …

Soul Contracts

Through each incarnation, our Soul (that is, us!) gets tested first, then we learn the presented lesson.

In our human life, we go to school to learn the lessons first, then we get tested!

Each incarnation is just like advancing to the next year in school. The lessons and teachers change, and the tests get harder each time. My advice comes from my experience, so let me save you a heap of heartache and anxiety – just learn them the first time they are presented and your earthly life will run a lot smoother. Trust me, don't postpone them!

When we are a young Soul, sitting on or around 5 ¼ on the awareness scale, you will encounter one or two Spiritual lessons in each incarnation.

Of course, it also depends on whether you learnt the presented lessons in a previous lifetime or not, as time and time again they present themselves, as agreed through your Soul Contract. Remember that you actually 'chose' these lessons for your Soul's learning. Many Souls get stuck on the proverbial mouse wheel in these early incarnations, and for obvious reasons – everyone else is always to blame, not them!

What types of lessons do we learn in our Soul Contracts? Great question. The biggest and hardest of all the recurring lessons is

Unconditional Love. Humans have a real aversion to learning this love, and it often takes all of their lifetimes to understand it.

Many place conditions on their Love, such as 'I'll love you if you do this ...' or 'I won't love you if you do that ...'

Many place their love in the wrong places. They pour their love into material possessions, their egos, their jobs, their homes, cars and accessories. The sad thing is that this love is temporary and only lasts while the love is new and shiny.

Others use or think of sex as love.

Pure, Unconditional Love is exactly that – LOVE with no conditions attached at all.

Unconditional Love knows no boundaries or judgements. It has no expectations or desired outcomes. It simply is.

I love everyone and everything, but I do not wish to own or control them. That's love with conditions.

Your Spiritual journey is the same as your academic journey. When you started in kindergarten, you knew very little. As you moved through each year, so did your learning. At the beginning of every new school year, lessons were determined for you according to the level you were at. In preschool, your lessons were basic reading, writing and arithmetic. Once you got to high school, you were able to choose the subjects/lessons you were interested in or drawn to. You had a choice.

Our Spiritual journey is the same.

In our academic life, we learn the lessons, then we get tested.

In life, we are tested, then we learn the lessons!

Before we are born into our lifetimes, we get together with our Soul Family. We choose who our teachers are and what role they will play. For instance, prior to coming into this lifetime, I decided I really needed to learn the lessons of forgiveness (finally), Unconditional Love, trust and patience. My Soul Family, Guides and I discussed the best type of scenarios for me to learn the lessons I had chosen (this would be reality TV at its best, wouldn't it! Imagine the ratings!).

Those coming into their very first incarnation also meet with their Soul Family and Guides. They may choose either a short or long lifetime. This will depend on the number of lessons.

Please remember that Soul Contracts are the ultimate ripple effect, and that each and every one of us has a Soul Contract and a Soul Family and these are intertwined throughout each lifetime. Each of us plays a pivotal role in each other's lives and has an impact on each other. Please allow your mind to expand to how big this concept actually is. It's huge, yet so simple and oh so perfect!

The role of karma in Soul Contracts

My Team shared a karmic secret with me this year! I couldn't believe my ears.

'Delivering karma' signals the end of yours! Yay, I hear you say!

It happens to you when your Guides say. It is never a conscious choice that you make, otherwise you will create bad karma.

Delivering karma is written into your Soul Contract in your last incarnation. By this time, you will be a spiritually enlightened Soul that is fully aware of Spiritual law and has completed the majority of your lessons in this life.

You have to earn the right to deliver karma. It is a Gift bestowed on you, and often you won't even realise that you have delivered it until after the fact! Delivering karma reminds you that, for all those times you experienced pain at the hands of others and you told yourself that 'karma would get them', you now know it really does happen! For every time you wished it would happen to others, the universe kept the score and allocated the task of delivering karma to Soul Contracts.

So, if you are reading this and have been a victim of abuse of any kind, please take comfort in this section. But know that you will never be the one to deliver karma to the person that has abused you – that's not how the cycle works. That will be up to another Soul.

Please also be mindful that if you have hurt someone deliberately (which means you are not yet a 6 and not in your last incarnation) and it wasn't associated with a Spiritual lesson, then karma will be neatly delivered to you by a 6 who is in their second-to-last or last incarnation.

Recognising mirrors

Spiritually speaking, a teacher comes into our life to teach us, the student, a lesson. A teacher may be a young Soul or a 6. Anyone can agree to teach us our lesson – the only prerequisite is that they have already learnt the lesson themselves.

We agree to the roles we play in our Soul Contract and the Soul Contracts of others.

Often, we are mirrors to and of each other, and this is where life gets to be fun! When a person acts as a mirror to you, they are reflecting behaviours in the 'I' that you are in this life. However, it is the Spiritual 'You' that acknowledges what you are seeing and/or hearing then looks at the lesson then enjoys the insight and subsequent growth.

If you are going through conflict in your life, stop for a moment and reflect on what is 'really' happening. Humans that fight never consider the Soul in the dispute. Step outside of the situation and view it from your Soul's point of view. Use the other person as a mirror and look deep into them. Ask yourself, 'What behaviour is this person demonstrating to me, and what is it triggering in me?'

If the other person is pushing you away constantly, perhaps they do not feel worthy of your love. Do you feel worthy of receiving Love? Do you Love yourself? If the answer is no, then the place to start is within you, not with them. Start Loving and caring for yourself. You ARE worthy of your own Love. You realise that, don't you? Once you start loving yourself, you will notice that the behaviour in the other person that was angering you will no longer be an issue!

In this case, you were the student, and the other person was your teacher. They reflected to you what you needed to see.

When this happens, recognise it for what it is and STOP!

Parents: look in the mirror that is your child.

What do you see? What is your child showing you? They are reflecting the chaos inside your head because you are oblivious to it or ignoring it.

Sit down and invite them to sit with you. Cuddle them or ask them to cuddle you. All they want is YOU, so give YOU to them – just five or ten minutes of quality time instead of rushing around and avoiding them. Once your mind is calm and back in order, theirs will be too.

They are a reflection of you!

People in our lives are our biggest teachers; they are also our biggest students and mirrors, mirroring back to us exactly what we need to see. It's beautifully designed, isn't it?

If you have this type of insight, you are well on your way to becoming a 6 and living your best life as a Spiritual being. You are also well on your way to having learnt the most important lessons in life. Seeing your lessons through others can be a wake-up call for many. Most prefer to blame others for being inconsiderate, impatient or snappy rather than stopping and reflecting that perhaps they are the ones that are being grumpy and short tempered.

It would also pay to look at 'who is who in your zoo.' What Soul levels are you fighting with? Young Souls, that is, predominantly 5s and 5 ¼s, tend to clash with older Souls, particularly if we are a 5 ½ and above. I must admit that sometimes I feel that I'm dealing with *really* low levels Souls, I call them 2s – people who can only see things/life through their own eyes!

When I acknowledge my role as teacher in a situation, I always ask for protection and for the words to be given to me that my 'student' needs to hear in order to change their behaviour. Please remember that change is of someone's free will. We can choose to change or not. I am prepared to help anyone and everyone. However, I cannot learn their lessons for them and, if they are not prepared to help themselves, then I will walk away too. It is not your job to fix anyone. You cannot fix me, but you can offer me suggestions and/or channelled advice that I need. It will then be up to me to choose if I want to listen or to ignore the lesson altogether, and there's not a thing you can do about that.

That has been one of the biggest lessons for me when it comes to communicating with others. Just because a Soul Contract is shown to me, along with shortcuts as to how someone can help themselves, if they don't want to do it, that's their choice. It would be the same as if you recommended a restaurant to me. You can suggest menu items you really liked, but you can't choose for me, and you shouldn't be disappointed if I don't order your recommendation. Taking advice from you is exactly the same. Many people try to avoid their lessons, hoping that out of sight means out of mind. What they don't realise though is that it's only temporarily gone!

If you are unable to make sense of your human predicament, now would be a good time to look at the situation from a Soul's point of view. Who is the teacher? Who is the student? What are the lessons being taught and/or shared?

Note: As Spiritual as we can be, sometimes we just have to accept that there are people in life who just Are Souls! (*Read those last two words together as one and you'll see what I really meant to write!*) These types of people you just can't help. Not our circus, not our monkeys!

> *Take a good hard look in YOUR mirror*
>
> *before attacking someone's behaviour.*
>
> *Ask what are they showing you.*

Spiritual development

The key to developing spiritually is to learn the lessons of faith and trust first.

It's simple. Don't overdo it or try too hard, because you will only end up pushing the learning further away from you.

Consider exploring what Spirituality means for you through window shopping! Using crystals, pendulums, oracle cards, reading books, listening to podcasts, learning or receiving Reiki, meditation, automatic writing, connecting with nature, tai chi, music and journalling will all help you develop spiritually.

Please remember that your learning in this lifetime is limited to your Soul level. Put it this way, learning Soul language is a bit like learning Japanese. It's no good trying to speak fluent Japanese if you haven't even mastered the numbers, the alphabet or 'good morning'.

Another way of looking at Spiritual growth and learning is to imagine that you are a human student in grade 4 and you want to learn what a student is studying in year 12. It just wouldn't sink in, no matter how hard you tried. Spiritual learning is the same.

So, the best advice we can give you is not to rush or force any learning. Everything will happen in its own divine timing. Look at your life to date and you will see how true that statement is!

It's simple and it works. Don't complicate it by overthinking.

Dark Night of the Soul

The Dark Night of the Soul (DNS) is the pits. You WILL absolutely know when you are in it – there's no denying the pain, the torment and the torture of your mind giving up. Your DNS may come out of the blue or follow the loss of a relationship, job or material possessions. It is during this DNS that life as we know it crashes completely. We have been through so much heartache, trauma and grief that we simply no longer function or cry! We have what is humanly called a 'mental breakdown'. I/we prefer to call it a 'breakthrough!'

It's a very, very dark place indeed, so dark that many don't come out the other side. Only people who have been through it will understand. It is not depression or sadness, as they are afflictions of the mind. The DNS is much darker than that and is of your Soul. The good thing to know is that it is only temporary and that there IS light after that long, dark tunnel.

The DNS is also a complete miracle, similar to the caterpillar walking its last steps to its final resting place, wrapping itself up in a cocoon made of the finest silk (how lovely!), only to emerge up to three weeks later as one of the most beautiful creatures in the world – a butterfly! And, like the caterpillar/butterfly that gets to lead two lives in one, so do we!

I mentioned before that many Souls are choosing to live multiple incarnations in this one; as such, Soul Contracts that would normally take two or three incarnations are being agreed to, attempted and/or completed in this lifetime. Once our Soul Contract is finished, we go Home where we are subjected to our Life Review. Sometimes, however, rather than dying or going Home, we go through a DNS, which is the equivalent of dying while still alive.

It will feel like the worst time of your life. You can't find anything resembling normal, and you may feel that the only option for you is to take yourself out of this life. You may feel like you are a burden to everyone. You will feel completely miserable and cannot stand your own company. You realise that the monsters inside your head are you! One of the hardest parts about the DNS is that it's not obvious to anyone else because it's all happening inside of your head. You even find yourself saying things like 'I'd rather have cancer because then people could feel sorry for me.' That's what I used to say. People understood cancer, but no one understood what they couldn't see in me because I looked 'normal' on the outside.

As much as I wanted to stay in bed, wrapped up in my cocoon, I didn't dare as I thought I would never get out of it again. I'm sure that there are many, too many, of you in fact who can relate to this. Hopefully, you will now understand more about what is happening or has happened to you. I was single and alone at the time, living in a place I didn't want to be after losing my life as I knew it in Perth. No one cared. I was the most alone I had ever been in my life.

I will spare you the details of my suicide attempt out of respect to my kids and for the simple fact of the energy it would take for me to go back into that headspace. What I can say is that I can still absolutely justify my attempts to this day. I felt like a complete burden and waste of space and was convinced life would be better off without me in it.

I also see no benefit in going over the details when I would rather tell you how I got over it with the help of Opa and my

Team. It seems that they had other ideas for me and my life in this incarnation!

I will share my personal story about my Dark Night of the Soul.

I had been unhappily married for many years. I loved being a mum, but Perth, where I lived, had never felt like home for me. After my husband asked me for a divorce in April 2015, I could not wait to get out of Perth. Yes, I had friends there, and yes, I had a job there, and yes, I had a business there and it was where my kids lived. But it was not where my heart and Soul called home. For way too long, I had felt a shadow of myself. I hadn't wanted to go to Perth when my husband first asked me, but I went where he wanted me to go. It was an adventure, after all.

Prior to my divorce, my beautiful son told me that he felt it was time for me to reconcile with my parents as he felt they didn't have much longer to live. We had been estranged for seven years and had lessons outstanding that we had both walked away from. My son was right. He flew from Sydney and I flew from Perth, and we met in Adelaide and drove to my parents' home in Clayton Bay. That was another of the hardest days in my life. The humble pie was choking me.

Moving back to SA and to my parents, who had not been in my life for seven years, was incredibly hard. I rented a house nearby, then the grief hit. Suddenly I was no longer a wife, a mum, an employee or a business owner – I was now a divorcee with no job, no home and no friends in SA. I felt completely alone. My parents were consumed with their health issues, and I was unable to grieve for myself around them. I would arrive in their driveway, walk into their house and suddenly be thrust back into being a daughter looking after my parents.

Have you ever lived somewhere where you felt trapped … not just by the people you live with but by the area as well? It's hard to explain, but that's how it was for me for way too long. I wasn't strong back then like I am now.

I did this for three years as their health deteriorated. During this time, I reconnected with an old boyfriend who I had grown up with in the area. His marriage had failed as well, and we felt that it was destiny that we were back together as we had been a couple when we were 16 years old. He asked me to marry him, but I couldn't answer him. There was something about him I didn't trust, but I couldn't put my finger on it. Actually … that's not true. I *could* put my finger on it, but when I asked him about it, he denied it. This caused me to doubt my own intuition and the visions being shown to me by my Team, which caused me a lot of grief.

I was really struggling at this time emotionally. I used to cry every day. I felt like a complete burden to everyone. Everyone had a life of their own.

I had always wanted to live and sail on the coast of New South Wales. The pull of all those little towns, bays and sailing clubs was a life I yearned for every day for years. Yet here I was in South Australia.

We were Spiritual people, and at times this could be incredibly hard because of the human element. We were Dutch, and we were stubborn. This is how I discovered it was time to deal with the agreed-to lessons in our Soul Contracts. They were the lessons of tolerance, forgiveness and Unconditional Love.

You know how you tend to put off lessons if they are too hard? Well, I'd done that, and now it was time to learn them once and for all … and YES! putting off lessons does indeed make them come back bigger and harder to learn – I can attest to that.

By now, I had truly accepted my ability to talk to Spirit and Loved Ones that had gone Home. I also knew that I didn't want either of my parents coming back to haunt and taunt me once they had passed, because I knew they would! I knew that could potentially end up in a 24/7 situation of seeing them and knowing they could see me, and I didn't want that. The best option available to me was to understand the role they played in my life and then thank them 'FOR-GIVING' me the opportunity to learn compassion and Unconditional Love.

It was a quick thank you of forgiveness between Dad and I, one that I had put off all my life ... It was over and done with in a minute flat! We both knew we had to face the lesson as Dad was losing time.

It's stupid, isn't it, how we avoid these lessons and aggravate ourselves about them during our life? We often waste years of emotion, tears and wrinkles avoiding relationships and lessons, when all we had to do was acknowledge them, thank them for their role, then wish them on their way. Done.

Is there someone in your life that you need to forgive? Be honest with yourself (and also them!), preferably while they are still alive. It's such an important part of your Spiritual growth. I will share my secret to forgiveness in a later chapter. It's helped many and I know it will help and give you comfort too.

Over the years, I had tried coming to terms with immeasurable loss, trauma and grief. However, as I also didn't have a job, money or a house and was living in a completely different state to the one I wanted to be in, I was miserable and tried to take my own life. The decision ended up being taken out of my hands.

Suicide was, in fact, the easy option.

Continuing to live was the hard option.

People told me at the time that there was obviously a reason for the Spiritual intervention. I believe that is about me helping you and others, through Readings, to live your best lives.

I believe it is part of my Soul Contract to inspire others to live, REALLY LIVE, their lives like I had to live, 'really live.' Of course it doesn't have to be the same way, but so many people are just living a life of slow suicide. Some think that they are invincible and will deal with their 'shit' ONE DAY! Well, guess what, reader? That day is TODAY!

In July 2018, I left Victor Harbor towing my 22-foot caravan. I cried every day. I was miserable. As I drove through a small town in New South Wales, I told Opa that I wanted to turn around and give up. Opa said 'No! Keep persevering. Persevere, we will always help you.'

So, I kept driving down the Newell Highway. I entered the town of West Wyalong when Opa said to me, 'Turn right in three streets from now!' I knew from experience that, when Opa asks me to do something, I should do it. I drove past one street, then the next and, at the third street, I turned right. Opa told me to pull over, get out and walk back to the corner. Once I got to the corner of the street and the highway, I said, 'Okay, what am I doing here?'

Opa said, 'Look up at the street sign!'

No way! I looked up and saw 'Perseverance St'. Located in West Wyalong, New South Wales.

I burst into both tears AND a smile at the same time! How could I ever doubt Opa? I can't, I just can't! I can, however, doubt myself!

So, I got back in the car, turned on my favourite music and started singing along.

It wasn't that far down the track when Opa again asked me to stop – this time on Albert Street in Forbes, New South Wales – then park and get out for a walk. Again, Opa stopped me at a corner. This time, it was the corner of Albert and Gap Street. It was here that he said to me, 'You are just taking a GAP year, lighten up and enjoy yourself. People are envious of you and here you are just thinking about how sad and lonely you are! You have us!'

He was right, of course.

I knew to trust Opa about these kinds of directions. Let me share a couple of other times he has also been 100% spot on with instructions, then I'll get right back on track. I share these with you so that you may understand my life better and in turn understand your life better and learn how to receive your own Signs.

In 2016, while living in Clayton Bay, South Australia, near my mum and dad, I thought it would be better if I moved to Victor Harbor as that's where I would potentially find a job, new friends and a new life. It was a Tuesday afternoon, and I was running late on my way to view a rental property. Opa interrupted my driving and said, 'Lieve meisje, turn the car around, turn left at the end of the street, then at the second right, turn right.'

'Opa,' I said, 'I'll run late for the 15-minute open home on the rental, and I really want to get the house!' Opa repeated the instructions. As I turned right into the street, Opa said, 'Not so fast! Slowly.' Then he said, 'STOP!' So, I stopped. After all, Opa always knows best! 'What am I doing here, Opa?' I asked. 'Get out of the car, cross the road and walk up the back of the block of land here.' So, I did. It was a really steep block, and the weeds were hip high! I wondered what I would do if I was bitten by a snake. 'Go right up the top,' said Opa.

So, I did.

'Turn around,' said Opa.

I was about to ask Opa what I was doing on the vacant block of land when I turned around and was greeted with the most beautiful view of Victor Harbor. The view of the ocean from the Bluff past Granite Island and around to Port Elliot was fantastic.

'Yeah, so?' I asked.

'Walk to the bottom of the block again.' I did, until Opa said, 'Stop! Look to your right at knee height.'

I did, and what did I see? A 'For Sale' sign. My first comment to Opa was, 'I can't afford this – it's right in town and the view is incredible! But I don't want to build a house!'

'Ring the agent!'

So, I did.

Turns out that the block of land was in my budget. I went in and signed on the dotted line ten minutes later.

Today, I am the proud owner of the beautiful white house I had often seen in my dreams while living in Perth. It seems it was beautifully manifested the day I trusted Opa and found the block. Oh, and I missed out on the rental house that I had been on my way to, and that was okay.

The moral of this story is to never, ever give up on your dreams and know that, if your dreams are in your best interest, your Guides are more than happy to guide you to them.

Yes, I know I've digressed again. It's because my Team want the story to go in this direction. It's about us giving you the confidence in yourself to ask and look for and believe in Signs shown to you by Spirit.

I have needed to share my stories with you because it shows you how faith in my Team works for me. They have helped me so many times, and I trust them with my life. This is all you need to do too! Trust, then believe.

Four months into my caravan trip, I was still crying every day, despite the Signs and divine help I was receiving. I was, after all, the one living as the human in this incarnation.

Very early one morning, while camping in a caravan park at Anna Bay, Opa woke me and said, 'Lieve meisje, no one is coming to rescue you, you need to rescue yourself!'

I asked him, 'But Opa, how? I can't turn my brain off, it has a mind of its own!'

He told me, 'We are going to start connecting people to you. You are to help them. Some can be done through paid Readings, and some will be your Gift to them. You will know which is which. You will only heal by helping others help themselves. As for your thoughts, you need to treat them like people and make appointments with them.' (I have included Opa's advice about making appointments with your thoughts in the section about worrying!) This was around the time that I started doing my free Readings 'live' on Facebook on Thursday nights. The messages that came through helped so many people, and Opa was right – helping them helped me.

There's nothing I can really say about my Dark Night of the Soul except that I never, ever want to go through it again. I'm pretty sure I've had a few practice runs throughout my life, but this was the worst. Every single cell in my body was in pain. I couldn't eat, and even breathing hurt. I was numb for months. I didn't want to live, but I couldn't come up with a safe way to take my life without Opa knowing. I felt so incredibly alone. I did what I had to do to function. I knew that if I went to bed, I would never get up again, and I just couldn't imagine how my kids would deal with me on the other side of the country and all my belongings in storage, so I continued to breathe. One breath at a time.

Maybe you can relate to this yourself, although I hope you actually can't!

I remember, before I left Victor Harbor the first time, that a lady I was working with expressed her extreme jealousy of my plans to travel. She was nasty about it, and I told her so. I told her that she needed to be jealous of all the shit I had been through, the trauma, the grief, the loss and the sadness, and not just the trip. Without the shit, I would not have gone away. I would have loved to be able to turn back the hands of time and try my old life out again. Ah! Hindsight! I'm sure you've met her.

She didn't understand, and we stopped being friends. She would never understand as she was a young Soul, a 5, and had never experienced such levels of loss.

Upon reflection, it's clear to me now that my caravan was my cocoon! I felt safe there. I travelled non-stop, towing my cocoon behind me till I reached Port Stephens, a place I had wanted to sail and live in for years. It was a dream. Once I settled, I joined the local sailing club as being on water, on a yacht, was my healing, my safe place. I was blessed to sail on a gorgeous yacht with a lively crew that remain my dear friends today. I lived for my sailing. It was my connection to my Spirit family.

As time went on, I found myself healing through each Reading I gave. I threw myself right into it. Many people were contacting me for help. Many had read my book, in all states of Australia and even Canada, America and Greece. I gave most of the sessions as a Gift. I felt that, if I did that, it would help to get rid of my bad karma.

Weeks passed and I found myself starting to smile again. Readings and sailing on beautiful Nelson Bay was all I needed. I felt like I could fly. I realised that I had grown through what I had gone through and morphed into a butterfly. Slowly, I trusted my new wings and stayed in the area for 12 months with a few side trips into Queensland.

At the point of writing this book, I have travelled 32,186 kilometres on my own while towing my caravan.

I then returned to Victor Harbor to build my beautiful home on 'that' block of land.

The DNS for children

It is becoming increasingly common for children to go through their own Dark Night of the Soul. As parents, we think that, because they are so young, their tantrums and anger are behavioural issues. Maybe they are at times, however, please consider the Soul that is 'them'.

These days, most kids being reincarnated are Old Souls, many with big lessons to both teach and learn.

Opa says:

> Let's look at it this way ... your child, potentially an Old Soul or a 6, is born into a family of young Souls ... 5s. From a very young age, these kids/Souls can see the lessons that their parents/siblings are contracted to learn in this lifetime. They also see that their family are 'choosing' not to accept

and/or undertake these lessons, preferring to avoid them. As an Old Soul, this child knows firsthand the benefits of learning lessons the first time they come around. They know how much bigger/worse lessons can get if they're not undertaken.

These Old Souls are still, in fact, human beings and, as such, can become easily affected by human feelings and frustrations. Their feelings and frustrations can be negative and thus quite destructive.

If you have an Old Soul child, then they are in your life to teach *you* patience and tolerance. My advice is to realise this, get this lesson learnt, then get on with having a great life with your child.

It's when our '6y' children are ignored spiritually that they are capable of spiralling into a Dark Night of the Soul. Trust me, this is worse for you as a parent as it will lead to your own DNS too.

You may be the parent, we acknowledge that, but these children are *your* teachers!

The nervous breakdown vs DNS – your breakthrough to you!

Years ago, when people became totally overwhelmed by the pressures of trying to fit into a 'normal', everyday life, they often became exhausted and experienced a nervous breakdown. Sound familiar? The feeling of overwhelming fatigue, sheer exhaustion and deep, dark depression has driven many to take their own lives.

If only they had been counselled through this as a 'breakthrough'! How many people would have been saved?

So, what do we want you to know? We want you to know that you WILL be okay and that you WILL get through this. You WON'T be who you were before, but you WILL be a much more grounded and confident human to navigate this illusion we call life.

The biggest issue around the DNS is realising and coming to terms with the fact that your life until this breaking point has been a complete illusion. Nothing will seem real to you anymore, because it isn't. This can be a scary realisation and will test your sanity. Please know that this is normal.

To simplify this with a 'nice' analogy, let's look again at the caterpillar.

Do you think the caterpillar would agree to being wrapped up in a cocoon if it knew it would have to give up having legs? How overwhelming would that be to the poor little caterpillar? It's always had legs, lots of them, and has always been close to the ground. All this time, it's trusted its legs. The caterpillar was grateful to get around in its little area – knowing it would take ages to get anywhere, so it stayed close to home and never aspired to be more, let alone fly.

The air has always been something it has breathed – one could not even begin to imagine flying. It's never had wings and would have no idea how or where to start using them. Can you relate to the caterpillar? I sure can.

A caterpillar can't choose to *not* go through this process of change. Do you think if the caterpillar could see the benefits of having magnificent wings, seeing new things and travelling to places it had never even thought of, that it would rush to get wrapped up? I sure would.

So the caterpillar surrenders and enters its cocoon where it stays, not moving, day and night for three weeks. The caterpillar had no idea what would happen as the silk threads started to wrap around it. The caterpillar had no more strength or willpower to fight and then came a knowing to surrender to the process.

Slowly, the silk threads protecting the caterpillar through the period of transition fall away. It tries to walk but falls to the ground. Then, after a few more attempts, something magical happens – rather than falling, it finds itself flying. It is exhilarating! Now able to go wherever it wants, whenever it wants, in much less time than it would take with legs – the old way.

The caterpillar thought it had experienced freedom before, but this newfound freedom was more amazing than the life it had left behind.

Your DNS is a breakthrough from the old you to the new you. See it as a bridge – a bridge to a new you, a new way of life. It's about discarding what isn't working anymore. It's about rebuilding the true, genuine, authentic, new you. The *real* you. You ARE emerging, just like the butterfly with your very own wings.

If you are going through your own DNS, wrap yourself up in some beautiful silk threads, also known as comfy bed sheets, and disengage from life as you know it for a minimum of three weeks, just like the caterpillar. Trust that the universe, with its lifetimes of experience in the DNS, knows exactly what it's doing and what's best for your highest good.

Watch the magic happen. They are not shoulder blades on your back, but rather the beginning of your very own wings. You too are destined to FLY!

Be careful what you ask for!

Amy owned the book shop in a gorgeous coastal country town near Byron Bay in New South Wales. If you haven't been, you must go!

I hadn't planned to call into this little village, but Opa had other plans for me. This is my recollection of that day in March 2019...

I was driving through the beautiful countryside on my way to a bookstore in Byron Bay to drop off complimentary copies of my first book *Caught Between Two Worlds*. I had no intention of stopping anywhere on the way because I had to be back in Kyogle that night, an hour and a half away from Byron. Opa and I always talk while I drive. It's the only time he really has me as a captive audience!

Opa: Lieve meisje, please turn right at the upcoming road sign directing traffic towards the coast.

Me: And do what there?

Opa didn't answer, but I followed his directions.

Opa: See that car park up there next to the café? Park in there, please. Then head back down the street, walk past the café and the shoe shop, and go into the bookshop! Trust me!

I did as Opa instructed me, as I do! I wasn't sure what was going to greet me once I got in the bookshop, and I wasn't sure what my 'assignment' was here.
    Then I saw Amy. She had her head buried in her hands at the register. She was sobbing. I said to her, 'Oh, looks like I'm just in time. Do you need someone to talk to or give you a hug?'
    Amy said, 'I'll take the hug first, then the chat.' We hugged, then Amy said, 'I just asked for an Angel, and you walked in my door!'

Me: Oh, I love that you believe in and called for an Angel. I'm happy to be your Angel! Have you got any tissues? We can talk now if you like – I'm free!

Amy: No, I can't talk now, customers will walk in!

Me: No, they won't. I can take care of that.

I quietly put Opa B, my Gatekeeper, by the front door of the bookshop, and no one came in the entire time Amy and I were talking. I love when that happens!

Me: I feel like I've been sent here to help you. So, while my Opa (indicating upstairs) is holding customers at bay so you can talk to me, feel safe to do so.

A beautiful peace and stillness came over us both and the shop itself and the light changed! I love it when it does that! I telepathically thanked Opa for bringing me here, then Amy started to tell me what had happened. I respect Amy's privacy and won't share the contents of our chat. Let me just say that I'm very glad that Opa got me there when he did or the outcome could have been very different! I also explained who I was and what I was doing in the area and asked if she might be interested in a few complimentary copies of my book, which she was.

Once Amy had gotten everything off her chest, her tears had either subsided or run out, and her breathing had gone back to normal, I knew we were finished as a customer came into the store. Amy was composed, and I excused myself to go out to the car to collect the books for her.

When I came back and handed Amy the books, she said to me, 'Marion, I asked for an Angel today, and no sooner had I said it that you walked in! I feel truly blessed that you trusted yourself to come into my shop today. You were the perfect person to help me! I am ever so grateful. Thank you. I will contact you soon for a full Reading.'

I knew that I would never hear from her again as she didn't need a full Reading … she just needed courage!

My resumé of Angel Assignments

When the TV series *Touched by an Angel* came to our screens in the mid-1990s, I felt that if they can make a TV series about this stuff that is exactly like my life, then someone, somewhere understands me!

Now that I'm older, I reflect that at every job I've ever held, I had been placed there for a specific purpose. It's only ever obvious in hindsight, normally when I've quit because the lessons got too hard or had, in fact, been taught!

In 2018, I had been travelling in my caravan and found myself based at Port Stephens in New South Wales.

For many, many years, I used to daydream and hope that one day I would live and sail there. However, as I was living in Perth and was married, I could see no way for that dream to ever see the light of day! I actually remember thinking to myself, 'I believe in reincarnation, but gee I hope that it REALLY is real, because I'll live the life my partner wants in this life, and I'll lead the life I want in the next!' Perth, while it was good to my family and me, and my two best friends lived there, had never felt like home. I felt like I was far away from where my Soul wanted to be. My Soul was sad. It's bad enough when your heart and mind are sad but when your Soul is sad, that's really sad.

Maybe you too have felt this feeling of not fitting in or feeling lost in your life too. It's an awfully sad feeling, isn't it? People on their true Spiritual path tend to be loners and lightworkers. For us, it's not about the human experience, but rather the Spiritual experience.

My life has been all about being the support system to so many people, right when they needed it most. I have been shown by my Team that, as a 6, I didn't come here to be supported. Growing up, I never felt supported by my family. It's because of this that I have an abundance of love and support for those on their Soul journey whose lives crisscross with mine!

Over the years, many people I have worked with have come to me for advice. It seems that I'm a magnet for those struggling to find their way in life, and it's these Souls that my Team offer their wisdom and Unconditional Love, guidance and acceptance to through me. Maybe this describes your life too, especially if you are an Old Soul.

When I look back at my life, including my working life and social life, I've attracted people who are suicidal or really struggling to take another step. I can receive three or four messages a week from people begging for my help or support. Opa tells me which ones are genuine, and I give them my time for free. Others, I will direct to my website to book a Reading. These people all feel like 'assignments' to me. So often, they have been unable to find help or support in their 'human world.'

When I went through my Dark Night of the Soul, Opa told me to throw myself into helping others as that will help me grow stronger. He was right.

That's why, when I was offered a full-time administration role in Port Stephens, I grabbed it. I remember walking into the office on my first day, and the first thing I did while waiting for the manager to collect me from reception was to 'scan' the office for my next assignment. There wasn't one! I was relieved – a normal job at last.

I found myself working with a beautiful Earth Angel named Natasha. Nat and I hit it off straight away. She was the most beautiful Soul, so kind and patient and an absolute joy to work with. I felt it was finally my time to be happy and that I could work in an environment where I could just be 'human' and my 'Soul' work would not come into it.

I should have known better.

The next day, I met Jodie. Jodie didn't work Mondays, which is why I hadn't met her the day I started. Turns out, I was there to help her.

As soon as I met Jodie, Opa showed me that she had two negative entities attached to her. We spent the first day getting to know each other as work colleagues then, the next day, the Soul work came into it. Jodie surrounded herself with crystals on her desk, which gave us something to talk about initially. I knew that my Team would work their magic between us by providing us opportunities to be alone to talk. We didn't have to wait long until Nat went home sick one day. At closing time, Jodie asked me if I would mind talking to her after work to help her with something. Of course I said yes! I told Jodie about my Gift and that I was able to pick up how troubled she was. I then invited her to talk to me if she felt comfortable.

Jodie told me that she had felt negative energies about her for the past few months. They taunted her by talking to her and telling her nasty untruths. She said that they interrupted her during the day when she was thinking and working and would often become very loud. She was even starting to doubt her own sanity, but she knew that she was normal. She had had several bouts of very disturbing sleep paralysis where she saw the entities with her eyes open – that must've been so scary!

Jodie confided in me that she was desperate and sobbed uncontrollably while we were in the carpark. She said that these situations and lack of sleep made her feel very depressed and exhausted and that she was struggling to cope.

I listened to Jodie and, most importantly, Jodie said she 'felt heard!' I'm glad. She said that some of the things I/we said to her were better than any counsellor or psychologist had ever said to her. I told Jodie that I would work with my Team tonight when I got home and that I would see her at work the next day.

That night, together with my Team, we were able to clear the two entities that had attached themselves to Jodie. We explained the benefits of moving on and asked my other Guide, Joop, to show them the way.

The next day, Jodie didn't come to work. Nat said that this was not uncommon, as she regularly missed one or two days a week. I checked in with my Team, and they were also unconcerned. They said that Jodie was enjoying the best sleep she'd had in years and not to check in on her.

Jodie came back to work the next day, looking refreshed. She asked me if I had worked with my Team two nights earlier, and I said that I had. She said that she could tell because she was not being bothered by the entities and had been able to enjoy a full night's sleep. Jodie then gave me a really big hug, and we got on with what we had come there to do – work!

Jodie worked until the end of the week then resigned. When I asked her why, she told me that it was as if she had been waiting for me to join the company so that I could help her. She said that no other counsellor had been able to help her in the same way I had. I told her that it's not me at all and entirely my Team's good work and, with all due respect, mainstream counsellors work on the 'mind' and I work on a Soul level. She understood this completely.

Jodie was a very Old Soul whose heart was very open. She knew that she also had a Gift of being able to 'see dead people', as she put it. However, she had chosen not to work with it. No one had ever taught her how to not use her Gift … that was, until she met me.

I explained to Jodie the responsibilities of working with a Gift such as ours, and that we have a choice whether we want to or not. Jodie has chosen to live her life as humanly as possible in this incarnation as she feels that she needs to rest, possibly from her previous incarnation and, potentially, in readiness for her next!

Jodie has since moved on to work in a veterinary clinic and is loving being with animals.

My notes to Jodie's situation

Sadly, there are quite a few of you who experience situations like Jodie's. If this is you, and if you feel brave enough, please know that you can deal with these entities yourself, after all, they are just us 'dead!' While they may show their fearful face, they are just lost Souls that gravitate to Love. Talk to them, share your love with them. You may feel silly at first, but just talk to them like you would any person. Send them to the 'light', if you have to.

If you need more guidance, please drop me a line.

I have worked in many supposedly 'normal' jobs during my life, and I always ended up in exactly the right place at the right time to help my latest assignment or lost Soul. On its own, my 'human' life didn't make sense – it was only when I looked at it spiritually that it did.

Just like Monica in *Touched by an Angel*.

Soul levels and the role of the ego

No one knows how many incarnations we go through. I guess it all depends on how dedicated you are to learning your lessons. The quicker you learn, the less you need to reincarnate. All of us are at various stages in our Soul Journeys. Keep in mind the next time you walk around the supermarket that you are sharing with Souls of all ages.

Once you incarnate into this lifetime, potentially as a 5 ¾ or above, there's a very good chance that you are now working in your Soul purpose in one of the many Spiritual modalities available to us as humans, having dabbled since you were a 5 ½.

Your Soul purpose is doing what you love

Your Gifts and Soul purpose will be becoming more evident to you now. You may already find yourself giving messages from Spirit through Psychic and/or Spiritual Readings or tarot cards. You may find yourself studying Reiki, Bowen and healing energy work and you may feel compelled to lay your hands on anyone and everyone to provide comfort to them ... but don't.

I once had an excited 5 ½ tell me how they had just completed Reiki 1 and believed that they had 'healed' someone through distance healing. When I asked whether they got the recipient's permission, they said, 'I didn't need to, I just sent it!' My Team always cringes when they hear this. They asked me to tell them, 'You must always get a person's permission before you send healing. Their suffering may be part of their Soul Contract, and healing may interfere with the conditions around that contract.' They may have agreed to experience suffering or ill health, physically or mentally, in this lifetime so that those they are in a Contract with will have the opportunity to learn their Spiritual lessons of compassion, empathy, selflessness and Unconditional Love. Once those lessons are learnt, the unwell person will go Home or get well again.

Or perhaps the contract is about you learning lessons from the person that is unwell. Lessons of forgiveness, acceptance and Unconditional Love, perhaps?

This must be considered at all times when working in our modalities. Many new 'healers' work as if they are the masters of the universe, when in truth they are just the master's apprentice!

The universe knows the correct way things need to be done. It's been done that way since before there were stars in the sky. Humans don't know, but think they do. This is where it becomes so very important to trust your own Wiredness, not your human brain, because it will know exactly the role it needs to play (or not play) in someone else's Soul Contract. Keep your mind out of it, along with your ego.

The universe asks for nothing more.

Sarah finally gets approval through forgiveness

One day, Sarah came to me for a Reading. Prior to Sarah coming, Karen came through to me and asked me to give Sarah a message. I wrote her message down. Karen's love for Sarah was incredible – she was determined that I got the messages right.

Sarah and I worked through the issues that had brought her to the session. She then pointed to Karen's note on my notebook and said to me, 'What's this about, Maz?'

Me: As you can see, your friend Karen came through to me before you even arrived today. She was very insistent that I understand her message and adamant that I give it to you today. Would you like me to tell you about it?

Karen: Yes, please tell her, Maz! And tell her that I am here.

Sarah: Yes, please.

Me: Karen came through before you got here and was adamant that I tell you that she is very, very grateful that you stepped in and looked after her three kids after she took her own life! Karen was very apologetic and sorry that she went when she did, but she said she just couldn't stand being alive any longer. She is very sorry but very grateful to you, and so glad that her kids have you!

I was about to ask Sarah if this message made sense to her, but I could see by her tears that it certainly did!

Sarah: Maz! Oh my goodness.

I let Sarah take in the gravity of Karen's visit while I reassured Karen that I would look after Sarah.

Sarah: But Maz, but ... it's been such a burden for me. I have felt guilty for moving into her house with her kids and partner ever since she died. Please ask Karen if she will forgive me.

Karen: Sarah doesn't need to be asking ME for forgiveness, I need to be asking her! Please tell her how grateful I am that she did everything humanly possible for my kids and family. Please tell her how very, very sorry I am and how, at the time, I truly felt that I did not have a choice at all. I just couldn't stand being alive any longer! Please tell Sarah that, if ever she needs anything, she can just ask me and I will help her.

Me: Of course! I will tell Sarah everything.

And I did, word for word. Karen then asked me to give Sarah a hug for her, which I did. So many tears were cried that day.

Sarah: Oh Maz! Oh Karen! I have felt so bad, so burdened, by what I've been carrying around since Karen's passing. I feel such relief now. I'm so glad that she is okay with what I did.

Karen then felt safe to leave Sarah and I, but not before thanking me for hearing her and sharing her very important messages with Sarah.

My experience of Sarah's Readings

I knew that Karen's message for Sarah was important when she came through before Sarah had even arrived. As a spiritual Soul, I understood my role delivering these messages for Karen; however, as a human, I hoped that the messages were accurate and would be understood by Sarah.

I am nearly always given the names of passed Loved Ones, and it is their name that connects with the person in situations like this.

It always feels like a great responsibility to deliver messages like this. I never really know how someone might interpret or feel about the message. That's what experience gives me. I knew it was safe for me to share Karen's message and that Sarah would accept it and understand it. To be able to witness such incredible contact and healing for both parties is amazing and very hard to put into words.

On the other hand, I personally know how special it is when you have known your Guide while they were alive. Sarah now knows hers and will, I hope, always feel comfort with Karen by her side.

The other thing I always make sure of is that I have plenty of tissues and chocolates handy for times just like these!

Kara's experience – turn your life around

Every now and again, I receive a cry for help like no other, and I know I have to pull out all the stops to help the person. A few years ago, a dear friend messaged to say she was sending me someone who was very close to being unable to take another step forward in her life. My friend knew that I was doing Readings that day as it was a Saturday. I asked her to give her friend my address and to come at 3pm.

Which she did.

Her name is Kara.

I call her my warrior woman!

Out of respect, I won't go into details about why Kara needed to come to see me that day, but let's say that I was her last resort! There was absolutely NO way I was going to let Kara out of my sight that day. When we finished many hours later after the sun had gone down, Kara had a plan, and I was relieved.

My notes to Kara's Reading

All I can say is 'Oh my goodness'! Watching someone go through their Dark Night of the Soul and come out the other end grabbing their life with both hands, physically and spiritually, is something I wish everyone could witness. Then again, it's a powerful experience and not everyone can deal with it.

I've seen many people who have come to me for Readings either partway through their Dark Night of their Soul or deep in it. This was the first time that I've seen someone deal with their demons in front of me and kick them to the curb.

Kara was back, and she was more alive and shining brighter than she ever has in her life.

This experience gave me a 'wee little' insight as to how a midwife must feel as she delivers another Soul into our world, straight from heaven! All that potential, all that incredibleness is what I felt with Kara.

To this day, I am so proud of everything that woman has dealt with and overcome. The power of the human spirit is Kara. I love this about her but what I actually love more is her wicked sense of humour! Kara keeps me laughing every day – she has come so far from the first time I met her.

What do you see for me?

Dylan rang me one day on the spur of the moment for a quick session. He only had one question.

Me: Hi Dylan, this is Maz. Thanks for asking to have a quick session with me. What is your question?

Dylan: I'm an accountant, and I'm sick of it. I was wondering what I should do instead.

Me: Do exactly what you are doing now!

Dylan: What? Being an accountant? I'm sick of numbers and figures and GST/BAS stuff!

Me: No! Look at what you're doodling! Look at the papers all over your desk. I don't know what you're planning to do with them, but I do 'see' that they would make great outdoor statues and garden features. Your designs would be perfect for small gardens, because they would make the garden look bigger. Does that make sense?

Dylan: Huh? How can you see what I'm doodling?

Me: I just can. Perhaps I'm looking through your eyes, or perhaps I'm watching telepathically. To be honest, I don't really know how I see it, but I do. Does it make sense to you?

Dylan: Absolutely! That's incredible! Now that I'm looking at it, I see what you mean. I think that I could turn the things I've doodled into life-sized statues and garden ornaments for small gardens! I didn't think you would be able to tell me anything, and the fact that you did because you could see me doodling as I talked to you is just weird, but I like it, and I love the information. I feel like you're giving me permission to change careers! Awesome. Thanks, Marion.

My notes on Dylan's Reading

You are not the only one fascinated by what I do – I am too! The other funny thing is that if I try too hard, it doesn't seem to work. But, if I don't try and treat it all matter-of-factly, it's so easy. Every Reading is new to me, and I always expect the unexpected.

Signs
– how the universe is trying to get your attention!

I'm up to my favourite part – SIGNS!

We use the GPS in our car to help us navigate to where we want to go. To get to your destination or goal, you need to put in a very specific address. If you don't, you could end up anywhere, right?

Well, the universe is exactly the same! You need to give the universe your specifics and it will very happily take you there too.

5s see coincidences.

5 ½s see coincidences and Signs and are unsure how to tell the difference.

6s see Signs and know exactly what they mean and what to do when they see them, as they've asked for them.

Me? I always look for Signs whenever I need to make an important life decision and can't make up my mind or am conflicted about the right decision for me.

I never make a decision these days with my brain! Why? Because it always lets me down.

I would like to share some of my experiences of how 'Signs' have played a very important part in my life's journey. I want to help you understand how I do what I do, rather than me just telling you what to do.

My parents used to live on the Murray River foreshore in beautiful Clayton Bay, South Australia. They used to love the pelicans that circled overhead then divebombed to catch fish. Dad always called them '747 jumbo jets'. They had pictures in their house of pelicans. Pelicans were their Team's Sign.

Years ago, I bought two gorgeous plush pelicans, a big and a small one, and they sat on my parents' bed forever. I now have them. I'm looking at them as I type, and it's like having my parents with me. When I travel, they sit on the dashboard of my car. I also have two pairs of ceramic pelicans that were given to me by a dear friend when I left South Australia. My home has six beautiful paintings with two pelicans in them. I cherish pelicans and the memories of my parents having them as their 'Sign of being in the right place at the right time!'

I needed to tell you about the pelicans because it took me a while to realise the TRUE meaning behind being shown a huge photo of two pelicans by a friend while up here in Airlie Beach. When I first saw the photo, I was speechless.

I had been seeing someone casually up here and enjoyed their company. However, there were many red flags that I ignored. I held hope that he would one day 'see' for himself that I could help him in this earthly life. After all, he was the one that showed me the huge photo of two pelicans that was in his storage shed.

'Oh my goodness!' I thought when he showed me. I was initially speechless because, to me, this was a Sign from my parents saying that I was in the right place at the right time, wasn't it? I thought so and continued to tolerate his ambivalent attitude *because* I had seen the Sign, right?

So, why did I feel so awful? Why did I feel disrespected? Why did I feel full of nerves and anxiety whenever I anticipated him coming to visit – I was never allowed to visit him!

Time went on.

In late February 2024, I got some advice from Opa. You will laugh at it, but there was simply no other way for Opa to show me how to put this guy in his place and teach him a lesson. What did Opa show me, I hear you ask?

I was typing away in the library one day when this person came to visit me. Opa gave me the words to say next and, after some initial chatter, the conversation went like this:

Me: Hey, when are you planning to see me next, as I never know?

Him: Oh, I don't know, Maz.

Me: Well, you know, it kinda makes it hard for me. I can't ring you or message you to find out when you plan to visit as you won't let me. We can't go out because you don't want people to see us together because you fear what they will say. You keep me hidden away for your own convenience because you are still in a relationship with the ex you say you have broken up from!

Him: Yeah, I like it that way!

Opa then put the following words in my mouth:

Me: Hey, how often do you fill up your car at the service station?

Him: Probably once a week.

Me: Do you ever ring your service station?

Him: No.

Me: Do you ever text your service station?

Him: No! What's this all about? What are you getting at, Maz?

Me: Well, it seems that I am your service station! I've now decided that I'm closed for business! I respect myself and will not allow you to use me any longer. I can't ring you ... I can't text you. You drop in unannounced and expect the same good ol' fashioned service that you are used to! Well, that service has now closed – it's been withdrawn from you!

Him: But, but, but ...

Me: No buts! We're over!

Thanks, Opa!

Messages come through to me based on exactly what someone needs to hear and in a way that makes the point hit home. If this message had been delivered to him in any other way, he would not have picked it up.

Despite the photo of the pelicans and thinking he was 'the one', I told him I didn't want to see him anymore because I had learnt the strength to be true to myself. I had been seeing the red flags for sexy underwear up to that point because I wanted them to be that. Sadly, they were just red flags!

I discussed this situation with my dear friend Lori. I said that I was still confused that this person had been holding up 'my Sign', but the relationship didn't work out. Lori and my Team have clarified that YES it was my Sign, but not in the way I had 'hoped' it was. It was actually my Sign to NOT be with him...yet!

You, me, us, we interpret Signs as being wonderful positive things to experience. I interpreted the Sign as us being 'meant to be!' and was thrilled that I, again, had found 'the one' in my life when, in fact, it was the opposite!

There's a huge difference to being alone and being lonely. I live alone, but I'm never lonely. I was, however, with this person and felt lonely – now that's an awful feeling! Maybe you are going through this and seeing sexy red underwear too. Look closer and see that they may actually be red flags. If they are, and you don't know how to stand up for yourself or end it, then Opa would be very happy for you to use his 'service station' analogy!

Maybe you need to become a 'self-serve service station' and put yourself first too!

I would now like to share a few more personal experiences about times when I asked for specific Signs to help me make a big life decision. Maybe it will help you differentiate between what is a thought and a what is a Sign for you!

2023 – my Signs to leave Victor Harbor and travel again

Working together with your Soul allows you to take shortcuts in your life that living only as a human can't. Signs are the perfect things to follow to make your way through life! By sharing my experiences, I hope to give you the confidence to ask for and receive Signs in your life too. Following my 2019 return to South Australia from my 14 month solo caravan journey, I:

- built my own home on 'that' block of land
- manifested full time work to build my house
- endured Covid twice which now leaves me breathless or is that life's energy?"
- gave Readings, sometimes daily.

I also endured a lot of trauma, grief and heartache. In 2023, I had been working very hard at work and dealing with a lot of family issues/grief. I again chatted with my Team about showing me Signs as to whether I should take a 12 month leave of absence from my job and go away in my caravan to recover and regain strength again, or whether I should stay and continue working. I felt very disillusioned about my life and completely directionless.

My Spiritual Team were doing all they could to keep me alive and going when all I really wanted to do was close my eyes in this world and open them again back 'Home!'

I know that many of you feel this way at times, and I understand, I truly do. We just have to keep going. There's a reason, they say!

Just like in my 2018 request to my Team, I told them that I didn't care what direction they wanted me to continue in, I just wanted to see Signs to help me make the decisions. I felt like a yacht without a rudder or centreboard ... or sails, for that matter!

Going away in a caravan and towing it thousands of kilometres alone is a huge decision! Each time I've seen a Sign to do it, it's resulted in a lot of hard work. Ignoring the turmoil that leads me to take the trip, even the journey itself, towing a 22-foot caravan to places that I had never been before, is incredibly tough. Exciting, sure, but tough. All those white lines! All that backing up in front of people! Argh! Never mind the preparation in packing up my house and putting it into storage – alone – then putting it all in the house after it had been built! *Please bear with me, there is a point to this story. I feel that if I share my personal stories, you can see that I am just like you and, believe me ... if I can do it, you CAN too.*

I knew what I was asking for in mid-2023, and I was prepared to get a 'No!' Here's an excerpt of my conversation with my Team while I broke down:

Me: Opa, Opa, Joop, Mark, Staven and Mum and Dad, please show me where I am meant to be. You have been showing me that you want me to write this next book, yet I am working 44 hours a week and helping people voluntarily as a Psychic. So many want to take their life, plus doing Readings, plus dealing with all the grief and stress in Perth. Work is stressful … when I get home, all I feel like doing is listening to loud music and flopping on the lounge.

If you want me to go to Airlie Beach, please show me Signs. Show me Signs on telly, set up a coincidental rendezvous with Mandy, who can help me rent my house out, help me find out if there are yachts I can crew on there, help me to find caravan parks that have long-term parking, help to find house sits in the area to help save money, help me to ask my managers for 12 months off!

Team: You have got to be kidding about the last one … now you're really testing US!

And then I started seeing the Signs. I recognised them easily. You see, when you are on track in your life and are shown the Signs that you have asked for and everything starts to fall into place effortlessly, the process feels very transactional, like going through the supermarket checkout.

The very next morning after this breakdown, the *Today* show was broadcasting from Airlie Beach in the Whitsunday Islands.

One tick.

On my way to work, I stopped at the post office. So did Mandy, my real estate agent contact!

Two ticks.

I approached my manager asking for 12 months leave without pay. The answer was YES, with 18 September 2023 the date that I would start my leave.

Three ticks.

Then I made enquiries with the Whitsunday Sailing Club and had a terrific chat with the receptionist at the time. She organised a full membership for me and told me that, once I arrived, they would easily find me a yacht to crew on during their year-round Wednesday twilight series racing.

Fourth tick.

Then I rang the Proserpine Caravan Park. Robyn advised me that they had long-term parking for permanents, and I could stay there for the entire 12 months if I wished.

Fifth tick.

Then I looked on the Mindahome website and found a house-sit in Airlie Beach for my arrival.

Sixth tick.

I would just like to add an additional note here to this sixth tick as I edit this book. It is now November 2024, and I have been at the house-sit for 12 months. I couldn't believe my luck when I took this house-sit 12 months ago for a local business family. Not only did I get to look after their beautiful home and puppy, but I also ran their business whenever they were away, giving me some extra dollars in the bank. Win-win.

I cannot even begin to put into words how magical life can feel at times. I started to believe that maybe all those hard, stressful and traumatic times were finally behind me and that my dreams could start. Never ever give up on your dreams. Mandy was able to rent my house out for the rent I needed in order to survive financially. I swear she hides her wings under her work shirt. Blessings to you, Mandy.

Seventh tick!

It looked like I was *really* going again! The whole process had been relatively easy and stress free, too.

The universe had ticked all the boxes that needed ticking, and the time was right for me to get back into my caravan before yet another Dark Night of the Soul crept in under my sheets!

My point is this: if you have a dream, follow it. If you are uncertain whether you should follow it, chat to your Guides about showing you the Signs. They are always happy to help. Please remember that it is in your Guides' best interest to help YOU and your best interest to listen to them. Dreams always come true.

There is absolutely NO way I would ever make a decision like this using my human brain. I didn't care what they showed me, to be honest. I just needed direction as I was sinking – drowning, not waving. But I asked my Guides for advice, and they showed me the way. I simply cannot imagine life without them, ever.

Everything fell into place, which is what it does when it is 'meant to be!'

To cut a long story short, I left South Australia on Monday 18 September 2023. After saying goodbye to my dear friends, my first destination was again Port Stephens, where I sailed with my 2018/19 crew again for two weeks then headed to Airlie Beach.

Am I going back to South Australia? Well, we will have to see what the signposts say, hey? For now though, they've given me a great Beneteau 35.1' yacht to crew on called *Lama*, after the Dalai Lama, at the Whitsunday Sailing Club, racing in their Wednesday night twilight series. I am sailing around the magnificent azure-coloured waters of the Whitsunday Islands, working on Hamilton Island for the airlines, making new friends every week AND finishing this book. All credit to my Guides, not me. I just turned up where they sent me.

Despite seeing all the Signs this time, it still took me a long time to make the actual decision to go! Why? Because, for the first time in my life, I couldn't '*see*' what was in front of me or what was going to happen! I actually thought I was going to Queensland to die!

After long, great discussions with people who knew and loved me, they reassured me that this is my turn to live a 'normal' life like everyone else does and to let the universe reveal itself to me every day, one day at a time.

So far, so good!

I share my experiences with you so you can see how it is for me. You already know how it is for you. Maybe you are nodding your head in agreement at a lot of the things I share, and maybe you aren't. I believe sharing experiences is important so that you no longer feel alone and can make sense of your own life, your own journey, your own Signs.

As I share my story with you I realise now that I no longer feel 'weird' but instead 'Wired'. Wired means connected to source and that's what we really are. Just like plugging your phone in to be connected to a power source, we can choose to be the same. But what I know is that we are NOT WEIRD.

Life *is* a mystery, so the best thing we can do is travel it together, helping each other out.

Just wait at the picnic bench for her

While I was towing my caravan from South Australia to Airlie Beach, I realised I would have to spend a night in Rockhampton as it was getting late. I had been driving all day and was hoping to be further on the map than I was. I checked the free camping apps and soon found one nearby. I had also been thinking about Mum and Dad a fair bit on the trip, and their two trusty soft pelicans were still sitting on the dashboard of my car, enjoying their return to Queensland.

I parked alongside everyone else spending the night. The park was next to some really beautiful gardens, and a walk was just what I needed. The air was refreshing, with the grass cool under my feet and the long shadows of the trees. It was warm but not humid. After my walk, I went back into my caravan. I had decided that I would walk across the road to the big shopping centre and have dinner there. Opa suggested that I simply make myself a fresh sandwich and a cup of tea for dinner. 'Hagelslag' or chocolate sprinkle sandwiches are part of any Dutchie's staple diet. We all grew up on them! My kids, their kids and me still love them today! It's as traditional as Dutch licorice, so that's what was on my sandwich that day.

I was considering where to eat my sandwich and read *Caught Between Two Worlds*, as I thought it was time to read it again. Opa made a suggestion:

Opa: Lieve meisje, go and sit at the picnic bench over there on the lawn in the shade. You will meet a lovely lady that you will click with. You will be very interested in her Gift too!

I did and began reading my book. It wasn't long before a lady walked up and asked to sit with me. Of course, I said yes. I then became very conscious of my sandwich and tried to hide the chocolate sprinkles! She laughed and said:

Lady: Ah! You must be Dutch. My husband, Henk, is Dutch too, and he eats them all the time along with the zwart/wit (black/white) licorice pastilles he eats every day! (Henk is my Dad's name. Turns out that he was travelling with me after all.)

Me: Oh my goodness! Yes, I am Dutch! I was trying to hide my sandwich from view as it feels childish eating it. I love them. And those licorice pastilles, I've just bought 250 grams of them – they are my favourite! And my dad's name is Henk too! What a wonderful coincidence!

Lady: Nothing is a coincidence, my dear. If there's something I've learnt from teaching Reiki and crystals to all the kids I've taught, it's that there really are no coincidences!

I just about choked on my sandwich! No wonder Opa wanted me to sit here! I'm so glad. I asked her to tell me more as I was very interested. Turns out that she had been teaching Reiki and crystal work to children for many years and had just retired. She showed me some photos of their amazing work. I was so very glad that Opa had brought us together that afternoon as I learnt so much from Cheryl and her gifted work with our Spiritual Children. I told her that I felt so encouraged that, with Earth Angels like her guiding our gifted young, the world just may improve Spiritually.

I told her about Opa's message about not going over to the shopping mall, then she said, 'Well, it certainly seems that Opa knows best, and that your dad is with you this afternoon. I've absolutely loved the past two hours that we've been talking!' She took me to her caravan to meet her 'Henk' and tell him about mine. I popped back to my caravan to get some more pastilles as she said her husband had run out! He was pleasantly surprised. I also asked Opa to write a message in the copy of my book that I was about to Gift her.

I absolutely loved our time together, and my life is so much better knowing that there are beautiful Souls like this helping our gifted young so they no longer get lost in our school systems!

The role of the internet and Signs

Do you remember when they used to say, 'Don't believe all you read about in the newspaper?' Well, that saying should now be, 'Don't believe all you read on social media.'

Spirit Guides are shaking their heads in disbelief at the brainwashing taking place via social media, yet people continue asking for Signs and expecting to see them there.

I/we wish that the internet and social media had never been invented. It is yet another money making, marketing/advertising avenue to bring you down. Sure, there are some great posts with Spiritual messages. I share many, and I also write them. However, they are in the minority.

Keep your wits about you and your mind open! Many people ask for 'Signs' in case they are real, but secretly they don't believe and keep their fingers crossed behind their back. Some would even freak out if they received the actual Sign they asked for, or a Sign full stop. But, most importantly, Guides tend not to show Signs on social media, so do yourself a favour and get off it and get your head back into the real world!

When Shirley (not her real name) first came to see me years ago, she was a sceptic! These days, she knows she has lived her own miracle.

Let me share Shirley's experience with you.

Shirley had been to see me a couple of times. During these sessions, we explored ways for her to ask for a Sign if she ever needed one. We discussed this for several hours, as I somehow knew that Shirley would only 'believe' in Signs once she actually received one or, in her case, three in one day. Signs are generally shown to us to provide us with important direction, clarity and guidance in our daily lives. They are not shown to us for sensationalist purposes. That wouldn't do us or our Guides any good at all.

Shirley rang me one day, many months later, asking for a session. I was able to fit her in that same morning. When she arrived, she told me:

> Maz, I have something I need to share with you, and I would like your insight into it. About seven months ago, while I was showering, I found a lump in my breast! I thought to myself, 'Oh, I need to go see Dr Roberts to get this lump checked out.' As soon as I'd thought it, I dismissed it.
>
> Two weeks later while on my way to an afternoon tea, I took a wrong turn. I checked out the Sign and it said 'Robertson Road.' I did a U-turn and went back to the main road, shaking my head at my silly mistake. About a kilometre down the road, a car rudely cut me off. The car had personalised number plates: 'ROBBIE'! I thought nothing more of it and honked my horn in annoyance. I rushed into the supermarket to buy bikkies, dip and cake only to be halted at the register while the assistant and a customer talked about the customer's husband named Rob! As I hopped in to start my car; something was ringing a bell for me:
>
> - Robertson
> - Robbie
> - Rob

Funny how I suddenly felt compelled to ring Dr Roberts. The secretary at the clinic told me that the doctor had just had a cancellation and that, if I could come in straight away, I could be seen.

Something was urging me to go and, for the first time in my life, I trusted something bigger outside of myself.
When I got there, I told my doctor about the breast lump. Well, to cut a long story short, they ordered immediate blood tests, X-rays and an ultrasound.

Turns out that the lump I had felt months earlier was in fact an early-stage breast cancer. Dr Roberts said to me that I was very lucky to have come in that day because if I had left it any longer, the cancer would have grown even further and become serious enough to result in a mastectomy, chemo and radiotherapy.

However, I didn't have to undergo any of that treatment as it had been caught early enough, all thanks to the Signs that I pieced together.

You too can learn from Shirley's experience as this is exactly how your Team of Guides will deliver messages to you – *not* by standing in front of you and telling you. One, because they can't and two, you may miss their message by thinking it's a thought. They will deliver it in a way that may feel obscure but is perfectly normal for Spirit.

I hope this story inspires you to ask for and watch for Signs for yourself and your family and never miss one again!

Do you know your confirmation sign?

As I write this, its 24 April. It's no ordinary day for me. In fact, it's a very significant day. Here's why:

On 24 April 1978, at the age of 16, my first boyfriend asked me to marry him. I said no.

On 24 April 1989, I met the man I married.

On 24 April 2015, after a 25-year marriage, my husband and I separated and I returned to live in Adelaide to care for my parents. At the end of 2017, they sadly both passed away.

By then, my kids were adults and lived their own lives in Perth. At the time, I didn't have a job or own a house and had no idea what I wanted to do next. I felt very confused and alone. I had a fair idea that I wanted to travel in a caravan. but I also wanted to work and stay in the town I was living in at the time and build a beach house with a view of the ocean.

I was again 'caught between two worlds.'

In February 2018, I was living on the oceanfront at Victor Harbor. I had been gazing out to sea and doodling on my drawing pad, drawings of a house I really couldn't envisage coming to fruition.

Suddenly, Mum and Dad walked in the back door behind where I was sitting and said to me, 'Just buy a caravan and go travel, would you?' Then they were gone.

But I knew I had just received direction from them. It was, in fact, the first time that they had made contact since going Home.

I put down my pen and had a frank conversation with my Team. Calmly and in Soul mode, I asked:

Okay, you have my attention. I need confirmation, please. Please let me meet women who have towed caravans alone around Australia, if this is what you want me to do, OR please show me a job here so that I can build my home here. I don't mind which road I go down, but this is what I ask for: clarification.

Mum and Dad's messages were so 'very real' and so very 'them!' I knew my direction but, as usual, my human self needed to explore it.

My prayers were answered an hour later when I received a phone call from Jan. Jan was calling to pick up the furniture she had bought at Mum and Dad's garage sale that I had held a few weeks prior. To be honest, and I never told Jan this, at the time I really wasn't up to visitors as I wanted to focus on manifesting the next step in my life. Of course, my Team knew better! They always do! Gosh, you must think that I'm a very slow learner! My Team do!

At 1:30pm, Jan knocked on my front door. Her car and trailer were parked across the front of my house and neatly reversed so that they didn't cross the driveway. I greeted her and asked if she had come alone or brought someone along who had towed the trailer for her. Jan replied, 'No, I've come alone. I know how to reverse a trailer, after all, I've just finished towing my caravan alone for two years!'

Oh my goodness! Jan was sent by my Team in answer to my plea. I asked her to come in for a cuppa. Then, for the next two and a half hours, I listened to Jan and drank copious amounts of tea while listening to her tales of towing her caravan around Australia, alone!

I knew it was what I wanted too.

Was this a coincidence? What do you think?

That was Sign #1

Two weeks later, I walked into a local health food shop. As I went to pay for my homeopathic medicine, the beautiful girl behind the counter looked at me with her eyes glistening and asked,

'Are you Marion Weatherburn?' I said yes, and she said, 'I knew you lived in Victor. I picked up your book in NSW as I was travelling alone in my van for four years. I've been asking Spirit to bring you into my store! May I give you a hug?' That's how I met Angel M and received a hug that I'll never forget as we both dissolved into tears of recognition that our Souls knew each other, but not from this life – tears for the magic that had brought us together as friends over the common interest of travelling in vans solo!

Dearest M, wherever you are, I know it is the right place for you. You are such a divine Angel and a true ripple effect in our world! I am still so very glad that we connected that day. You changed my life and inspired me!

That was Sign #2 and confirmation that I had to buy a caravan and run away in order to heal.

I had thought I would head to the Port Stephens area in New South Wales. I knew that all I wanted to do was find a decent sailing club and crew on boats as a volunteer. Sailing was my life when I was young. It waned through my married life as it just didn't work out for me. I knew that if I sailed, I would heal, but I had no idea how it was all going to work and how long I would go for. In the end, I spent close to 12 months in Port Stephens and crewed on yachts during their Wednesday and Saturday series racing. It truly was the time of my life and a dream come true, one that I never thought I would realise in my lifetime.

A few weekends later, I went to visit my dear friend Maxine. She lived on Encounter Lakes and had friends down from Adelaide for the weekend, whom I had never met before. Given the gorgeous weather and location, we all hopped into kayaks and paddled away from the shore. One of the ladies paddled over to me and said, 'I don't know what makes me want to say this to you, but I feel compelled to tell you that whatever it is on your mind at the moment that you want to do, you should just go do it!' I thanked her for the message and, when the rest of the group had caught up to us, the conversation was dropped. She had said exactly what I needed to hear

That was Sign #3

While enjoying a glass of wine a while later, I told Maxine what her friend had said to me along with my encounters with Jan and Angel M. I told Maxine that I had made the decision to go looking for caravans that week with a view to leaving on 4 July – Independence Day in America. Until then, I was going to have to get my head around how to put my plan into place.

However, I always knew my Team had my back.

On 24 April 2018, I bought my caravan and decided to embark on a massive exploration of New South Wales and Queensland and my life ... alone!

Part of getting ready to leave South Australia meant that I had to find a storage shed for my belongings. So, when I found myself out one day during May 2018, inspecting storage units in which to store my furniture, I could no longer deny that I was meant to go on this journey. However, I had checked out three units and didn't feel happy with any of them. I was driving home feeling very despondent, thinking maybe I wasn't meant to go on this trip after all!

Suddenly, and as if I had a passenger in the passenger seat, I was given an instruction by my Opa to, 'Turn right, turn left, turn right, turn left, STOP! Look across the road!' I've learnt to trust the feeling when this stuff happens. And, of course, what was facing me across the road? Brand-new storage sheds! I was so excited. It *had* to be a Sign that I was meant to leave South Australia!

I rang the number on the fence and enquired as to whether there were any units available. I was told that they were all occupied. Deflated, I turned the car around and headed home to continue my packing.

Less than an hour later, my phone rang. I was greeted by a rep from the office I had enquired with earlier. 'Hi Marion, a gentleman has just come in and handed in his keys to his storage unit and it's now available, if you would like it?' Gingerly I asked what number it was. You can probably guess his reply...

'24!'

The number 24 has always been my trusted Sign whenever I need confirmation. I took this phone call as a Sign that I *was* indeed meant to go on this journey and accepted the storage unit.

The day before I left Victor Harbor, while packing my caravan, my dear friend Maxine rang to invite me to lunch at a local café. What table number were we allocated? You know it – 24!

After lunch, Maxine and I wandered down to the local pub and ordered a glass of champers each, as girls do! Again, we were given the table number 24.

Maxine and I discussed what name I should give my caravan. She suggested I get some of those letterbox number stickers and stick them on the door. The next day my caravan had the numbers '24' stuck on the door in letterbox numbers. They are still there today.

24 is my go-to number. I trust this number to always show me that I am in the right place, at the right time, all the time. This number gives me complete faith that I am on the right path in my life. I hope it inspires you to find your very own special number and it's very personal meaning for you!

EXTRA: This information has been taken from my webpage, which was created on 24 January 2020 – ha! I only just realised!

https://psychiclikenoother.com.au/why-the-number-24-is-so-important-to-me

On 24 June 2019 (again, 24 = right time, right place), I flew to Adelaide from where I was staying in New South Wales at the time to sign the paperwork for my new home to be built in Victor Harbor. Then the acceptance papers came through and were signed on 24 July, giving me much-needed comfort that I was indeed 'meant to be' building my home.

Two days later when I flew back to Port Stephens, my seat number was 24A.

In the first week of November, I received my final house plans and contract in the mail. The council approval documents were dated 24 October 2019, and my planning approval documents were dated 28 October (which was my wedding anniversary)! The tears were bittersweet as I was building my home alone, but that was okay because I KNEW I had the universe on my side this time.

Once, a good friend of mine returned a book she had borrowed. She pulled out one of my old boarding passes that I had used as a bookmark. It showed the seat number 24A from a flight I had taken to Perth years ago. My friend returned the book to me with the boarding pass, knowing that the number was important to me!

There's that number again! The number 24 always confirms for me that I am in the right place at the right time. I trust this number with my Soul.

Do you frequently see occurring or repeating numbers? If so, what are they? Do you make a note of them? Do you make note of what you were thinking when you see them? Do you see them as a Sign or a coincidence? I'd love to know what yours is!

I'm considering getting the number 24 tattooed on me – it's is one of the Signs I ask for whenever I am asking.

By the way – a friend posted this on my Facebook page after hearing my story:

> **Angel Number 24 and its meaning:** When the angel number 24 keeps appearing in your life, don't ignore it. This is a message from your guardian angels, and they want you to pay attention! The angel number 24 is an indication that whatever you are doing now is getting you closer to your goals.

I have many, many stories that I would like to share with you about Signs just like this that I have received, but what I would prefer to do is inspire you to live your own truth and ask for your own

Signs. Ask for them, then look for them, believe them when they are there and never, ever doubt that you can do this 'weird' stuff too. You just have to get your silly mind out of the way and trust the universe to show you how to be Wired.

Maybe it's time that you started looking for your own Signs before you miss too many more!

Why did I ask for more proof?

I'm human, you know that, right? And, just like you, I am my own biggest sceptic. One day, I asked for extra proof from my Team that they really ARE real. I hear you ask why do I feel the need for more proof. It's because my human brain 'doubts' what I receive, I guess, because it's so normal for me to question, anyone would.

One Saturday, I had a bunch of beautiful 6s from my Soul Clinic group come over for an afternoon of support, love and friendship. These afternoons are a great way for us to recharge our energy banks and to chat about stuff that has been happening for us as we fly about the world trying to put it back together again!

So, picture this... we are sitting around the table talking, sharing our stories. When it came to my turn, I shared the Signs about my mum and dad, Henk and Louise! As I told the story to the group, I also shared that my mum loved the Doris Day song 'Que sera sera'. However, my mum always preferred her version, which went, 'Kiss my arse, my arse, whatever will be, will be!' Mum always got laughs for singing this version, and today was no different. We also sang her version at her funeral (at least some of us did)!

Lori gently reached over, took my hand and said, 'I can add to your Signs, Maz!'

I was curious!

Lori said, 'Maz, my Opa was Dutch, and his name was Hank, or Hendrikus, just like your dad! And look at this.' She rolled up her sleeve and tattooed in plain ink, plain as day, were the words

'Que sera sera'! Lori added, 'I have your mum and dad as Signs too, further confirmation that you are on the right track, right here, right now, with us as your family and friends!'

I love that woman! I knew she was Special, now I know why. I will never have doubt again.

Thank you, Mum and Dad, for these incredible Signs and proof that you are indeed with me, exactly as you said you were. Every time I read this story back as I edit and polish this book, I am filled with 'truth bumps!' and that beautiful, magical feeling that I get every time they are around!

My mum's message to the world is, 'Kiss my arse, my arse, whatever will be, will be, the future's not ours you see, kiss my arse, my arse!' I still hear her laughing!

I now have the words 'whatever will be, will be' tattooed on my left forearm as the continuation of Lori's tattoo and my mum's anthem!

Animals as Signs

What are your animal Signs? Do you have any? Caterpillars? Butterflies? Dragonflies? Bees? Cats? Bats? Bears? Deer?

As you know from my earlier story, mine is pelicans – to be specific, two pelicans always standing proud together.

I had never told either of my kids about the meaning I attached to pelicans. However, they both knew how much their Opa and Oma loved them, so when this next situation happened, I was as gobsmacked as my son.

I flew my son over from Perth in August 2023 to visit prior to me leaving South Australia for my trip to the Whitsunday Islands. He hadn't been to the area since my mum's funeral in December 2017, and he hadn't seen the house I had built in the three years I had lived there. When I asked him what he really wanted to do with his time while he was with me, he said that he wanted to go to Clayton. He needed to go and feel his Oma and Opa's energy there.

I thought it was a great idea, so we picked a huge bunch of daisies from my backyard and drove to Clayton.

Over the past seven years, since losing his Opa, my son has experienced several visits from my dad. My son struggles knowing that his Opa has seen firsthand the troubles he has been through. He's embarrassed. He also knows that the visits are real.

I remember asking my dad once whether he spends any time with my son and, if so, to let me know how he was doing. Dad told me he spent more time with my son than with me, and that I shouldn't be offended by that. My dad accepted his grandson for who he was, and my son accepted his Opa in his life. It seems there were times though when no matter how strong my dad came through to him, my son's mind was stronger and rejected him.

Just because we, as a family, are so spiritually connected, it doesn't always mean that we believe all the time. Like all other humans, we are sceptical. We are constantly tested by our brains to understand our Spiritual experiences. My parents understood and continued to provide my son with a safety blanket, protecting him from himself as best they could.

As my son gently placed the daisies in the Murray River out the front of my parents' house, they slowly drifted out to the channel marker where his Oma and Opa can watch the daily sunrise and sunsets, just like they loved to do when they were alive from the comfort of the home they lovingly built together on the water. My son decided that he wanted to walk up to the top of the cliff we had always walked up whenever we stayed with my parents. He wanted to overlook the Murray River and contemplate his life, and he wanted me to come with him. We walked up together, hand in hand. We 'get' each other, my son and I – we always have. The silence was comfortable, and I knew that we were not alone and that his Oma and Opa were with him. My parents were glad that he had finally decided to come before I left South Australia.

We sat at the top of the cliff on the bench and watched the shifting weather. We found it really curious that just as we thought the clouds were going to dump a whole lot of rain on us, they instead parted and the sun came out. Mum and Dad always said this happened right over their house. It was a very curious fact. We knew they were with us. After an hour, he said he wanted to walk around their house as it was empty at the time.

Or was it?

I sat in my car while he walked over to the beautiful home they had designed and built together. It had the best view in Clayton of the Murray River as it flowed down to Goolwa. Clayton Bay had been our sailing playground when I was growing up. It holds a very special place in my heart.

I decided it was the perfect time for me to talk to Mum and Dad. I cried, as I always do, and begged my Team to show my son a Sign that he could not deny when he saw it.

I asked my parents to show him a Sign that would stay with him forever with its truth. I asked them to touch his heart and Soul while he walked around their house. I asked them to remind him who he was – to remind him of his Spiritual self and his Gift of connection, which we always saw as our true self … not the human form that makes all the mistakes, but the Soul Self. I asked them to give him a Sign to tell him that he would get through all the trauma he had been going through.

I was not prepared for what came next.

I drove up towards the house and parked nearby on the side of the road where I could clearly see it. It wasn't long before my son came around the side of the house. As he walked towards the car, I could see that he was visibly shaken and crying. He got in the car and just sat.

So, I sat too.

I held his hand as tears rolled down his face!

I waited.

He looked pale and couldn't speak for about five minutes. Eventually, he said:

Mum, something really strange happened. I loved it, but it's upset me. When I was looking through the windows of the dining room into the house, I saw a big reflection of two pelicans. When I turned around, I could see nothing behind me. But they *were* there! When I looked inside, I could see nothing inside. But they *were* there! Am I going mad, Mum?

I replied, 'You are NOT going mad at all! Let me explain something to you.'

I told him about what I had asked of my mum and dad, how I wanted them to show him something that would stay with him forever ... something that would change his life forever!

It seems they did!

We cried together, and I asked him to ask his Opa for help as he was now in the perfect place to help.

My son said that he had asked his Opa for help in the past but that he hadn't lately as he felt bad for the choices he had been making. He said that he will ask again and that the day's reunion was something that he would never forget.

I hope not!

Warning Signs

Even I don't listen sometimes and think I know better. Ignoring a Sign may cost you dollars and sense! Warning Signs are presented to you for your own wellbeing. I will share a couple of my experiences to help you understand what I mean.

Do you remember my story earlier about my decision to take a particular road to the airport and dismiss my Team's advice? Well, ignoring those very obvious Signs to take a different road cost me $486 and three demerit points! Argh! What is wrong with me! I have the help that so many people wished they had, and I still don't listen!

Just after my first book was published, I was living with a 'friend' who had asked me to marry him! I won't mention his name because, to be honest, I want to forget it!

I remember coming home from a day doing Readings. It was a long day, and I felt exhausted. He hadn't done anything about getting ready for dinner and it was already 8pm. It was the middle of summer and extremely hot. We were standing together at the kitchen bench. He had been playing some very loud music that was grating on my nerves. As my legs were aching, I didn't feel like walking all the way to the other room where the music was playing to change it. I asked him, 'Would you please turn the music down for me?', to which he replied, 'No, I'm really enjoying it! I love this band!' I said, 'I know, but I have worked all day while you have been at home, and I would love some peace and quiet. Please turn it down for me?' Again, he said no!

Telepathically, I asked Opa, half-joking, 'Can you turn the music down for me please? I've been doing Team work all day and just can't stand this intrusion into our energy!'

Now, this is weird, but true! The music went off, and all the heat in the room was replaced with extreme cold, to the point that we could see our breath!

Telepathically, I thanked Opa for turning it off. I was grateful. I was even too tired to work out how he had managed it. Out loud, I said, 'Thanks Opa!', to which my friend replied, 'You're a weirdo! I'm getting out of here!' He left the house and didn't return until the next day.

That night I slept like a baby! Opa obviously didn't like my friend, and he soon made that obvious in a way that I thought was amazing.

Sometimes, we are given warning Signs by our Guides but, because we want to believe we are right about a situation, we ignore them, just like I did in this situation. Eventually, my Guides made it obvious to me that they did not approve.

Have you seen the plaques that hang on walls that say 'Live, Hope, Love'? I had these three words on three separate plaques hanging on the kitchen wall in our house as framed prints held up with Blu-tac. One word kept falling off the wall, and I kept picking it up. Each time this word fell off, I would add more Blu-tac and stick it back up. Initially, this happened maybe once a week, then twice a week, then every day. Each time I would put on more Blu-tac. I even bought an extra packet thinking the packet I had already used wasn't working properly. I took off all the old Blu-tac and replaced it with the new stuff. Beauty, it worked! However, as soon as I turned my back, down it came again.

The day my friend and I broke up, he said to me, 'Have you noticed that it was the word LOVE that always fell off the wall?' Such a great observation from a sceptic, I must say. Until it was pointed out by him, a person incapable of loving anyone except himself, I hadn't realised. After he left the house, I put it up and it never fell down again!

I wasn't surprised. I don't think you are either!

Here was a Sign that LOVE was not a part of my life. I had been trying to force it to work by continually putting more Blue-tac on it so it would 'stick!' Now, I'm glad it didn't.

I share this with you so you can see that, underneath all these words, I really am human just like you! You may say that you would be grateful for the Signs I receive, and I am, but believe me, you too may be tempted to question the Signs when they come through. This is especially true in the beginning when there is still a lot of doubt in your mind. Doubt usually comes because of your expectations – you don't really know how this all works, and you might be expecting Signs to be different to what they actually are. This is completely normal.

Remember that you only have one mind and all our Spiritual messages come through to be processed by it. Our brain, as good as it is, won't ever understand these types of messages or know how to interpret them correctly until you get used to the 'feeling' they come with.

Whenever I get a 'Sign', it always comes with a feeling of 'incredible love!' It's hard to describe – it's like knowing that someone out there REALLY cares about me and loves me! So, if I get that feeling with a Sign, then I know for sure that it's real. If I don't have that feeling, then I either ask for another Sign or wait.

Most of all, it's the feeling I trust.

Trust your training wings

Trust, faith, whatever you want to call it ... how do we do it? How do we get it?

Life experience, that's how.

Tonight, hold a lit match up to a wall so that it casts a shadow. You will see the shadow of your hand and the match – the flame, however, will not cast a shadow! Does that mean it's not there? Of course it's there! If you 'touch' it, you *will* feel it.

Trust and faith are the same.

You first have to believe it's there, even if you can't see it. Once you put your trust and faith in the 'unseen,' you *will* start to feel it.

I commonly refer to trust as having Spiritual training wings (formerly known as training wheels!)

Trust plays one of the biggest roles in Spirituality. It's one of our biggest lessons! Furthermore, if you are prepared to trust, the universe will reward you in more ways than one. The more you trust in the universe, the more you will see, experience and come to know in your world. It will open up in the most magical of ways. By relinquishing your need to control and trust the universe, so much will come to you.

It's okay to have training wings. You may wobble or have 'wing' failure at times, but there's a whole unseen force encouraging you to go on. It's a force that will eventually help you to fly through life smoothly. That force is your Soul, and you can find it by letting go of your expectations of others and situations and by turning up in your life every day to be guided by the universe. How much easier is that? You've always said that you wanted to find an easier way, well here it is, right here in this book written just for you! It's a shortcut to navigating this incarnation.

That's what I do, and that's why it's so aMAZing! The universe knows me way better than I know me!

Please remember that your Soul has lived many lifetimes before and is very patient. It's just that you, housed in the human body/vehicle in this lifetime, have forgotten. You will be presented many times with circumstances where suddenly you will start to remember all that you had forgotten in this incarnation. All previous learning will come back to you. You haven't lost it; it's just waiting for everything to align perfectly for you to remember. It will turn up at exactly the right time. You will see! Trust!

3 Little Pigs Retreat

It was late on a Friday afternoon in 2016, and the weather had turned nasty. At the time, I lived on the beach at Encounter Bay, and it wanted to huff and puff and blow my house away! How appropriate the weather was for my reading that day. You'll have a little chuckle at this session.

Rebecca texted me to say that she was on her way but that she had been delayed due to the weather. I told her to drive safe and that I would see her when she got here. When she arrived, I made cuppas. Opa had already shown me why she had come today. I was keen to find out if it was true and wanted to get started quickly so that Bec could make her way home safely!

Me: Bec, before I start, let me show you the drawings that came through about an hour before you got here. This first one shows what I can only describe as a wedding chapel. My Team called it 'Weddings by the Sea!' They are also telling me that this business will not work as well as the other business. I found this next drawing interesting. It's three little cottages set into the side of a hill. The hill looks like it's near Mount Compass (a town nearby). To the left of the three cottages is a large house, which I would call the caretaker's house, and an edible garden fringes the house! Look here on the wall, they've named it 'The 3 Little Pigs Retreat'. It seems that this is a resort for people wanting to 'try out' experimental eco-housing solutions prior to commencing their build. There's a house of straw bales, a house of clay blocks and a house of bricks, all of which are handmade. They are telling me that the resort-style eco-accommodation is an absolute winner, and you must progress this. These seem like businesses to me. Do they make sense to you?

Bec: Oh Marion, this is incredible. I've only just sat down and had a sip of tea and you've already given me everything I need! I came here because my husband and I want to start a business in Mount Compass where we have land. We have already actually started on the eco huts that we are going to call, exactly as you said, 'The 3 Little Pigs Retreat!' That's incredible. We've also been considering a wedding chapel overlooking the sea on the way to Deep Creek National Park, but we're not sure. Oh my goodness! Ian will be really, really excited! This is quite amazing!

Me: Oh Bec, I think it's amazing too! It's such a fantastic idea. How great that someone can come and experience what each house offers insulation-wise prior to building their own home! This business is going to be a big success, and we're thrilled that you've shown it to us today. The wedding business was just an option to consider, but it's not the way you will progress.

Bec: Thank you so much again. Now that I've gotten what I came for, I'm going to leave so that I can get back before this front comes in.

Here she gestured to the view outside of the angry ocean across the road! I told her that was a great idea and wished her and her husband every success for their new business.

My course in miracles

In September 2023, I left South Australia, towing my 22 foot caravan for Airlie Beach. There were many times when I was consumed by worry. Will I get there safely? Am I meant to be going? Will I be okay? Will I make friends? Why am I going again? When you travel alone, you become your own best friend, enemy, critic and audience! There are some songs I sing along with and I think 'Yeah, I can go on *The Voice Australia*!' and then my critic says, 'Not with that voice!' I talk to myself all the time. I argue. I laugh. I cry.

When I drive long distances, I like to listen to podcasts. I also talk to my Team pretty much all the time. I ask them questions about things I would like to learn about from their perspective. I also like to ask for Signs. This road trip to Airlie Beach was no different. Tens, hundreds, thousands of kilometres went past, and I had to do something to keep myself awake. I would play games with my Team, like guessing the last digit on the number plate of the car coming towards me or what colour the next car would be. Podcasts were the best as they were so engaging. I just escaped into them.

Over the last 20 years, I have been trying to read the book *A Course in Miracles*. Have you read it? It's extremely thick, the paper it's printed on is extremely thin, the text is extremely small and its chock-a-block full of information that does not sink in for me. It's a real test to read it, but I felt like there were keys in there to unlocking the mysteries of my life. So, I decided to listen to it instead. I tried to persevere but, by the time I got to Mackay, I'd had enough of the man's flat voice. Instead, I turned it off and sat in silence.

Then, no less than five kilometres from the Mackay turn-off to Proserpine, it started … it seemed that my Team wanted to show me I was on the right road having the right journey at exactly the right time, because they sent me Signs that confirmed everything for me. It all started when I saw a Sign for 'A Course in Miracles' on a billboard in a paddock on my driver's side. I was completely shocked! In all my travels and everywhere I have been, I have never, ever seen a sign promoting a course in miracles!

I thanked my Team and promised that I would try listening to it again one day on a long drive. They were telling me, it seems, that there is indeed information in there that I need to know.

I drove on with a smile and soon came to a small town called Take Leap! Whenever I am uncertain about my direction in life, my Guides constantly tell me to 'take a leap' of faith and trust them. Sure enough, when I do, everything works out perfectly, as if by magic!

I began to laugh out loud. My Team can be very playful at times, and this was one of those times. How on earth had they arranged for me to see these physical Signs in my outer world?

Out loud, I said to them, 'You really are magical, you know that? And you really make me believe in Angels!' Well, if I didn't hear it with my own two ears I wouldn't have believed it, but the music I had been listening to changed and decided 'of its own accord' (or did it?) to play the Robbie Williams song 'Angels'!

I burst into tears!

Why do I doubt? Stupid human!

I began talking to my Team: Opa D, Opa B, Mum and Dad, Joop, Mark and Staven. I thanked them over and over again. They told me to be quiet! They said that one day I will see for myself how this magic works! I can't wait to go Home and see how everything is orchestrated for our benefit.

I was less than an hour from my destination when I saw a huge green signpost declaring that Proserpine was straight ahead, and that 'Marian' was on the left!

I had NO doubt that I was meant to be on this journey. I was feeling incredibly excited, electrically so! I even wondered how I could drive straight! I felt high on life and incredible love. Those two words on that sign indicated to me that I, Marion, was on the right road to Proserpine! Incredible.

My car and caravan had made the almost 6000 km journey over four weeks safely without any incident whatsoever! I know for a fact that Angels are real, and I hope that you are starting to believe this for yourself and that reading about my experiences will inspire you to see what you too can manifest.

I also hope that you are starting to get excited about your own journeys! I'm excited for you!

When I arrived at Proserpine Caravan Park, Robyn the caretaker greeted me warmly. 'Maz, welcome to Prossie, you made it. It's so lovely to meet you finally after all our chats! Oh, and I have some mail for you!'

Robyn went into the office and came out with a large envelope. I knew intuitively that it was from my friend Sarah! Sarah always thought of everything! Inside Sarah's envelope was a sheet of A4 paper full of photographs of her beautiful fluffies and lots of messages and cut-out hearts. Sarah has this 6y way of knowing exactly what's needed before it's needed, and opening her envelope and having all the hearts fall out made me cry! Bless ya, Sarah, for knowing how much I would love receiving your special Gift when I arrived.

Prior to leaving South Australia, I asked all my friends to gift me a small heart. I was calling this trip my 'Hearts & Hugs' tour! I received a lot of hearts and cards before I left and stuck them everywhere in my caravan. Each time I look at a heart, I feel a hug. I set my itinerary from Victor Harbor to Airlie Beach, visiting towns where I knew a hug would be waiting. It all made sense on my first drive into Airlie Beach where I saw a huge tourism sign saying 'Home of the Heart Reef' with a huge photo of the pristine heart reef. How could I not smile? To me, it felt like coming home. I am a really blessed person to know each and every one of you, and I thank everyone who has supported me through all my traumas and tears. Thank you for all your support, kindness and friendship.

I still ask for Signs to help me along my journey. I always will. We all need them.

I hope that this chapter has inspired you to *really* think about the direction you are heading in in your life. Are you on track? Or off-track? Do you feel like you need some guidance? I share my experiences with you so you can see it really *is* easy to ask and receive from the universe. Please remember that if you would like to help yourself in this way, I am only a Reading away, and the universe always has your back when it's for your highest good!

Let me inspire you to believe!

Pay attention

One of the most important things you can do for yourself and your Guides is to *really* pay attention! Don't just ask for a Sign and promptly walk away. Be specific about the Sign you want to see and when you want to see it. Give your Guides something to work with. Then pay attention!

Stop taking life so seriously!

Too many people take life and people at face value! That's what the Awakening is *really* all about! *Nothing* is as it first seems. The Awakening is all about realising that life as a human is a complete illusion. You are *not* who you think you are.

To start with, there are two of you!

You are the I, AND you are the Me!

How often do you say something to yourself like 'I have to tell myself XYZ' or 'I wish I had listened to myself'?

There you are – there are two of YOU!

There is 'you' that is the body, which is as old as you are physically, then there is 'you' that is the Soul, who is as old as all the incarnations that you have ever lived.

Look around you. I am a Soul, you are a Soul, we are surrounded by Souls! There are Souls everywhere you go. You work with them, you play sport with them, they're the parents and teachers at school and you shop alongside them, and they ALL have their own energy!

If you are at a 5 ¾ and above, you will be very sensitive to energy everywhere you go. The energy comes from the Soul, *not* from the human body that you get around in. It's our energy that introduces us to others, not our words or appearance. It's this energy that we rely on when meeting new people.

So, my/our advice to you is to stop trying so hard, you stupid human! Stop taking your life and everyone in it at face value, and look beyond the skin. Let yourself feel the energy of the person in front of you. 'Read' them and see what you pick up.

Life is an illusion, and you will progress far quicker spiritually the sooner you realise and accept this fact! This is part of your learning and growth – we all have to go through it at some point in our incarnations!

BP service station lady

This story is about Elizabeth. It's another time when Opa put me exactly where I needed to be without me knowing I needed to be there! Who knows, maybe she had been asking for a Sign too and I came to deliver it. I totally trust these situations or assignments and look forward to them. This is exactly the kind of work I like doing – being in the right place, at the right time, giving the right words to the right person to help them, without them even realising they needed help. This is an excerpt of my encounter with Elizabeth:

The year was 2018. My friend and I had driven to Lakes Entrance in Victoria on the east coast of Australia, a beautiful place I had always wanted to visit. It's so gorgeous there. I had arranged to give two presentations: one at Lakes Entrance and one at a little town called Koroit with a really big New Age store. I love sharing my stories, and I love hearing other people's stories even more. We had decided to make a little holiday of it.

We spent a night in a motel in Mount Gambier on the way home. My dad had taken very ill, and I wanted to get home as soon as possible.

We got up early and headed to the local BP service station to fuel up. It was 6am, and there was no one else around. I pulled in, fuelled up and paid the woman behind the counter. I walked back to my car, then Opa got involved. I didn't mind, of course, but he had never done this at 6am before.

Opa: Lieve meisje, please give that lady working in there one of your books and write this message in the front of it – she will understand it!

Once I had written the message in the front of my book, I knew exactly why Opa had come through so early in the morning. I thanked him, then I went and lined up behind another guy who was paying for his fuel. Once the guy left, I walked back up to the counter.

Lady: Hi again, did you forget something?

Me: No, well not really. You see, I have a gift for you. I'm an author, and I'm in the area doing presentations. I've been urged to gift you a copy with this message in the front – I hope you understand it. I cautiously watched her face as I slid the book across the counter and she read the message. Gulp! My lesson in trust continued.

Lady: Oh my goodness! It's incredible that you have just done what you've done! You don't know what this means to me! It's EXACTLY what I need!

Boss: What's going on out here? What's all this shrieking ... it's only 6am!

Lady: It is, and what's going on is I'm outta here! I'm sick of you yelling at me at all hours of the day. You are a complete bully, and I'm sick of you. I quit!

With that, she dumped her apron, got her bag from under the counter, stormed out and drove off. By then, I was back in my car, where my friend asked, 'Are you responsible for that? I saw you get a book for her. Tell me what happened!' I told him, 'That, my friend, was the perfect example of a woman standing up for herself and no longer taking shit from a bully of a man!'

This woman gave me the courage to do the very same thing to my own 'friend' a month later! Remember what I said before: never lie to a Psychic? Well, my friend had lied to me for months. After this encounter at a service station, I was also motivated to quit the situation, and I'm very glad I did.

My notes to the BP lady's scenario

What I absolutely love most about my Gift is when I am put in the right place at the right time. I give the message in whatever way it comes to light, then disappear, leaving people to work through their situation. Many Earth Angels may relate to this. My life has always been a series of 'assignments'.

I drove away from that service station unsure who had been the teacher in that situation. Time taught me that the BP lady was my teacher. I'll be forever grateful to her.

One of the most important things to remember is that life is a complete illusion! Don't ever take anything at face value. Look beneath the surface energetically, and all will be revealed.

Trust it!

The judging of others

We know all about Soul Contracts, right? We all have them, but many do not realise and live their lives oblivious to the fact. Knowing that we all have Soul Contracts, it should be obvious that you cannot judge others for what they say or do in their lives. It is the human in us that does the judging. Judging is a human predicament – having and holding expectations of others, often unrealistic, often without them knowing – a standard we hold everyone to. It's an arrogant trait and one that will only lead to disappointment and broken relationships. Judging is predominantly from the ego.

This is where your faith in Spirituality will help. Ask for and receive guidance, clarity and understanding. Ask your Team of Guides to show you the bigger picture in tiny, bite-sized chunks.

Please remember that you are only an observer on the outside looking in to other people's lives. You have no idea what their Soul Contract looks like.

Words that need to come out of the dictionary

I believe that the following words need to be removed from all modern dictionaries:

Should – I *should*, you *should*, we *should* …
If – I had done this, or done that …
I will love you *if* …
I won't love you *if* …
Who, what, where, why and *how!*

These are all words that are conditional and lack faith and trust in the universe. They can all be so easily replaced by saying nothing at all!

Children as our Spiritual Teachers

Our children are leading the way. In my articles and videos, for years I have talked about how children are our Spiritual Teachers. I love sharing time with families where the mum and dad are the parents, but the children are their teachers. Gratefully, some parents are even listening to their kids more and more and realising that Old Souls is truly what they are! Some kids' Souls are way older than their parents'!

Finally, there are kids in the playground that can communicate, hear and also deliver messages from Spirit and Loved Ones to each other.

I remember a seven-year-old telling me during a Reading that she heard a message from another child's grandmother in Spirit at the school playground one day. The other child was bullying a smaller child when his grandma came through and said, 'Grandma Bubba is watching you and doesn't like the way you are treating [name] and wants you to stop!' Well, the child certainly did stop bullying, and while they couldn't quite comprehend what had happened, they started to bully less.

We hope that this awareness has continued into her adulthood!

Soul language shared amongst children is palpable. Everything changes energetically when someone channels true messages from Loved Ones back Home. If you feel no change in energy when someone is giving you a message, then I would be questioning their 'source.'

The truth is always seen by a Psychic. Remember that! It's a big responsibility to carry, especially when you see others completely wrapped up by their lies and games with innocent parties.

That's the hardest part about this role and also the best.

You are WIRED
You are Connected!

'Oh, they're such an Old Soul!'

Have you ever heard these words as someone bends down to check out the baby in a pram?

Do these people even realise what they are saying? Most people who say this are just a 5 themselves! How do they even know an Old Soul when they are just young Souls themselves?

Great question!

The universe, in her wisdom, is allowing and encouraging Souls to learn lessons quicker than ever before. Our world is so far out of balance that the only way forward is for Souls to accumulate wisdom and learn lessons quickly so that they can come back to help during this, one of the most important times in history – the Awakening.

Opa told me that some Souls are living two or more incarnations in this one. That's why their lives seem so chaotic. Rather than choosing one or two lessons in their Soul Contract and subsequent incarnation, then dying, going through a Life Review, choosing new lessons and being reincarnated for the next round of learning, some are choosing two or three lifetimes worth of lessons to learn back to back in this one incarnation. It is the Dark Night of the Soul that then splits the two lifetimes, rather than returning home and reincarnating.

You may have seen the faraway look in those gorgeous big eyes as an Old Soul in a very young body as it greets you with *'that look!'* You know the one! We fall into the depth of those eyes and fall in Love with their very Soul. We feel safe with them. We feel like they have come to help us in this lifetime. They feel like Angels.

That's because they are!

These children will astound you with their wisdom, and the stories they share of their memories will truly leave you believing beyond doubt that there really IS more to life ... more than you ever suspected to be true or real.

You may find that you are the parents of these children; however, *they* are *your* teachers and have actually lived many more lifetimes than you. They know that they are here to put our world back into balance one family at a time, probably starting with yours (no wonder they came into this world screaming! Can't blame them, right?)

I would like to share a few stories with you now about these special kids. I am very blessed to do so much work with these young Earth Angels, these 6s disguised as children.

First, I will share a couple of stories about my own son.

James' story

When James (name changed) was five years old, he used to taunt his four-year-old sister by taking her teddy bear away and teasing her with it. As a parent, I was over it! Time out, the naughty corner, star charts and empty threats didn't work. I had no idea how to help the situation. My Opa did, though!

One day, Opa said to me, 'Bend down to James's height, look him in the eye and say, "Listen to your heart!"' I replied, 'No way, he won't listen to me.' Opa asked me to trust him, and I knew to, so I did.

As his sister was crying, I bent down to James and repeated exactly what Opa had said to me, then I walked away. I hid behind a wall out of their sight.

What I saw next shocked me! James actually gave the teddy bear back to his sister and walked away!

Yes!

It worked every time after that, and the game soon had no fun to it anymore and it stopped. Thank goodness.

My son, who is now an adult, has rung me many times over his lifetime to ask about decisions he has to make. My answer has and always will be the same, 'Listen to your heart …' His reply is also always the same, 'I knew you would say that!' then he hangs up, hopefully to listen to his heart. His own Soul Contract has been a nightmare to the point where we had to cancel it! Yes, this can be done and is sometimes very necessary! This is a very specialised field of work.

The teaching that I do nowadays based on colours, shapes and numbers comes from that particular situation. By 'listening to his heart', my son was actually listening to his Soul. Over time, Opa encouraged me to share this teaching with others so that they too could learn how to listen to their own Soul and allow it to guide them through their life. This teaching has now been shared with hundreds of people who all use it, and it has changed their lives. We call it the 85/15 principle and I will explain it later in this book.

Here's another scenario, when James, a toddler at the time and still in nappies, was the only person that could stop his sister from screaming with colicky pain.

Louise suffered terrible colic when she was a baby. Her brother was about three-and-a-half when this incident took place. I was sitting together with my husband, exhausted from trying to calm her down. My parents were also sitting in the same room with us. Louise was lying on my knees on her back, and her head was at the end of my knees. She was still crying. We had tried all we could to calm her down. Any parent that has ever had a child suffering with colic understands how exasperating this situation is.

James had been asleep in his cot, or so we thought. He waddled into the lounge room still wearing his nappy and no T-shirt or singlet. He stood in front of Louise, that is, at the back of her head. He never looked at anyone else except his baby sister. He gently, but deliberately, swirled his hand in the air around Louise's head three times then placed the same hand on her heart, and she went to sleep! Yes! She went to sleep! Once she was asleep, he walked back to bed and fell asleep again, and the four of us just looked at each other in disbelief.

We had witnessed a true miracle.

Yes, my son has the Gift, and so does my daughter. They both know it's real but choose to exercise their rights to live as human, unlike their mum! Maybe one day they will truly embrace it.

I wrote my first book for them.

I write my second book for You!

Blessings to you, my beautiful, gifted children.

Talea's story

My next story is about Talea. Talea was the first child I experienced talking to me telepathically! While I have used telepathy my whole life, my experience with Talea was a different experience again. Let me share our story:

Back in 2015, I was doing a Reading for Talea's mum Samantha in the Adelaide Hills. Halfway through the session, Samantha's beautiful five-year-old daughter walked in. As she did, my Opa said to me, 'Please pay attention to this little girl as she is going to teach you something that you will teach to others later in life.' I told Opa that I couldn't possibly be taught anything by a five-year-old, could I? Nonetheless, in she walked. She was very comfortable in her own presence, with big brown eyes and long brown hair in ringlets. I found myself straighten up as if in the presence of a teacher. An Archangel, even. Even as I type this, her energy still makes me sit up straight in order to pay respect to her. Powerfully, gently, aMAZingly!

She said, 'Hi, I'm Talea,' but her lips didn't move! Talea's mum then said, 'Talea, please say hello to Marion.' I just looked at her mum as Talea had already said hello to me.

Opa told me to answer her telepathically, so I said, 'You are really special, aren't you?', to which she replied, 'I'm Mummy's teacher.' I asked, 'What are you here to teach Mummy?' (neither of us moved our lips during this conversation; we kept our eyes locked on each other's and had the most extraordinary connection I had ever had with someone else's child!) Talea then replied, 'I'm here to teach Mummy how to Love and forgive people! Can I go outside and play now please?' Out loud, I said, 'Umm, yes.' So, she did.

Samantha then turned to me, smiling, and said, 'Did she just talk to you telepathically?' When I said she had, Sam said, 'She does it with me all the time!'

I was completely astonished at what had just taken place. I'd used telepathy before, but only to put my thoughts into other people's minds, asking them to do something for me!

I have some fun stories to tell about my other experiences with telepathy, but that's for a whole other type of book ... wink wink!

Anyway, Samantha went on to tell me all about her special daughter. Opa was right – my work did change. I never looked at children the same way again and started doing more work with them and helping parents to work with their gifted children.

Quite often, between the ages of three and ten years old, our gifted children present to paediatricians with their parents who are at their wits end about their child's behaviour. Some 6s who are children use their Gifts in a variety of ways, including bad behaviour, just to get their parents' attention. They haven't yet learnt how to interpret what they are seeing or knowing. All I can recommend is to pay attention to your child.

Quite often, due to their behaviour, they are mistakenly diagnosed as having ADHD or ODD, among others. These kids are then put on medications to calm their behaviour. However, this medication doesn't change the gift that the child is carrying in this incarnation. It does, however, make those around them, including parents, siblings, family, teachers and students, more comfortable in their presence as the child has been numbed by the medication.

I implore you to consider the contents of this book before embarking down traditional medical practices. Get in touch with me. I have been through so much with kids on a Spiritual level, and I understand. I share as much as I can in my books.

You might be the parents; however, children are your teachers! We are so blessed.

Blessings to you, beautiful Archangel with the long dark brown ringlets and all-knowing eyes. Thank you for showing you to me. I honour you.

Jackson's story

I asked Jackson's mum for approval if I could use their story in this book if I changed their names, and she agreed.

I received a call from a young mum one day almost at her wits end with her son's disturbing behaviour. I was invited to her house to see Jackson in his own environment, and we 'connected' immediately, Soul to Soul. I chatted with him then played my colours game with him. The game started with the story about my son and the teddy bear and listening to your heart. Opa taught me to streamline this craft to share with children and their families so they can learn to hear and know their own messages. With the colours game, I am able to find out if someone can hear me telepathically. Jackson heard me straight away. If he could hear me, then there was a very good chance that he could hear his Guides too!

Because Jackson could hear me telepathically, I knew he was a 6. He was one of us. For most of my life up to this point, I had never had any real connection with anyone like me. Now here I was working with children who were exactly like me. I had company at last! It was fantastic to be able to help parents understand their kids.

Helping kids on this level meant I was then able to help parents parent their gifted child without the need for medication. Once kids are understood by their families on this level, they feel like they belong. Until then, they fight for their very existence as they feel but don't understand the difference between their families and themselves.

Because these kids have all their senses intact, they often get overloaded as everything becomes too much for them. You know how you say that you are an 'Empath' and struggle to cope being around people? Well, these kids are Empaths on steroids! Imagine for a minute what their life must be like!

Families have no idea until we have a session together or someone teaches them the shortcut about how to 'deal' with the outbursts and tantrums. These kids are extremely sensitive and pick up everything seen *and* unseen, spoken and unspoken, felt and unfelt, and it overwhelms them. Once I have been able to explain this to the family, I am able to give their parents the tools to help them all live together happily under one roof. Jackson's mum recently told me two of her experiences with him:

> Jackson had a really good habit of always being ready for school on time. But, on a couple of occasions, he had refused to get ready. I thought he was being defiant but, because you showed me otherwise, I looked at the situation through his eyes and senses and trusted him. It turned out that there was no coincidence – on the days that Jackson had stalled getting us to school, we ended up avoiding an accident that, had we been on time, we would certainly have been involved in.
>
> There was another time when Jackson asked me to go down a different street on the way to school. I told him that if we went that way, we would be late. I was a bit frustrated with him on both of these occasions, so this time I went the usual way to school (after all, parents know best, don't they?) Turned out that there were roadworks on our normal street and we were late by over 30 minutes. The road that Jackson had wanted to take would have gotten us there right on time!

Sometimes our gifted children show us their Gifts through the most amazing of childlike ways:

I would also like to tell you a funny story that happened one day on the way home from school. I (Mum) had picked up Jackson from pre-primary school. At the time, he was still in a booster seat in the backseat of the car. He started asking me to drive to Bunnings on the way home. He kept saying, 'Mummy, we have to go to Bunnings. Bunnings is our local hardware store. Mummy, we have to go to Bunnings!' I told him we weren't going to Bunnings, but he kept repeating himself. I asked him why, and he told me, 'We have to get a long white thing with four holes,' and used his hands to demonstrate the length then putting something into the holes! I had no idea what he was talking about. I told him, 'Jackson, we have to go home because we are going to put up the Christmas tree together!' Well! Jackson knew best, didn't he? Turns out we had to go to Bunnings that afternoon after all, because we needed a power board for the lights on the Christmas tree! Yes! A white power board was what we bought at Bunnings and yes, with four holes to put all the power cords into! I now know to listen to Jackson whenever he mucks around getting ready for school or at other times. Jackson has taught me so much.

Jackson's mum rang me a couple of years later to tell me how things were going and told me that she wanted me to know that the time I had spent with Jackson had been very valuable for him and her family. It had helped turn perceived bad behaviour into valuable messages.

The message in this story is for parents – please do not jump to hasty conclusions that your child is being naughty. Maybe, just maybe, they sense something you can't. It's worth noting! Remember that life is just an illusion!

Blessings to you, Jackson, the boy with the world in his eyes and at his feet!

Levi's story

Ah! Levi! What a kid! What a bright, shiny kid! Well, that's how I saw him.

His mum would say, 'Ah! Levi! Why did I ever have you? Be a good boy, go to sleep, go to your room!'

Levi was five years old when his mum first came to see me for a Reading. It was about her personal life and her love life, not her life with her kids!

However, her Guides and mine ganged up on her, and out came a whole lot of information that she needed to hear.

Through her Reading, we also told her about Levi's special 6th sense and how I was being shown how Gifted he was. She said she didn't believe it, and instead proceeded to tell me he was severely autistic with ADHD and would sometimes take hours to go to bed.

Some months went by, and I didn't hear from Levi's mum. Then, one day, I ran into her at the shops. She looked haggard for her 34 years. I asked if I could give her a hug and, as I did, she started crying. She told me, through her sobs, how difficult Levi was to live with and how it had been affecting the whole family.

So, we sat.
And talked.

She said that she had been thinking about what I had told her … that it had stayed with her. She then said that they have walked along the beach past my house many times after school and that she points my house out to Levi.

I made an offer to her. 'How about we arrange that you walk past my house after school tomorrow, and I'll be sitting on the sand. You can stop and chat with me, and we'll act as if it was unplanned. You can introduce me to Levi, and I can take the rest from there, if you like.'

Levi's mum thought it was a great idea.

The next afternoon found me sitting on the beach, watching Levi and his mum come closer on their daily walk.

Mum gave the appropriate, 'Oh, what a surprise. Look Levi, it's Maz!'

No response.

'Maz this is my son, Levi. Levi, this is Maz.'

No response.

I tried to chat with Levi, but he just wanted to fill the hole he had dug with seawater. Obviously, this kept him busy for a long time. I tried to make 'normal childlike human' conversation with him but couldn't get through. So, I asked Opa for help.

Opa then showed me a damned sexy guy on a green motorbike! (I wanted to ask if he was here for me – but, alas, he wasn't! He was great to perve on though, I'll tell you! I am only human, after all!) Anyway, this guy was probably in his early thirties and shirtless (I'm pretty sure those muscles wouldn't have fit inside a shirt anyway ... he was gorgeous, just saying!). Dark hair, tanned skin, sinful smile ... wait? He was saying something about Levi!

Putting my Psychic hat on, I asked him to repeat his message, which he did. 'I'm Levi's Guide. Ask him now about how he makes his mum stop before driving into their driveway so that I can go in first on my motorbike!'

So, I did.

As Levi was walking back with yet another bucket of water, I asked him, 'Hey Levi, who's the guy on the green motorbike, and why doesn't he wear a shirt or helmet? He just said hello to me.'

Levi made eye contact with me for the first time, then replied, 'Can you see him too?'

Mum: Oh my goodness, can you see him, Marion? I thought Levi was making it up or that he was an invisible friend. Levi always makes me wait so that this guy can ride his motorbike up our driveway before we drive up. That's crazy. Who is he?'

Me: Yes, I can see him, Levi. He told me he is your friend, your Guide, and he likes to help you go to sleep at night-time, but you don't listen to him. Why not?'

Levi: 'cos Daddy says it's just my imagination and he's not real. I know he's real. He's always with me when I feel angry and sad. He tells me how he used to feel angry and sad when he was my age. He told me that he used to bully kids at school, like I do, because they didn't understand him. I told him that I get mad at the kids at school because they don't understand me and then they are nasty to me. He told me that once he was old enough, he got his motorbike licence and bought a motorbike – a green one, just like you described. He said he never wore a helmet. One day, he was angry at his mum and dad and he took his motorbike for a ride. It had been raining and it was very cold. The roads were slippery, and he lost control of his bike and crashed into a fence. He said that the accident was his fault because he was so angry at his parents and also at the kids at school. He wanted to show them that he could ride really fast. They always told him not to, and that day he told them he didn't care about them and off he went.

He knows how angry I get. I can't ride a motorbike yet, and I'm pretty sure he doesn't even want me to have one. He helps me when I get really angry and sad inside and I feel like I'm going to explode. He talks to me about how he spends time with his mum and dad because they are still so sad he died in the accident. He tells me he is very sorry for what he did that day and he didn't do it on purpose but he should have worn a helmet. He keeps trying to help them, but they don't listen. He tells me to listen to him, and he helps me go to sleep. I always feel better when I listen to him. He doesn't want me to get so angry that I end up hurting my mum and dad by doing something silly. But I won't. He makes me feel sad. I wish he was alive so I could go on his motorbike with him.

Levi's mum and I sat awestruck as Levi told his story – please remember he was only five at the time.

The outcome of this visit was so lovely. Mum had a much better insight and understanding of her son, and bedtime was no longer a time when Mum had to fight the animals in her zoo! I never saw them again after that day. Levi would be 11 now. Levi's sexy hunk Guide showing himself to me was the breakthrough I needed when Levi was initially ignoring me.

I told the guy on the motorbike that I'd be happy for him to guide me any time too!

Blessings to you Levi, keep shining and listening to your spunky guide!

So! You think you gave birth to a weirdo!

Congratulations! You have been blessed. But that's the last time you call them 'weird' – they are 'Wired', and 'Wired' means connected to Source.

This means they are a Gift from the universe to you.

Children don't come with a manual, and they definitely don't come with a manual if they've come into this world with all 6 senses intact.

Old Souls don't come with a manual, because they don't need one! They know EXACTLY what they are here to do! Life with them will be full-on for you, expect that. But it's all very worth it.

If you are ever struggling with issues like some of the parents I've mentioned were, please keep an open mind and reach out to me. There are many things you can do to help your family to live with, nurture and encourage your Old Soul or Gifted child.

You don't know everything just because you are the parents! Ouch, that comment hurt, didn't it? But it's true. That may be why your very special child, with all their 6 senses intact, chose you! They are your teacher. Trust them – they will show you the way.

It's part of your parental responsibility to 'teach'. However, you don't need to teach them how to see, hear, taste, touch or smell as its part of the growing process. The 6th sense is different because it develops with us each time we are reincarnated.

While these children were born with all 6 senses intact, they, like me, may not know how to integrate that sense into their 'human' existence and life, at least not until they remember. They are simply not aware of it and may also feel that they don't belong or are weird compared to their friends. It's like we were born spiritually and need to learn to be human.

If your child has the special gift of 'knowing', please embrace them for being Wired. Some children may be like this from day one, while others may take more time to start their Spiritual journey in this incarnation. We never know when it will be or what will trigger it. What I am shown is that we are links in the chain, and everything else needs to be in order before our link can be added.

You may also like to look at it as a jigsaw puzzle. Each piece has its position, but it can't be put there until every other piece around it is in place. Your Soul has been with you through all your incarnations. Your Soul has the picture of the puzzle you are assembling, lifetime by lifetime. Unfortunately, you can't see it. You have to complete the puzzle a bit at a time.

Sometimes when doing a puzzle without a picture, we can fit a few pieces together easily, usually the edges, only to find that the puzzle gets 'stuck' and you cannot continue. That's when you need to take a step back and look at the puzzle from a different perspective: a Soul's perspective.

Margaret's story

Margaret rang seeking advice about her 12-year-old daughter who 'saw dead people and often made predictions that came true'! Margaret herself was a believer and proud to be Tiffany's mum.

Margaret wanted to know how best to support Tiffany's Gift. We agreed on a time when I would chat with Tiffany over video, as they lived in a different state to me.

The following evening, after connecting with Tiffany via video, I undertook my normal testing of colours, shapes and numbers with her. It is worth noting here that I don't need to physically be with a child/person when undertaking this. Tiffany proved to me instantly that she was telepathic and gifted. Tiffany heard and knew all the shapes, colours and numbers that I was sending her telepathically from 3000 kilometres away over the internet! Just for a minute, imagine all the images that were between Tiffany and me, yet the telepathic ones that I sent were the ones that got through! That's how powerful this skill is.

After a while, I asked Tiff to explain to me what her life was like at school. She told me she was always alone and didn't feel like she fitted in with the other girls or kids in her year.

While I was listening to her, Opa showed me visions of her at school. I love this part of my Gift. My Psychic vision is incredible when people explain things to me – it's like I'm right there with them! Opa showed me a boy in her class called Tom, and that Tom wore an unusual leather bracelet. Opa asked me to ask Tiffany to look for him at school the next day and to introduce herself, as he too was a 6. Opa asked Tiffany to comment on Tom's bracelet and that would start their friendship. It would reunite two beautiful 6s: Soul Mates.

I explained my visions to Tiffany, and she confirmed that she did indeed know a boy in her class called Tom and that he, too, was always alone. She left the video call feeling more excited about going to school than she had been for a very long time.

The following night, her mum asked me to call them. Tiffany was glowing. Mum told me that Tiffany had some exciting news to tell me. I couldn't wait.

Tiffany told me that she had gone to school that day and, at the break, had indeed gone up to Tom and asked him about his bracelet. She told me his bracelet had a crystal on it, and that his mum had given it to him. Tom told Tiffany that his mum lets him use her oracle cards and that he is regularly guided by his grandma to give messages to his mum.

Tiffany thanked me profusely for telling her about Tom and was really excited to tell me that he was her new best friend!

I was so excited for them for finding each other at such a young age. Regardless of how long their human friendship lasts, their Souls were united in their 6yness and they were no longer alone in this world. Oh, how I wish I'd had a friend like Tiffany or Tom when I was at school, it would have made my life so much more 'normal!' I am, however, very glad for them. I also give great credit to Tiffany's mum for arranging this very special session for Tiffany and me. How blessed they are to have each other in their lives. One day, I hope the two mums meet and share their experiences from this beautiful story.

Blessings to you, beautiful Earth Angel Tiffany, and your friend with wings, Tom, and also your parents for their incredible support of your Gift.

Scenarios like this are becoming more and more common. Maybe your child is a 5 ½, a 5 ¾ or even a 6, or maybe they're not! Regardless, parents, please keep an open mind as there is more than only the human way to help your child navigate this incarnation.

This next story is about two very special people in my life. Because they are so special and this story is so very real, they have given me permission to share it. I have, however, changed their names.

Sharing Granny Y and her granddaughter's beautiful experience together

My dear friend Y used to look after her granddaughter, and a very GRAND granddaughter she certainly is. One day, while sitting quietly together with her granddaughter on the floor, Y was thinking it had been a while since she had sung to little kids and she racked her brain trying to think of a nursery rhyme to sing. She came up with 'row, row, row your boat' but found that she couldn't remember all the words. Remember that she did not sing the song out loud … she sang it in her head. Then her granddaughter started singing out loud, 'Row, row, row your boat, gently down the stream. Merrily, merrily, merrily, merrily, life is but a dream. Is that the one, Granny?' she asked innocently looking up at my friend Y with all the sweetness that a beautiful three-year-old's eyes could shine with. With tears in her eyes, Y said, 'YES, that's the one!'

Granny Y simply could not believe what had just taken place between them. This is a true Soul Connection with Soul Family. Granny Y is a dear friend of mine who, like many of us, has had devastating trauma in her life. Little G is her Angel here on earth, with little Angel wings sprouting in the place of shoulder blades! What joy she brings to Granny Y's life!

Again, it is so beautiful to witness. Very humbling.

Blessings to you little Angel with the perfect name for an Angel! I love you so much for sharing your incredible experience with me and other parents that are reading this story, with tears in their eyes, nodding in agreement as they too have experienced these types of miracles that are very hard to explain.

Telepathy IS real. I suggest you try it for yourself! Be kind though, and never use telepathy as a weapon, or it'll bite you on the arse! It is, however, a great tool for your spiritual toolbox when trying to discipline kids that just don't listen – start out by singing a song in your head and watch it catch on! You can do it easily with adults too; I usually do it when I'm in a lift and there's that awkward silence. This is how you will know for sure that this stuff works, as you will have your own proof!

My little Johnny story

This following story comes from my own children's childhood, and it illustrates the potential misdiagnosis of our children's mental health and behaviour patterns.

Scenario 1:

Johnny is a little boy in year 3 at school. Johnny is an Old Soul, a 6. All of Johnny's 6 senses are fully intact. He is a really warm, compassionate and empathic Soul. His kind nature is infectious, and this makes him popular at school. He is very well balanced and lacks ego. His friends at school and his teachers love him. Johnny, however, likes to cheer kids up, teachers too, and hasn't yet learnt the empathic art of detaching.

Sadly, the same cannot be said for his mum. His mum is a 5, a very young, immature Soul. She is a volatile and often angry human being, bitter at the world because she doesn't understand why Johnny's father left her. She has no capacity for self-reflection, preferring instead to lay all the blame purely on him and feel like a victim.

No wonder he left! This mum often resents Johnny's presence and interruptions into her avid scrolling while on social media. It is obvious to him that she doesn't understand him or want him around.

But Johnny's love for his mum is unconditional; he is a 6, after all! He tries to please her every day … but not as a people pleaser, just as her son. His role in their Soul Contract is to teach her about Unconditional Love.

One day Johnny comes home from school and goes to shut the front door, which slams shut. He then throws his school bag down near the door.

Johnny's mum is a 5 or very young, immature Soul. She is seated at the kitchen table, smoking a cigarette and drinking her daily glass of wine while texting friends on Facebook. She exclaims:

> Oh Johnny, there you go again, slamming the door and throwing your school bag on the floor. It really annoys me when you do this. You did it yesterday too! Go pick up your bag and take it to your room and don't come out till dinner time … I don't want to see you!

Johnny has a clear conscience knowing that he hasn't really done anything wrong. If he had, he would own his part of the blame. He does as his mum asks and goes to his room to do homework until his mum calls him out for dinner.

Scenario 2:

Now picture this: same little Johnny, but this time he comes home to a mum who is a 6.

So, Johnny comes home from school, goes to shut the front door, which slams shut, and throws his school bag down near the door.

His mum is a 6 and, as such, 'tunes' into Johnny throughout the day. By doing so, she already knew that her son wasn't his usual self. She called out to him, inviting him to come and share her fruit platter with her. There was no phone, alcohol, cigarette or distraction in sight. She gave Johnny her complete focus and attention (how validated he must feel with her as his mum, hey?)

She doesn't ask Johnny how his day was, or even why the door slammed or why he threw his school bag on the floor. What she did instead was ask:

'Johnny, who were you with today that was sad or angry?'

Johnny thought before replying, 'Um, only Sarah, I think. Sarah was crying, so I gave her a hug. Is that okay?'

Mum's response was warm and empathetic. 'Yes, it's lovely that you did that. Why was Sarah crying?'

Johnny responded, 'She was sitting by herself and crying because she was sad that her mum and dad were splitting up. I knew that my hug would make her feel better.'

'Okay, and how about yesterday? Who were you with yesterday that might have been a bit angry?'

Johnny had to give this one some real thought. 'Um, my teacher, probably. She was angry, I just knew…'

'What did you know?' Mum asked.

'I just "knew" that my teacher had had a fight with her husband at home. I saw it in my mind. She was angry at him, so I told her some jokes and she ended up laughing. It made her face look nice, smoother. Is that okay?'

'Oh, Johnny! Thank you so much for remembering these things. You are such a special Soul. I checked in on you today while you were at school, and I knew it would be really helpful for you and me to talk when you got home. The way you dropped your school bag on the floor and shut the front door also told me that you needed to talk. You are not a naughty boy, so I knew this was not normal for you.

'Now, there's something I need to share with you. You have a Soul, we all do. Your Soul is the 'you' inside of you that is caring, loving and strong and knows the difference between right and wrong! You are also an Empath, which means you feel other people's emotions as if they are yours. Let me explain it like this… after I use a sponge to clean the mess on the kitchen bench, I rinse the sponge out to make it clean and fresh again. You are, in a way, a sponge cleaning up other people's messes when they don't know how to make themselves feel better. Their sadness and anger are stuck to them like the dirt is to the bench. Your empathic nature is to take away their pain for them. Like my sponge cleans up the dirt, you take away their sadness and their anger. And that's a beautiful thing.

'When you help other people, the best thing you can do is to come and tell me all about it. I love to listen to you and, this way, the sad and angry feelings you have absorbed from people around you won't stay with you, just like the dirt doesn't stay in my sponge when I rinse it under the tap!'

Johnny replied, 'Is that all I have to do? Talk to you about it? Okay, thank you, I will.'

Johnny's mum shared some further information with Johnny about energy and what it feels like to feel the energy of the people around him. Johnny accepted his mum's information without question as it felt right for him.

Johnny got his homework out of his school bag, sat back at the kitchen table, nibbled on some apple and started on his homework. Johnny and Mum enjoyed chatting about their day while Mum got dinner ready, which they later ate at the table together.

I share this as you may be able to relate it to your children.

Going back to the little Johnny in our first scenario, Johnny's mum knew nothing about her son's 'special 6th sense' and would have scoffed at it or labelled him as 'weird!' (sound familiar?). By the time this little Johnny is 13, his mum will have taken him to numerous doctors to find a diagnosis for his 'emotional behaviour and outbursts' and 'ADD tendencies', for which he will be given a prescription for Ritalin.

Sadly, Ritalin has squashed his special Gift, and he no longer uses it.

Mum still sits at the kitchen table, drinking, smoking and checking her social media accounts, ignoring her responsibility as Johnny's mum.

Johnny in scenario 2, however, thrived in his home and school environment.

So did his mum.

If you are interested in finding out more about this beautiful work with children, please feel free to contact me or watch my video on YouTube entitled 'Children as our Spiritual Teachers'.

I would like to share a few more stories with you about other children that I have had the absolute pleasure of sitting with. All stories are real; however, the names have been changed to protect their identity.

Siena's story

To this day, this experience still takes my breath away.

During my very first session with Siena's mum, I said, 'Do you have a daughter about this tall, approximately six years old with very long, dark, straight hair, whose name starts with S?' Mum said, 'Yes, that's my daughter Siena, but I'm not here to talk about her!' I said, 'No, you're right, we don't have to talk about her, but I feel I need to talk about her. You see, Opa is showing me how special Siena is. Before she turns ten, she will have already talked to you about 'stuff' that you know she hasn't experienced in this life … past-life stuff. Siena remembers parts of her past life during flashbacks. Siena "knows" things before they even happen. She is also extremely sensitive to anyone feeling angry or sad. I need you to know this about her, because some of her behaviour "could be" interpreted as her being a drama queen or suffering with ADHD. However, we know these interpretations aren't right. I just wanted to ask you to keep this information in the back of your mind! She is in your life to help keep you grounded and to see things for what they really are!'

While Siena's mum thought this was interesting, she struggled to believe it or even talk about it. That was until something happened, and now Mum has no doubt whatsoever.

Many months after our session, I received a phone call from Siena's mum, asking for a quick chat. I had been waiting to receive a call just like this one! She told me:

> Marion, I have to tell you about what happened the other day! My mum, who lives across the road, wears a very special ring that she rarely takes off. She had been at my house in the morning and went home after lunch. The next day, she came back and was very upset. She had lost her very special ring and came over to see if she had lost it at my house.
>
> We hunted high and low, then back at her house, but the ring was nowhere to be found. It left us feeling awful, to be honest. When Siena came home from school later that day, I was listening to her read. I remembered what you said and, figuring that we had nothing more to lose, asked her, 'Siena, you know Grandma's ring that she wears all the time? Well, she's lost it. I wonder if you know where it is.'

Siena looked up to the ceiling (much like I do) as if searching for the answer through images being shown to her. Then, plain as day, she replied, 'It's in Granny's little shed, at the back in the corner, right down the bottom inside the white bag in the corner.' I asked her how she knew that, as she isn't allowed to go in Grandma's garden shed, which is always kept locked. She replied, 'You asked me if I knew where Grandma's ring was, and I told you.' Then she got up, got a piece of fruit and went to her room.

> Excited, I phoned Mum, and Siena and I went over there. Initially, we walked from room to room, asking Siena if the ring was in each room as we entered it. Siena always said it wasn't, repeating that it was in the white bag in the corner of the garden shed. So, Mum and I went out to the garden shed

and unlocked it. Siena said, 'There, in that white bag in the corner … look in there.'

Well, 'that' white bag in the corner was a bag of potting mix. Yesterday, Mum had been potting pot plants, she said. She promptly upended the bag on the floor and, while sifting through its contents, found her ring twinkling in the soil! Siena had just smiled.

'Thank you, Marion,' Siena's mum said to me. 'If it wasn't for you telling me about my daughter's special Gift, we would never have found Mum's ring.'

Siena was six years old at the time.

Again, I share these stories with you so you keep an open mind about your own child's Wired behaviour at times. You might be the parent; however, they are our teachers!

Blessings to you Siena. I will always remember you and our very special connection with Love.

Sharing K and M's story

This brings me to K and M, another beautiful mother and daughter! M was just five when I met them both and already her angel wings were fully grown.

I met K and M after they arrived from interstate following the end of a very toxic relationship. Since our first session, K has now come to rely on M's special Gift. While this may seem demanding of a child to most, it's not – it's actually K's lesson of acceptance. K's traumatic life had left her doubting herself. Now that it was only the two of them in their new home and life, K often found herself talking out loud and asking M's advice. While never expecting an 'answer', K always got exactly what she needed to her simple yes or no questions from M.

In the four years I have known and guided these beautiful Souls in their relationship, I have become fascinated by the wisdom that M shows to her mum. It's very natural between them. Quite often, when K asks M a question, I have the answer already and sit on it, awaiting M's response. Time and time again there is confirmation of my abilities and confirmation of M's.

M and I often exchange a knowing look. It's powerful for me to experience, and M's love for me is so unconditional and accepting, as is mine for her. As 6s, we 'see' each other.

At times, we have both answered K at the same time with the same answer when she asks yet another self-doubting question, then we share that knowing look between us. Sometimes I wink, and sometimes M raises her eyebrows. We 'get it!' She's only nine!

We both know who is who here in K's zoo, and K loves it too!

Their relationship is the perfect example of daughter teaching Mum through agreed life experiences and guidance in their Soul Contract so that Mum can move from self-doubt to self-confidence.

I feel that sharing stories like this is vitally important as there are many families where 6s can be found. It's important that we recognise them and why they are here! It is my hope that M will continue to use her Gift for her highest good as she grows older. I'm sure she will!

Blessings to you, you pair of Angels connected by wings and silver threads. I love you both.

Sharing K and S's very special story

How did I meet S? Well, like most of the kids I meet, I met her through her mum, K, who had come to see me for herself. A few years after her session, I saw a message on my phone from K. She sounded really upset and asked me to ring her.

So, I did.

S was being bullied at school by other girls. It was an all-girls school. She was also finding it hard to fit in as they called her 'weird!' Sound familiar?

S was a child on the spectrum, according to her teachers.

S was a child with all 6 senses intact, according to her mum and me.

Gifted, certainly.

A 6, absolutely.

S had started refusing to go to school ever since she 'saw' a face come at her through the shelves in a department store. This didn't happen just once; it happened a couple of times. S was upset for the girl who kept showing herself to her because she was very bruised, as if she had been beaten up, which it turns out she had.

K asked if I would come and spend time with her, and we arranged for me to visit the following weekend.

K had explained to S that I would understand her, and she was so excited when I arrived. She couldn't wait to talk about her visions and hear what my Team and I had to say about them.

First, we talked about the girl in the shelves. I asked Opa the reason behind her showing herself to S. Opa showed me a young girl. Some might call her a ghost. Us? We call her a Soul choosing to be with S. Both girls were loners, and they kept each other company. Opa showed me that S was safe with this girl, who was around the same age and whose name started with L.

It seems that S had been entertaining 'disembodied' Spirits for a while now. K told me that there was in fact a girl around the same age as her daughter that she talks to a lot and that her name was L. L, however, was a Spirit.

Opa said the main reason L showed herself was to let S know that she wasn't alone. L understood how S felt as she had also been bullied.

S went on to tell me about the first time she saw L. It was in the toy section of Kmart. L had literally jumped through the shelves! L was trying to get S's attention. S said that L looked like she was about 12 and hadn't washed in ages and had blood on her face. S explained that L tried to make herself look scary, but S wasn't scared of her because her energy was sad rather than scary! This made perfect sense to me.

Opa also said that S wouldn't see her again, as S had acknowledged L fully a few weeks before and told her to go to the 'light'.

Good girl, S.

But K really wanted to talk about the two girls bullying S at school.

What to do, I thought to myself. I didn't have any answers, so I referred the issue to Opa, who asked me to play the 'game' he had taught me, the one with the colours, shapes and numbers. I asked K's permission, and she agreed. She even took part – S got all of them right, and K got all of them wrong. Not on purpose either ... she did actually try.

This game cannot be done light-heartedly as the person 'transmitting' the image must have nothing else in their mind at all so that the recipient can easily read it. Fortunately, for me, it's quite easy to have nothing in my mind! I then send images to the other person for them to receive. There is a lot of learning that goes hand in hand with this skill. If you are interested in learning it yourself, telepathy is intrinsic to the nature of older Souls.

S was 100% accurate every time. Of course she was. She is in her last lifetime and was blessed with a Gift to deliver karma and justice through her Psychic senses.

It was a long, yet very enjoyable, afternoon. I feel so privileged to be able to work with kids at this level. They make me feel 'normal', or should I say 'Wired!' We knew that S wasn't going crazy and that everything she was experiencing was real to her. It didn't matter than no one else in her family could see it. It was now time to ask her a very important question.

I explained to S about the evolution of the Soul and that, while she might be in primary school, her Soul was actually much older.

After explaining to S that she can see these Spirit children because she is an Old Soul and that no one else in her family can, I asked her, 'S, do you want to see these Souls? Do you want to help them? Because you do have a choice.'

Her answer was a resounding 'YES!' with absolutely no hesitation at all. It came straight from her Soul; she didn't even access her brain to think about it.

I was also there to help S take care of her bullies using her Psychic Gift of telepathy. I taught her how to talk to these two girls through their minds. I asked her to explain in very simple, straightforward language how she felt when they bullied her and what she would like them to do with their bullying.

Opa wanted to be sure that I trained S properly and that she understood the boundaries of the task she was going to undertake. Telepathy is a skill to be respected. Abuse it once, and you will lose it altogether.

Two or three months later, K rang to give me an update. She told me that S was the happiest she had seen her ever since our session together, and that she was relieved to have her daughter back. She then told me that S wanted to talk to me about something special that had happened. She asked me if I remembered the bullies. Of course I did. She laughed and told me that she had talked to them telepathically and asked them to leave the school. Guess what? They DID leave the school!

Apparently, S had spoken kindly to the bullies on a telepathic level daily, asking them to leave her alone and to stop being a bully as it affected her more than they realised (this was something L had shown her!). She also planted the 'seed' that they leave the school altogether so she could get on with learning her lessons properly. She told the girls telepathically that they were being unkind and should listen to their hearts.

Life's funny, isn't it! I absolutely LOVE THIS STUFF.

Coincidence, you might say.

Perfect, I say.

Wired is what it is.

S would be midway through high school now and, when I check in on her telepathically, I know she is doing just fine!

The message S would like to share is, 'Sometimes us kids just know things. It's like we remember what all the adults have forgotten! Start remembering, I say.'

Blessings to you, beautiful girl with the golden hair and golden wings.

The DJ thought she could catch me out!

Gotta love a sceptic! Well, Greg wanted to, that was for sure, but she didn't want him, it seemed!

Back in 2016, I was interviewed by a local radio station. At the time, I had done interviews for ABC Radio, 6PR radio station in Perth and written for a few newspapers and magazines here and overseas. A couple of local radio stations had offered to interview me about various stories in my book. This one didn't feel right, but I had agreed to do it and I was a woman of my word, so I went there!

I would love to say that I was 'warmly' welcomed by the staff and DJ at the radio station, but I wasn't – I would have needed a bulldozer to knock down those brick walls! I don't know if it's because people are scared that I will 'read' them. These people needn't have worried – they weren't that interesting anyway.

The interview started with the usual questions. How long have you been a Psychic? What's it like being a Psychic? Do you get scared? What if you see things for people that they don't want to see – do you still tell them? How do you know you're not making it up (why would I?). Can you give me the lotto numbers (why would I?). When did you first start writing your book? The list goes on.

The female DJ at this radio station wanted proof. Not surprising – they all do! Here's the scenario for you:

DJ: So Marion, what can you tell me about me? Do I have any 'visitors' here?

Me: Well, Andrew is here with me. He's in Spirit.

DJ: I don't know any Andrew in Spirit!

I asked my Team for specifics, which they sent to me.

Me: It seems that Andrew went out with your sister, Antoinette, in high school. But he cornered you in the kitchen one day, trying to kiss you and telling you that he was only going out with your sister so he could be close to you!

DJ: Oh! That Andrew!

Me: Yes! THAT Andrew!

DJ: I heard he had died. Does he have a message for me?

Me: He does. He wants to know why you didn't cry at his funeral like your sister did. He also wants to tell you that he still really likes you and wish that you hadn't played hard to get with him. That's it!

DJ: Yikes! Interesting that he just stayed with my sister so he could be near me. He was nice enough … he just wasn't my type. I couldn't have been his type either, because my sister is nothing like me. It's all too late now. I still wouldn't have gone out with him though!

We wrapped up our session, I left a few copies of my book and left. The energy in there was so awful. I couldn't put my finger on it, and neither could my Team. Maybe it was a clash of our energies. Never mind … or, as my good mum would say, 'Que sera, sera!'

The Key is always LOVE

When you don't know what to do or say, or where to go to find your answer, look within.

You will always have You, and your Soul knows way more than your mind. You are never alone when you have your Soul to guide you, which you always will.

If you are still stuck and feel like you are drowning, not waving, always ask, 'What would Love do?' My dear friend Michelle T gave me this pearl of wisdom. God knows I love that woman!

When you ask that question, you will always get your answer. It will be up to you to follow it.

What happens when we die?

I remember having a conversation with Opa and my Team about Soul Contracts and what happens when we die.

All I can say is that I'm glad I'm not a sceptic, because I'd hate to die with all these unanswered questions … as a 'human', that is! Our Soul already knows more than the mind and it knows exactly what happens when we go Home! and always looks forward to being released from its human form.

Please remember these two important facts:

1. We have died many times before and been reincarnated many times before.

2. None of us, no matter how special we may think we are, get out of this life alive!

My Team of Guides showed me that, at the end of each lifetime, we go through a Life Review, together with our Soul Family, teachers and Guides. We are shown the lessons we were meant to learn through our Soul Contracts and who we chose to learn them with. We see the lessons we learnt successfully and the ones we avoided – which ones we can tick off and those that will need to be attempted again because they were avoided (gotta hate that!).

My Team showed me a vision of us sitting in a private 'classroom' environment. We go to this classroom after we have recovered from leaving our human body and arriving Home. We all have our own classrooms that we share with our Soul Family and Team of Guides.

People we chose in our Soul Contracts rejoin us and share their part in our Soul Contract and journey. If we reneged on a lesson, they show us how they presented the lesson to us and how we chose to either learn or not learn it. You may wonder … what if some of these Souls are still alive? How can they be there in your Life Review? Please remember that all we really are is energy! The 'me' in you is this energy, not the bag of skin and bones known as your body.

My main Guide is Opa D (Mum's dad). So, my Life Review for this lifetime may look like this:

Opa: What lesson/s did you choose to learn in the lifetime you have just left behind?

Me: Trust, forgiveness, self-acceptance and Unconditional Love.

Opa: Who did you choose to learn these lessons with?

Me: Myself, my dad, husband and others (not named in this book).

Opa: Have you learnt them?

Me: Yes, I believe I did.

Opa B confirms that I did, in fact, learn them this time. Fark it was hard, let me tell ya!

Opa: Over what period of time did you choose to learn these lessons?

Me: One hundred years, because some of the teachers and/or students were not available until later in my life, so I had to choose a long lifetime this time.

Opa: Are you aware that you lived two lifetimes in the last one?

Me: No … what do you mean?

Opa: Rather than coming Home through the dying of your physical body, you agreed to transition through the Dark Night of your Soul. This means that you agreed to live two lifetimes worth of lessons in this one lifetime. We were concerned at first, however, it has accelerated your growth spiritually and, with the onset of Covid, we needed you to grow all you went through. And you did.

Me: Is that why it's been so traumatic for me?

Opa: It was traumatic for the human body you were in. Your Soul is very resilient and understood and accepted the undertaking. Your brain thought your life was over, and you experienced severe mental breakdowns. Your Soul was always strong enough to bring you out the other side. You could say that you 'died' while you were still alive.

Me: That makes perfect sense! This must be the same for many Souls in this lifetime.

Opa: Yes, many, many have agreed to this in this incarnation. It's all part of the big Awakening. Now, what lesson/s did you agree to teach others?

Me: Funnily enough, the lessons I taught were the same ones I had to learn and master.

Opa: Who did you choose to teach these to?

Me: My family, friends and work colleagues. The 'leaves' on my tree (I'm referring to the tree that Opa showed me many years ago).

Opa: Do you believe that they learnt from you?

Me: Some, yes, and some hated me for it. I believe I also inspired and/or influenced others. However, once I realised that they were not members of my Soul Family and that I was not in their inner teaching circle, I backed off. This was a lesson in itself. I wasn't their teacher. I was the observer. Not my zoo and not my monkeys!

Opa: Did you recognise the role of karma in your life, good and bad?

Me: Yes, and I consciously attended to my bad karma to make it right.

Opa: Yes, we saw that you did this. Such massive lessons and such a massive debt. You have been able to clear the debt from your ancestors who chose not to learn particular lessons in their various incarnations. A huge responsibility fell on your shoulders to clear and work through, and you did it. The path is now clear for generations of Soul Family that will follow you. We supported your human body and Soul throughout all this lifetime. We know you are exhausted in your mental and physical bodies. Your Soul and Spirit, however, are thriving.

You were born aware and awake in this incarnation. You went over and above to ensure you learnt all you needed to and have earnt good karma as a reward. We thank you for the role that you have played in our Soul Family. We have admired your tenacity and stoicism as a human and Soul. We were pleased that you agreed to do this for all of us and, because of this, we agreed to support and love you as your Guides. We would never have left your side.

You were also the bringer of karma in this lifetime. That was something you never knew about before. You may only deliver karma to someone once you have learnt your own lessons. It is your Sign that your lessons have been learnt. Well done!

You have reached the end of your incarnations and lessons. It is now time to put all you have learnt into practice as a Guide.

For those who haven't yet reached their last incarnation, the Life Review conversation would go something like this:

Team: What lessons would you like to learn in your next human incarnation?

You: Well, let's look at what's left to learn.

You would both then discuss what lessons were left to learn.

Team: What type of scenario or circumstance would you like to learn this in?

You would then discuss this.

Team: How long do you think you will need? How many years would you like us to allocate to you and your Soul Family to learn these lessons? We will need to see who is available to teach you. Do you have any preferences as to who you learn it with?
You would then discuss this.

Team: Do you also wish to play a role in another Soul's inner circle as their preferred teacher of their lessons, regardless of the circumstances?

You would then discuss this.

Once your past life has been reviewed and plans have been put into place for your next incarnation, such as the start date, Soul and Blood Family members including pets, completion date and so on, you are scheduled to arrive into your new family.

One of the hardest things you have to do as a human is to recognise the energy of your Soul Family member dressed in a different earthly form. This will confuse you. As a Spiritual being, however, it won't take long to recognise the situation – *hopefully*. We agree to take on different personas in order to teach lessons. It is very important to remember and our job to remind you of your Soul's purpose for the incarnation.

Remember that you are *never* alone!

Each lesson we learn, regardless of how many incarnations it takes, will eventually help our Soul to grow through the acquisition of wisdom through life experience.

> *We grow through all we go through*

One of the most important conversations in life

If you are sharing the very important time of transition in a Loved One's life, please do not let them struggle with the process or their thoughts. Invite them to keep an open mind and to talk to you about what they see.

Loved Ones in Spirit tend to come forward before the final transition. These periods of contact will jog their memory of the last time they were Home and provides a great deal of comfort.

They may even show themselves to you in your mind's eye so that you can share their presence with your Loved One.

Reassure your Loved Ones that, when they arrive, they will be met by members of their Soul Family. Tell them that, once they transition, they will no longer carry the burden of their human form, mind and emotions. They will no longer feel pain, physically or mentally. Initially, they will see their Soul Family coming forward to greet them, just like they did last time they died, combined with an incredible feeling of Unconditional Love and peace.

Many who are dying are scared to meet people they fought with in this life. It's important to differentiate between Soul Family and Blood Family. Soul Family are our soft places to fall. They 'get us' without explanation. They love us without condition. They are in every single one of our lifetimes in one form or another.

Blood Family, however, are the people we share our life with. They give birth to us and often provide us with lessons in this incarnation. That is their only role. We won't see that person again when we die. Blood Family are only connected to us while we inhabit our physical body, not when we are back in our Soul. There's a lot of comfort in knowing this, as many people fear they will see the people they hated in this lifetime when they go Home. Fortunately, it doesn't work this way.

It's crucial to talk to your Loved Ones about what their Sign will be when they 'visit' after they have gone Home. It can be a short chat, but it's the most important chat of your life. Having this conversation takes all the guesswork out of wondering whether that butterfly or dragonfly is actually your Loved One.

If you are both informed, then you will both know when contact has been made. There will be no denying their visit and, when it happens, you will both receive so much comfort from the contact.

More and more of our Loved Ones are going Home with the knowledge that there is, indeed, life after death. This brings them much comfort and eases the transition.

Julie and Neil – a Love that knows no bounds

There comes a time when we ask the question: is there life after death?

This question tends to come as we get closer to death, or if we have been given a diagnosis that will take us out of this life and into whatever is next.

I am not here to convince you that there is or isn't life after this life. I can only share my experiences with you, and there are many, many that I wish to share. However, the experiences can only be understood through where you are at in your life, your incarnations and your Soul's age.

Julie has given me permission to use her real name in this beautiful Love story. I feel like Julie has always been in my life, even though she lives in Canada! I actually cannot remember a time when I did not know her. Perhaps we are Soul Family and have been together in other lifetimes. It certainly feels like it.

Julie is one of the most beautiful and loving people you will ever be blessed to meet. Neil thought this about Julie too. They were each other's second marriage, and how blessed they were to have found each other.

Julie is a believer. This isn't surprising, as most Earth Angels believe that there is more to life. Julie is an Earth Angel and has well and truly mastered her earthly lesson of Unconditional Love.

Neil was a sceptic but, once his physical body became ill, he started to wonder whether there was, in fact, more to life. He shared his thoughts and questions with Julie. Julie knew she could talk to me anytime about living and dying. It is my favourite subject, after all! Julie also asked Neil if he would like to talk to me. After giving it some thought, Neil said yes.

Like many of us, I have sat with those who are dying. Their deepest fear is that they will be forgotten by their Loved Ones, and that's more painful to them than the actual act of dying or going Home.

I was working in the office one Tuesday. Julie and Neil had been on my mind all morning when I received a message from Julie asking if I was available to sit with Neil as he was close to going Home and wanted to talk to me.

As it happened, it was close to my lunch time. I had been giving sessions out of a cottage near where I was working and immediately went there. A friend had also just dropped in to see me at work, and it was timely that I could invite her beautiful energy to be with Neil too.

Once we were connected with Julie and Neil via video, Neil's Spirit Family immediately let me know that he was close to going Home and that they were ready to receive him. The energy in both rooms was one of complete Love. It was so beautiful. I let Neil know who was waiting for him before asking my Team to be with Neil's Team and Loved Ones in Spirit. Together, we sent healing energy and Love to Neil, clearing his path, reassuring him that he will be fine and reminding him that even though he couldn't remember, he had done this several times before. It was a combined Earth and Spirit Team effort to help make Neil's transition a peaceful one.

Julie said that at the actual time of Neil's passing, both she and her daughter saw a spiralling energy leave Neil's body. They took photos, which they shared with me. How special for Julie and her daughter to witness. How special it was of Neil to share this moment with them. Julie knows when Neil comes to visit her, and she describes the feeling as the same as the moment he left – words cannot explain it.

I love this for Julie and Neil.

How your Loved Ones may show themselves to you

Everyone has different expectations of what they will hear, see or know once they start dealing with their Loved Ones and/or Guides. It is my experience that people expect to 'see' their Loved Ones exactly like they were when they were living, in human form.

They expect the same from their Guides. Sadly though, if this were to take place, most people would die in shock or contact the local media to say they have a real live Spirit / Ghost in their house! People would not cope and Spirit cannot lower its energy to meet ours just because it suits the human or what the human expects of the Spirit. It just doesn't work that way.

Loved Ones who have gone Home have merely stepped out of their human body. Energy is the Soul, us, not the body. That's the illusion.

A couple of years ago, I received a message from a person regarding a Spirit who had shown themselves to her. Basically, a Spirit had literally stood in front of her and, as soon as she acknowledged the Spirit, it left as quickly as it had arrived. She was confused because she didn't recognise it. This experience left her startled and confused. Did this Spirit need her help? If she didn't know her, why did she show herself? What actually happened here? I'll explain, as it could well happen to you!

Once they go Home, the Souls of our Loved Ones are given opportunities to 'show' themselves to their families before moving on or reincarnating. They learn how to manipulate their energy to do so, as sometimes they only get one chance. Just like we go through lessons and training here while we are living, those who have gone Home also continue to learn.

Many Souls that have gone Home know how much their Loved Ones, who are still living, miss them. Please remember that the Souls that are already Home no longer carry human emotions, feelings or baggage – those all died when the human body died.

Sometimes our Loved Ones have not been able to teach us the lessons that our Soul Contracts described. For example, say they were a teacher in a Soul Contract with their still-living Loved One, yet the Loved One chose not to learn their lesson. The Soul that has returned Home is shown how the Loved One feels about the situation now that their Loved One has died. The Loved One is then given the opportunity to 'show' themselves one more time. The acceptance of their 'visit' helps to heal the Loved One still living and also to close off the Soul Contract for the one already back at Home.

So … the Spirit that returned Home is shown, after much practice, how to show themselves to their Loved One still living. It's all about energy, you see. In this case, this Spirit showed themselves to my friend but was unrelated to her. As soon as my friend acknowledged that she saw her, the Spirit and her Team knew she was ready to show herself to her own family member as she had mastered the art of being seen! Fascinating, isn't it?

Will someone be there to meet me when I go Home?

The answer is yes and also no.

This is going to be very hard for me to share. I've never told anyone this, but my Team really want you to read and feel this experience for yourself and your own situations.

Earlier, I shared Julie and Neil's experience with you. It is quite common, especially for people who have never had a religious faith or are sceptics, to question whether there is more to life after death. Those preparing to go Home may suddenly want to find out if there will be someone waiting to greet them when they get there.

It is very hard to explain to someone at the end of their life, when the brain has often begun to lose its sharpness, what it will be like for them to go Home. Telling them that they have died a few times before will make no sense to them as this is the first time dying in this incarnation.

Mostly, when I sit with people who are preparing to die or go Home, I don't talk. If I do talk out loud, it's for the human family members in the room who want to know what's going on, mostly out of curiosity so that, when it's their time, they will know what to expect too.

I hold their hands and transmit all the messages to their Soul telepathically and through energy. I share my visions of who is waiting for them. They may say the name out loud when they see the person for themselves prior to leaving their body.

Members of our Soul Family are there to greet us when we come Home. They have been expecting you and are ready for the next stage in your life and journey.

I knew this. So, when it was my mum's turn to go Home, I wasn't surprised to see her family with her – brothers, sisters, Opa, everyone. Everyone that was, it seems, except her mum. I looked everywhere for Mum's mum; my Oma D. Mum's mum had died during the war when my mum was just 14. She had to leave school and take care of her dad and six siblings. All her life, she desperately missed her mum and always wondered why her mum wouldn't contact her, given that they both had our 'Gift!'

It's very hard to read this story back – I can't see the words because of my tears!

I 'looked' everywhere for Mum's mum while she was getting close to going Home. I was about to lose my mum and wanted her to have her mum there to meet her. Mum had always told me that she hoped that, when she finally died, her mum would come to meet her.

I begged Opa D, Opa B and my Team – if anyone could talk to Oma D and bring her to meet her daughter, then please do it. I asked them, 'Why won't Mum's mum come to her? Please ask her to come meet her last surviving daughter.'

But she didn't. I was heartbroken.

I knew Mum was close to going Home. I begged and I pleaded for Oma to come. Mum's brothers, sisters and her dad were already waiting for her. One of my uncles had even managed to snaffle some freesias from somewhere, which were Mum's favourite flower and had been in her wedding bouquet, to give her when she arrived.

But Oma D would not come to be with them.

I was absolutely beside myself. What could I do? Imagine what this was like. What's the point of having a Gift like this if the one person you need to hear you ignores you?

Then I saw Oma D, Mum's mum, standing a long way away on a hill with her back to us. Her hair was in a bun, and she wore black. But, try as I might to get her attention, she wouldn't turn to me or her daughter coming Home.

I cried hysterically. I was gutted for my mum. She was passing, and I couldn't share any of this with anyone! Everyone was in their own private pain.

Mum and I had talked a few times about her wanting her mum to meet with her. It was important. I had always promised Mum that I would make sure her mum would be there to meet her. I could not imagine going Home and not being greeted by my mum! It's just too sad!

'Oma, Oma, Oma please …' I begged.

And, right before my mum went Home, her mum turned to me. She was holding freesias too and said, 'I will wait my turn. Let all the others see her first – they haven't seen me either since coming Home. I didn't think they wanted to because they were so young when I died. Your mum was the eldest at 14, and she had to bring those kids up during the war. She was their mum, not me, and now she is reunited as their mum and their sister. My turn will come, just not yet.'

Then Oma D was gone.

And so was my mum.

I cried all the way home, all that night and all the next day. I'm crying now too, as I recall the emotions of not being able to bring Mum the one thing she wanted her whole life – to be reunited with her mum.

I felt like I had let her down. Out of everyone I knew, I should have been able to bring her mum to her.

But I couldn't.

The first time I heard from my mum and dad after they had gone Home was that day in February when they walked in my kitchen door and told me to 'just go buy the caravan and do the trip, would ya!'

Then I knew that all was well again.

Pat

This story is hard to write, but we will share it!

Every now and again, Opa and my Team 'take me over' and put me exactly where I need to be. I never question this as I trust them completely and have had quite a few experiences like this one. When they 'take over', I am filled with a feeling of complete trust and love. They always know where I am needed, and I didn't question it on this day.

We had lived in Perth for eight years. The first house we rented was in Tuart Hill. Living in Perth really took some getting used to for me. There was one lady who truly understood. Her name was June, and her husband's name was Pat. June had moved across the country from Sydney years earlier with Pat. He was a Chinese immigrant who came out from China in the early '60s with two timber storage crates filled with their possessions. I still have one of those crates today.

June and I both felt that Perth was not home for us. We had this in common and comforted each other many times when we yearned to live back on the other side of Australia. My son was four at the time, and many mornings I would see June chatting over the fence to him as he stood on the wall happily chatting back. I was glad they had each other.

Over the years, June and Pat became like family to us. Even once we moved houses, we still stayed in close touch with them. Pat was special to me as he was extremely Spiritual. He felt a lot like Opa does to me. Pat was a wise Old Soul and always explained things to me in a Spiritual way so I could understand. He was ageless, or so I thought.

One day, in 2003, the morning started like any other. The kids were up and breakfasted, ready for school. My husband was at work, and I was getting ready to go to work. After dropping the kids off at school, I drove down the Mitchell Freeway in the direction of Nedlands where I worked as a secretary for private investigators.

Suddenly though, I turned left off Hutton Street, up Royal Street and parked out the front of June and Pat's house. I messaged my office manager and told her I wouldn't be in that day. I didn't know why, but I knew I wouldn't be.

Everything became very matter of fact, transactional, like it always does when this happens. This type of feeling reassures me that I'm in the right place at the right time.

June and Pat did not know I was coming that morning but somehow it seemed that they did. June answered the door and said, 'Come in, he's ready to go to the hospital!' I said 'Okay' then said hello to Pat. He replied, 'Good morning, I need to go the hospital.' He was dressed and ready to go, with his bag packed. It was almost as if they were waiting for me. I scoured my brain to see if we had talked that morning and that I had offered to take him, but I know for certain that I didn't.

Me: Would you like me to take you? Are we going to Charlie's Hospital?

Pat: Yes please.

Me: Okay. Do you have everything you need?

Pat: Yes, I won't be needing much. I won't be there long!

Well, Pat knew before June and I did that he was very close to going Home. In fact, Pat passed away very peacefully with us at his side two days later at the age of 87. Pat was the first person that I had lost that really mattered to me. His strength at the end really endeared me to him. He was very calm and transactional, as if he remembered all the other times that he had died and knew intuitively that he would wake up at Home! This gave Pat enormous comfort.

Pat was one of those rare people you meet in life when you know, as soon as you meet them, that your life just got a whole lot better for knowing them! The one thing my kids and I will always remember about Pat's last days was how cold he always felt … so cold, in fact, that June knitted him a beanie for his nose – it was bright red, but Pat loved it!

It's times like these that I love my Gift and my Team so much. It's where my heart and Soul know exactly where they need to be and why, and the mind stays out of it completely. Pat was so comfortable with his situation that I couldn't be anything else as I sat by his bedside and didn't go to work that day, or the next five days.

Dawn walking down a road to nowhere

Dawn's story is another one of those beautiful times that my Team put me exactly where I need to be, and I have no need to question any of it.

I moved to Victor Harbor in 2016. At this point, I was working casually while also taking care of my parents, who were both very ill. My friend Dave invited me to fill in on his lawn bowls team one evening, and that's where I met Dawn. Dawn was an older lady who fell in love with me and told me so every time we played lawn bowls. I was touched.

One day, I received a phone call from her husband, J. He told me he wanted to tell me something very private about his wife, and I wasn't to tell her that he had told me. I agreed as I was curious.

J told me that his wife believed that I was the daughter they lost at birth, reincarnated!

Far out! Try and process that as a human, why don't you? I couldn't and, because I couldn't, I asked Opa for help. Opa said, 'Trust, just trust!'

So, when Dawn and J invited me over for lunch one day, I again trusted. Dawn opened up to me over lunch and told me how she felt. Personally, I did not feel connected in any way to the daughter she had lost but, if she felt that way and knowing me was helping her get over the loss of losing a daughter at birth, then I was very happy to know her.

Dawn and J came to my parents' funerals after they both passed away in 2017. Dawn helped me with a garage sale at Mum's and gave me a lot of comfort during those early, dark days.

While Dawn could never take the place of my mum, she certainly went a long way to helping me through my grief. Our connection was a Soul connection, one of those, 'I know I know you, but not from this lifetime' kinds of connection.

I remember the morning distinctly – it was early 2018. My friend Dave had stayed the night. He had been helping me through my grief, and I was very grateful for his company at the time. It was a cold, windy morning. After brekky, Dave said to me, 'Hey Maz, do you have to go out this morning, because my car is parked behind yours in the driveway and I'm going back to bed!' I told him, 'Nah, I'm not going anywhere. I'm working on some blogs for my Facebook page!'

Then …

Opa: Quick, get in the car and drive!

Me: Where am I going? Can I get changed out of my jarmies first and put shoes on?

Opa: No! There isn't time! Move Dave's car – don't take his!

I trust Opa, so I grabbed my keys, yelling to Dave that I was just going out, hopped in my car – in my jarmies and barefoot – and asked Opa for directions.

Opa: Go down the end of the road then turn left, then turn right onto the main road where you will see Dawn having a heart attack while she's walking into town!

I accelerated madly, and Opa was right, again! I drove up onto the footpath where Dawn had collapsed. There was no one else around. She was alive, thank goodness, and I was able to get her into my car. We raced Dawn to the hospital and through the emergency doors. Opa had gotten me there right in time. I knew I was leaving Dawn in good hands and went home to change and update Dave on what had just happened!

All he said to me was, 'You're weird, I know, but good on you for trusting it and going to rescue her!'

Dawn was released from hospital two days later with a new treatment plan and medication. She is still very much alive today and quilting her heart out!

The truth comes out in a Reading – are you ready?

These messages often hit a nerve, and I know this when I see your tears fall. I/We then know that we have got through to you, and we are grateful to your Soul for the acknowledgement.

I chat with my Team every day. There have been plenty of times when I myself have copped a good telling off and been shown the truth in a situation that I've had to accept and learn from. That can be pretty confronting. I also know how much better my life is when I do accept the truth shown to me. Trust me, it's not all about Angels!

It can be very hard at times to give people the truth as it is shown to me. Sometimes, I try to share the messages I receive, and they are rejected. People then wonder why their lives don't improve!

Be careful what you ask for if you don't want to hear the answer. Even bad news gets delivered, but my Team have trained me very well in delivering these types of messages. After giving thousands of Readings, I know how to deliver bad news. At times, there is some news I just won't share – instead, my Team and I counsel you towards the change.

Sitting with someone in a consultation is a big responsibility. It's not all fun and games or proving that I can do what I say I do.

That would miss the point completely. I don't need to tell you I see you cheating on your partner or lying to get what you think you want in life. However, I see the shit, and it's usually not pretty! That's why I hate crowds and public places. The games people play to maintain the illusion of their life are painful to watch. For things to change in your life for the better, you need to own your shit!

I don't tell people what they want to hear – I tell them what I get, what I'm given. Often, your Guides will bring messages through to you via my Team. You may not know how to accept what they have to say, but that may be part of your lesson and/or Soul Contract.

From me/us, you will always get the truth.

The movie *The Five People You Meet in Heaven* beautifully captures what happens and who we meet during our lives and why.

My Team of Guides bring you everything that is right for your Soul's growth and journey in this life. They see the bigger picture – the whole you!

Take your messages away, and let time reveal all. The messages don't need to make sense at the time – they generally never make sense to me either! It's lovely to receive your emails and messages down the track when things *do* fall into place and make sense to you. Please keep sending them as they are important for me to receive.

People often ask me if I get tired doing lots of Readings back to back. I don't – it's the opposite, actually. I get very energised! It's the shitty real-life stuff that makes me tired! Spiritual work is so uplifting, energising and fascinating. Half of the time, I feel like I'm on the most aMAZing high! It's just beautiful. I wish, wish, wish I could do them all the time, and I could share the lessons and the journey all the time too. I would feel so complete and wouldn't have to juggle my two worlds: human and Spiritual.

That's my dream, anyway.

I find it very interesting too that, when information comes through, many of you say 'Oh I knew that' or 'I've been getting that too!'

If that's the case, all you need from me is to know how to tune into your own messages for yourself. Confirmation. It's worth it.

Please, people, trust this stuff. It IS real, and it's there for your benefit.

If I'm confirming what you already know, then you don't need me at all, except to possibly reassure YOU!

**Mum J says,
'But I can't wait five years to see my daughter again!'**

In *Caught Between Two Worlds*, I shared a story about Sophie and Peter. Peter came to visit Sophie during her session with me. Peter was alive, not dead! If you don't remember this story, you may like to read it. It's the most profound Reading I've ever given and has helped me enormously in sharing my Gift through Readings for others.

Many people mistakenly think that my Gift is to talk to those who have gone Home! That's only partially true. First of all, I *can* talk to them, if they want to talk to me! I don't go wandering the aisles looking for dead people to talk to! Lordy, I don't have that much time on my hands. That would be like knocking on every front door of every house in every neighbourhood to talk to the people living there. I could imagine nothing worse.

In many stories that I share, the session revolves around someone who is still very much alive. In Sophie's story, Peter shared with me that we are all energy – dead or alive, it doesn't matter. To me, helping people in this life is what matters the most as this is where we learn our lessons, not back Home!

If you receive messages from someone who is still alive during your session with me, it means that there is a Soul Contract in place.

We can help you work through it so it gets completed in this lifetime.

J's story was exactly the same.

I'm a mum, and I know how hard it is to parent kids! I also know how hard it is to parent kids when there are two parents who parent differently. I have seen the devastating effects when one parent uses their child as a pawn against the other parent out of spite when relationships fall apart.

This happened to this beautiful family. Mum J came to see me for a session. She had been referred to me by a friend, and J has now become one of my closest friends. I've seen the road J has had to walk following a spiteful allegation made against her that resulted in her losing custody of her daughter. J, her daughter and her son are all Earth Angels, which is why this story makes no sense on a human level. This is a story about their Soul Contract.

J: Maz, you have to help me. My ex had my daughter taken away from me because I was suffering from depression as he believes I'm not a fit mother! She's eight years old, and it was a few months ago. I need to know that I will get her back! How can I get her back, Marion?

I pleaded telepathically, 'Opa, you need to help me on this one please!' J explained the circumstances that had led to the situation she found herself in. It was gut-wrenching and heartbreaking, and she had every right to feel like a victim. J is a very Spiritual person and lives her Spirituality, quietly moving about her life on a day-by-day basis. J was trying to survive without her daughter but was struggling big time, as anyone would when an unfair decision has been made about their life.

Opa: Lieve meisje, this is going to be incredibly hard for you to tell J, but she is not going to get her daughter back for five years. She will get her back when she turns 13. Until then, she needs to do her very best for her own mental health, strength and her son. This is now out of her hands, and it's unfair as it has been done to her, not with her!

Me: Oh! Bloody hell! I can't tell her that! It'll kill her! Can't I have easier assignments?

Opa: Lieve meisje, out of anyone, you are actually the perfect person to give J this information, because she respects you and will accept it from you. No, she won't like it, but who would?

So I told her. And then yes, J fell apart. She took herself outside for a smoke, three actually, one after the other. She was inconsolable. I really wanted to be wrong this time. I wanted desperately to fix this for her. I would hate to be given this news.

I promised J with my life that she would get through it and that, once her and her daughter were reunited when she was 13, they would be a really happy family of three. I promised J that her daughter needs to be with her dad at this point in time. Her daughter is a 6, an Old Soul, and so is her son! They have chosen very hard lessons to teach in this lifetime. I told J that once her daughter is back with her, she will stay with her, and there will be no ongoing hostility or resentment between her and her daughter. As her daughter is an Old Soul, she is capable of demonstrating Unconditional Love, and they will enjoy a very close relationship for the rest of their lives.

And this is exactly what has happened.

My experience of J's session

Opa was right that J respected me as a Reader and as a person. While J knew that there was no way I would ever make things up and was shocked at being told it would take five years to get her daughter back, I supported her the whole time as her friend. I loved J as a sister, and she knew I had her back.

Earth Angels have some of the hardest Soul Contracts out of anyone. J's was no different. As a 6, J has, like many of us, been a victim of the cruel behaviour of 5s. We go through life teaching lessons to others without realising what the situation is. It's not until after the fact that we can see, with clarity, the role we played.

If there were more Earth Angels and people in the world like J, our world would be a much, much lovelier place to live.

This was the hardest Reading I've ever given, and one where I wanted to be wrong.

I now count J as one of my best friends, and I know she counts me as one of hers. We have been through so much together and so many synchronicities. We even ring each other at the same time sometimes! We're only ever just a thought away for each other.

If you are going for a Psychic Reading, please be prepared to accept the messages that come through because they are for your highest good.

Rather than spending the next five years sitting around, waiting for the day to come when she would be with her daughter again, J worked on herself and has become one of the strongest and most resilient women I know. Her daughter will now benefit as she grows into the beautiful woman she is becoming, just like her mum.

I feel privileged to be a part of this beautiful family's life.

Sometimes Spirit knows best!

Yes, sometimes Spirit knows best ... especially when you think you do! This is what Billy's reading was like in January 2017.

Me: Hi Billy, thanks for having a session with me today. Where would you like to start?

Billy: Well, you have been recommended to me, and I wanted to come and see you for myself.

Me: Okay! *(Great, I thought to myself. I never know what people have said about me, and I always worry that I can't bring through what someone is hoping for.)* Where would you like me to 'look' for you, Billy?

Billy: Well, I'm going to ask my girlfriend to marry me, and I came to find out if I should and what her reply would be!

Me: Okay.

Frigging hell! Opa showed me straight away that he, in fact, shouldn't ask his girlfriend to marry him, and that in fact he should leave her! I asked Opa how I should deliver this message, and he said to let him. Here goes!

Me: Billy, my Opa is going to give you the message straight! Are you ready?

Billy: Yes.

I took a deep breath and begged Opa to be gentle! I don't know why, but I needed Billy's approval for some reason. Probably because he had been recommended to me and I didn't want to let him down, but here I was, about to let him down big time!

Opa: Billy, your girlfriend might be your girlfriend, but she is not right for you. She is the wrong girl to marry. I recommend that you break up with her!

Billy: What a crock of shit! What on earth do you mean?

THE TRUTH COMES OUT IN A READING – ARE YOU READY?

Opa: Just as I said, you need to break up with her.

Billy: I just don't understand! I want to be a husband and a dad. She is right for me!

Opa: Billy, let me tell you what we see. By breaking up with her, you are going to meet the love of your life! You will meet her exactly two months after breaking up with this girl. You will recognise the new girl by her electric blue eyes ... oh, and she will be two months pregnant ... but not to you.

Billy: Now I've heard everything! I don't want to talk about this subject anymore ... it's complete shit! Can you tell me if my bunny rabbit is happy in Heaven?

Me: (*What the? And he said Opa's conversation was shit!*) I don't channel rabbits!

Billy: Okay, well, I'm going now. I am very disappointed with this Reading!

Billy tried to pay me for the Reading, but I told him not to worry about it, then he left. Once he was gone, I had a chat to Opa. I asked him if the messages he had told Billy were true! Opa said they were. I told Opa that I was very embarrassed and that it had been a complete waste of an hour. Opa didn't respond, and I left it at that.

It's funny how things happen though, isn't it?

Four months later, I was cooking dinner for a friend on a Sunday night when the phone rang. Here's how that conversation went:

Me: Hello, Marion speaking.

Billy: Hi, it's me Billy? You gave me that shit reading at the beginning of the year, do you remember?

Me: Yes, I remember … how are you? *(I was silently hoping the ground would open up and swallow me!)*

Billy: I rang to let you know how absolutely shit I thought your Reading was at the time.

Me: I'm really sorry that that was your experience. I don't know what to say, to be honest *(nothing like honest feedback on a Sunday night!)*

Billy: Well, your shit turned out to be true!

Me: What?

Billy: Yep, exactly like you said, word for word! I wouldn't have believed it if I hadn't lived it myself!

Me: Okay … so what happened?

Billy: Well, I left my girlfriend and, two months to the date, I met my new girlfriend, exactly like you said. Marion, can I show you a photo of her, particularly her eyes? I've never seen blue eyes like it! Billy took my breath away. He showed me the photo, and her eyes were blindingly blue. I had never seen eyes like those either! Just as I was wondering whether she was also two months pregnant,

Billy interrupted:

Billy: And guess what? I'm going to be a dad! Well, not a real dad but, just as you said, she was two months pregnant when I met her! I've asked her to marry me, and she said yes! We are so happy!

THE TRUTH COMES OUT IN A READING – ARE YOU READY?

Me: Billy, I am thrilled for you! That's amazing. I'm gobsmacked, to be honest!

At this point, I told Opa telepathically, 'Blimey you certainly had me with this Reading! This is incredible! Thank you so much for giving Billy the messages that day in January!' Opa just smiled and said *lieve meisje!*

Billy: Marion, I would really like you to meet her.

Me: I would love to meet her too! I will be at the Body and Soul Psychic Expo next month. Would you be able to bring her there to meet me? That would be incredible.

Billy: Yes definitely! So, the reason I'm ringing is to tell you how amazing I thought your Reading was, and to thank you for sharing your Gift with people who come to see you. It's because of you that I've met my girlfriend and I'm going to be a dad. We're so in love and feel so blessed to have met each other. My girlfriend knows about you and would like to meet you too.

Me: Well Billy, thank you so much for saying so. I have to admit that I'm really, REALLY relieved that this Reading, which seemed completely unrealistic at the time, has now happened for you. I couldn't be happier!

Billy: Righto, we will see you at the Expo. I look forward to seeing you again.

Me: Me too.

Billy and his girlfriend did in fact come to the Expo. His new girlfriend was exactly as Opa had described. They both looked so incredibly happy together, and we took a photograph to capture our meeting forever, which I will always treasure.

My experience of Billy's Readings

I can't help but take it personally when someone says to me that their reading was S H I T! The information is not from me, and I feel very defensive of Opa's messages. It's not like I would make messages up and, if I did, I would make them way better than the one given to Billy. And, while I didn't think it at the time, fortunately the message that did come through was actually perfect! There's absolutely no way I, nor you, could ever make up a story like that, tell someone then have it come true exactly point for point.

I admired Billy for ringing me to tell me his story – he didn't have to. Their visit meant the world to me at the Expo. It gave me confidence to keep going and to know that even when the messages come through for someone that are hard to hear, they are also perfect.

Sharing Readings with you

I shared many Readings with you in *Caught Between Two Worlds*. Thank you to everyone who sent me feedback and wrote reviews on Goodreads. I loved hearing from you. If you are yet to leave your review, I would love to read it. Just google the Goodreads website and *Caught Between Two Worlds* and leave your review. Once you have read this book, please leave a review for it too – I would love to hear your thoughts!

I initially wrote my first book for my two kids to help them understand who I was and who they are. It was going to be my legacy. Hand on heart, I never expected anyone to want to read about my life. I know I don't sound like much of a Psychic when I say I honestly thought that people could do this themselves.

How wrong I was! I have received many messages from people thanking me for writing *Caught Between Two Worlds*. One letter was handwritten and read like this:

Dear Marion Weatherburn,

My name is XXX and I live in YYY in northern New South Wales.

I was given your book by another patient here at the nursing home where I live. Your book has given me, and many other patients here, so much peace. We have all loved it, and we talk about it in our book club. Your book is now very creased and dogeared. It has coffee stains on the cover, but I want to tell you what someone wrote inside the cover. It was this:

Please read this book – it will give you comfort. When you have finished reading it, please pass it on to someone that you think will benefit from reading it too! But whatever you do, do NOT throw it out, ever!

I believe that message right there is the real reason I wrote the book. As there were no contact details or return information, I was unable to thank the sender, so I've done it here.

Dear sender of the beautiful 2018 letter,

I hope this message reaches you, and you are still able to read it. Mind you, if you have gone Home already, then you already know my message. When I received your letter, I was going through a huge period of sadness and self-doubt. Your letter literally lit up my life. I am so very grateful that you took the time to find me and write to me. Your letter arrived at the perfect time and has given me the courage to keep walking this path. I hope you get to read my next book too. If you are reading this and would like me to send you a copy as my Gift to you, please contact me again.

In love, light and blessings,
Marion Weatherburn

I remember times when I lived in Perth, my son lived in Sydney, my mum in Adelaide and Opa was in heaven. As 6s, we are really sensitive to the energies around us, seen and unseen! Sometimes, one of us would just feel 'weird' with no explanation. We were able to determine that the 'weirdness' didn't belong to us. I can now see that we were just 'Wired' into what was happening around us or to someone in our family, somewhere.

We knew to trust this Wired feeling.

If the feeling grew, we would get on the phone to each other and the conversation would go something like this:

Mum: Marion, are you okay? Something's wrong again somewhere. Do you feel it too? It's not with me, is it with you?

Me: Hi, Mum. No, we're all okay here. I was just about to ring you to see if it was you or Dad. Okay, I will ring my kids.

Mum: No, we are all fine here.

Me: Okay, good to know. Bye.

Me: Hi, son. Are you okay? Oma and I are getting the 'feels' and trying to find out who it belongs to.

Son: Nah! I'm all good, Mum. I was just about to ring you as I've got the same feels.

Me: Good, I'm glad you're okay. We're all okay too.

Later that afternoon...

Me: Mum, are you sure you're okay? The feeling is getting worse. Something's wrong somewhere!

Mum: No, we're okay. Are the kids okay, Marion? I'm going to ring our family in Holland as this feeling is just about making me sick.

Me: Yeah, me too. I can't even concentrate now. My kids are fine! Ringing Holland is a good idea. Please let me know if something is wrong.

Mum: Yes, I will. I hope not though!

Son: Mum, are you sure you're okay? Shall I ring Oma and Opa? Something is really wrong somewhere, and I don't like how I'm feeling. It's giving me a massive headache, and I feel like being sick!

Me: I'm glad you're okay. Your sister is too, as are Oma and Opa. It must be someone in Holland with something wrong. I'll let you know when I know more.

Son: Thanks Mum, love you.

Me: Love you too. We'll work this out, I promise. I'll let you know if I hear anything.

There were no more phone calls that night. The next call came early the following morning from Mum.

Mum: Marion, the feeling should go now. It belonged to my sister. She died last night. My dad, your Opa was letting us all know that things weren't right. As Opa has gone Home, the only long-distance call he could make to let us know was via telepathy. Mum's sister passed peacefully. But, even though she was related to my mum and Opa, she did not join my Team of Guides as she is not part of my Soul Family.

I share this story with you in the hope that perhaps you and your family experience similar things. I want to help you recognise them when they happen so that you trust them for what they truly are – messages from heaven … an advance warning that we need to be ready for 'news'. We do not see this as a bad thing at all.

Phone line work

Here's a look at some light-hearted Readings I gave back in the 1990s.

At times, I would engage in Psychic phone line Readings to earn extra money. This didn't work out for me because the companies I worked for wanted me to drag out the phone calls for as long as possible, a minimum of ten minutes, to be exact. At $3.30 a minute, it was a lucrative business, but I didn't agree to dragging out phone calls just to make the business more money. For me, the truth can be told in much less time than that – in 30 seconds, in fact! A bit like this one:

Me: Hi there, you have come through to me for a Reading. Where would you like to start today?

Caller: I am going for a job interview today. I'm wondering if I should wear my red lucky knickers or my blue lucky knickers to the interview?

Me: (*Seriously? Oh well, may as well tell her the truth*) You may as well not wear any knickers – that's the only way you will get lucky as you won't get the job today!

Caller: *Beep beep beep*

She had obviously hung up – I was paid 35 cents for the call!

Note to caller: Please accept my apology for all those years ago. I was going to tell you to go for a different job that was a little further from home that I saw you getting before you hung up on me. I hope that destiny took your hand in its own and you got that job.

Me: Hello, you have come through to me for a Reading. How may I help you today?

Caller: Can you tell me if my boyfriend is coming to see me tonight? He's four hours late!

Me: No. He's home with his wife having dinner!

Caller: *Beep beep beep*

Later that week…

Me: Hello, you have come through to me for a Reading. How may I help you today?

Caller: Hi, is my boyfriend still coming over today?
Me: No, he is home sick, and his wife is taking care of him.

Caller: *Beep beep beep*

The business owner, who had been listening to our call, said to me, 'Marion, you MUST keep the caller on the line for a minimum of ten minutes so we get maximum payment.' I asked, 'But why? She asked me a question, I gave her the information … end of questions.' They replied, 'Marion, I am going to cancel your contract with our services. You are not the kind of Reader we want working for us.' I replied with, 'Maybe you would like a Reading with me. I only give the truth though, think you could handle that?', then I hung up as I already knew her answer.

Me: Hi there, you have come to me for a Reading, how may I help you today?

Caller: I'm going to propose to my girlfriend tonight and I'm wondering what she will say.

Me: Okay, I see two things. Which one would you like to hear about first?

Caller: The first one, please.

Me: Okay. I see that this is the fourth time you are proposing to someone, and each time has been to a different person. I/we would actually like to recommend that you look at yourself very closely before you ask this next lady to marry you. Be really honest with yourself, because you are already married and the last three relationships have all started in exactly the same way, in that you were already married when you asked the next person to marry you.

Caller: How do you know this about me?

Me: Did you mean to call the Psychic phone line or the R-rated phone line?

Caller: Okay, I accept what you're saying. Will it be worth my while to take a look at myself?

Me: Yes. If you do this, I promise you that you will never have to ask another person to marry you. It's definitely in your best interest, and in her best interest as well.

Two weeks later...

Me: Hi, you have come through to me for a Reading today, how may I help you?

Caller: I asked to speak with you personally as you are the first Psychic person that's ever picked up on my issues. I want to thank you for being upfront with me. Because of you, I actually took a good look at myself and I can see where my last three relationships have gone wrong, and I've taken ownership of that. I have since had an honest conversation with my soon-to-be-ex-wife, who was actually understanding. She told me that I had beaten her in asking for a divorce. I've also explained my situation to my current girlfriend in a very honest conversation and she has given me her wholehearted support and love. She said yes to my proposal, and we are going to be married. I can now sleep at night, and I'm having the best sleep of my entire life!

Me: I'm so glad to hear this. You have made my day. Congratulations on your fourth and final wedding! You are both going to live happily ever after, and I'm really pleased to tell you that!

This next story was incredibly frustrating for me as a Reader. In 2021, during Covid, I decided to contact a reputable Psychic phone line business to offer my services. My business had slowed a little, and I wanted to keep my Reading skills up. I sent an introduction email to the Psychic phone line and received a reply from Janet, asking me if I was available at 2:30pm that day to chat. I said I was and, at 2:30pm, Janet rang and introduced herself to me. She said she had worked for the company for over 20 years and nobody got past her unless they were genuine – she reminded me of a matron in a hospital! She said that she tested everyone for authenticity before they were accepted. She wanted me to do a Reading for her and would ring me at the same time the next day, giving me 24 hours to do it.

I told Janet that was fine, as I had pretty much been shown everything already! We rang off, and I got to work. I wasn't happy in my job at that time and really wanted to impress this woman so that I could quit. I saw and wrote the following so that I could email it to her in time for our chat the next day:

I was shown that, just that day, Janet had interviewed a Psychic named Nancy who had impressed her. I was shown that, next to her driveway, was a paddock of horses that she would feed grass and talk to.

I was shown that Janet's dining room table was a mess with photos following the death of her mother nearly two years ago. Janet was trying to put them into albums but found the task too overwhelming. I was also shown that Janet had been considering leaving her husband but couldn't summon the courage as it was actually her that had stopped trying in their relationship, not him!

I figured that was enough.

After I gave her the above information, she emailed me. 'I don't know how you got all that, but it's 100% true and accurate. I will let you know what decision we come to about putting you on our books.'

Two days later, I received an official 'Thank you for your application, but no thank you.'

I was so confused as Janet had confirmed everything and had told me more details about each of the facts, confirming them. I replied to the official response.

I never received an answer.

My notes to this situation

I shared this experience with my dear friend Leonie as I felt quite pissed off. How much more proof did this lady want! Leonie channelled the following message through for me. 'Maz, you are NOT a Psychic prostitute. The information you give people is genuine and of a Soul level. You do not need to prove yourself to anyone. This has been an exercise in confirming how accurate you are. Psychic phone lines are not about Soul work – your work is too precious to prostitute! Talk to your Opa and Team about getting more work sent your way. After all, a lot of people are waking up spiritually and need good value, quality and helpful Readings. That is what you offer!'

Leonie was able to make sense of the situation, and it was a huge lesson for me. Thank you, Ms Wings, AKA Leonie L.

So, there you have it.

If you are specifically after information about your past, present or future that's not on a Soul level, contact a phone line. However, if you are after information about your past, present or future that IS of a Soul level, then please contact me as my Team and I will be only too happy to guide you. Our Readings offer insight, direction, information, clarification and guidance for you on a Soul level as we believe that the life right here, right now is important!

Honestly though, I would rather you spend your money getting in touch with your own intuition and Guides rather than spend money on Psychic hotlines.

I have been doing Readings since the 1990s. For the first 15 years or so, I didn't charge at all. Then Opa taught me that people are more likely to learn from their Readings/sessions if they contributed somehow. This is because people who are prepared to invest in themselves are in fact ready to hear and learn.

Here in 2024, my sessions remain the same price they were in the 1990s because I charge for my time, *not* my Gift. My Gift comes from my Team of Guides, and I am the instrument to bring the information through to you. Over the past 30 years, I have given close to 7000 sessions. These sessions have been held in a variety of ways, including full and partially timed sessions, casual sessions and conversations, email Readings and 'live online' sessions. Not a day goes by where I don't receive communication in one form or other from people wanting to 'just get an opinion on something' or 'just run something' by me. If I can help, I will.

I remember once receiving a nasty message telling me that I was rude for charging people for my Gift. I said that I hadn't charged for over 15 years, and I now only charge for my time. I then asked her how much time she dedicated to volunteering during the week. She told me that she didn't volunteer her time at all – she worked full time, ran a house and family! I responded that I volunteer as a Psychic at least ten hours a week and that I also offer extra sessions following an initial session with me, and that I work full time, run a house and family as well.

She never replied.

How my Readings have changed over the years

In the 1990s

During my early years offering Readings, it was all about Loved Ones who had passed over wanting to connect with and reassure their living Loved Ones that they had made it to the 'other side.' I share many of these Readings in my first book *Caught Between Two Worlds*.

I saw myself as the 'Psychic postie', just delivering messages, sharing the images shown to me by my Team as I experienced them and reassuring those still living that yes, life does go on!

This was a time of real learning for me. Prior to each consultation, I would connect with my Team and let them know the name of the person coming to see me that day. I would then ask for any messages and/or information that the person coming needed to hear from their visitors in the Spirit world. I wrote these messages down word for word, rolled them into a scroll and placed them on the table for the person coming to their appointment. The messages were always shared throughout the consultation, and the proof of life after death was undeniable. Messages were always confirmed as accurate, which was chilling sometimes. It fascinated me. In fact, it's taken me 400 pages of writing to even try and find the right 'human' words to explain something that isn't part of the 'human' experience.

After a session, I used to sit for hours, often not sleeping, as I revisited it over and over in complete awe of the power of Love and the Spirit world.

It all fascinated me and continues to!

In the 2000s

Life was busy for me as a mum, daughter, wife and employee. As I didn't have a dedicated place to offer consultations, I would either do them in my lounge room when my partner was at work, or I would go to other people's homes. Neither was satisfactory to my partner, and I sadly began to offer fewer appointments.

For the first 20 years or so, I never charged to meet with and talk to people, which is all I thought I was doing. To me, I was just doing the same that any good friend would do for their friend – offer advice – except these people were strangers to me, even though I knew all about their lives! Again, I thought it was normal.

The sessions continued to be those of mediumship as healing on both sides of the veil.

In the 2010s

Life was still busy – in fact, it was getting busier.

People were coming to me all the time, not just for sessions, but also in daily life. Some I knew, and some I didn't. It was as if I was carrying a neon sign above my head saying 'bleeding hearts welcome'! I found that, regardless of where I went, people would tell me their troubles and seek my advice.

And I would give it.

Just like, I thought, anyone would.

People always told me that I had told them exactly what they needed to hear or what they needed to do. They would seek me out after they had taken my advice to either thank me or ask me what to do next.

This happened everywhere I went, and I saw more and more the inner workings of people's minds – their emotions, their feelings, their motivations ... their everything! It was a fascinating way of being taught by my Team – always putting me in the right place at the right time.

It wasn't always nice.

I didn't question it.

And still they came.

And still I gave.

And gave and gave because that's what I do. Helping people was my way of paying back my Team for having my Gift of 'Knowing!'

My husband and I divorced in 2015. He told me I needed to go back home to Adelaide after living in Perth for 20 years. He said that I needed to share my Gift with others and continue to touch the lives of many and write my book, so that it, too, could touch the lives of people.

Such a Gift he gave me.

And here I am, no longer 'caught between two worlds' but living my full life as myself – as my 'me!' ... no longer justifying the air I breathe or the space I took up in the world to make him or others comfortable. No longer did I have to apologise for being me.

Suddenly, I saw I had a Gift, and now I was going to learn how to truly harness it and to work with my Team one on one.

I am blessed. I know it.

Just on the topic of suicide – I know you may wonder why I would even attempt it. It takes such incredible strength to accept that life as you knew it is something you can no longer cope with. I have worked with many people who have reached the same point in their lives. I realise now that it was because I was looking at my life through human eyes. I thought that was all there was, back then. It was the beginning of a massive journey through my Dark Night of the Soul – a journey that spanned three years.

I went through a couple of years when I felt I had nothing more to lose. During the years after Perth, I had been visiting a lovely doctor who knows what she means to me. She helped my human self deal with all the grief and trauma I had been going through. I trusted her. So, one day, I had an idea and thought I would test her. I didn't care if I ended up in a psych hospital, as I knew I would have a lot of company there who would understand me – psych hospitals are full of Psychics by the way.

It was early 2018. I made an appointment with her, then attended it with a copy of *Caught Between Two Worlds*. I had written a dedication to her in the front that only she would understand.

When I walked into her room, she looked at me in surprise and said, 'Marion, you look so calm and peaceful, almost serene. May I ask why?' All the other times she had seen me, I had been a complete mess of sadness, grief and despair. This time was different.

'I've finally published my book!' I said.

'Congratulations! What's it about?'

I took a deep breath and faced my darkest fears, which had been there for many years. Then, I said, 'I have a Psychic Gift that I have lived with all my life. I've never told a doctor, psychologist or psychiatrist for fear that they would lock me up! My book is about feeling "caught between two worlds!" – my life, my experiences and my Readings. I wrote it for my two kids.'

We chatted about the book for a while, as I hadn't actually come in for a consultation.

Then I waited.

Dr K stood up, and immediately fear set in!

She opened the door, and my fear got worse … she *was* going to get the straitjacket and security. She wasn't going to let me back out in the community among 'normal' people again. (How far I've come! I share this because I'm sure there are many of you who have now awakened and feel the same!)

Then she spoke. 'Marion, congratulations on writing your book. You have a very important story to share. I am so very proud of you! You have a Gift, and the world is waiting for you!' As I write this, my eyes fill with emotion as I recall the incredible feeling of Unconditional Love that she showed me that day! I simply cannot thank that beautiful Earth Angel enough!

Her eyes glistened with tears … mine simply ran down my face!

I had just faced the worst fear of my life! Nothing would ever scare me again as much as trusting her that day with my whole life.

I stood. No words were needed. Instead, she hugged me and opened the door wider.

That's when my life truly started.

I haven't seen her since. I don't need to. She played her role in my life beautifully.

She is an Earth Angel amongst us.

It was after this that I bought my caravan. It was during this trip that I met a good friend, a beautiful Soul that I will call E. While I was in my caravan, I continued to give lots of Readings via phone, video or in person. I visited places on my travels, including meditation and healing centres and Spiritualist churches. I left copies of my first book and introduced myself to many bookstores and groups. I was kept very busy with Readings. I was starting to feel my purpose for living.

It was then that E suggested that I should go 'live' with sessions on Facebook, offering oracle card Readings and guidance. This was all new to me and a huge learning curve. I kept saying to E that I just wanted to give messages as I had no connection to the cards at all. That was until I started using them on the live sessions.

I would always give my message to someone online then follow it up with a card from one of the decks I felt drawn to. I have many. It was uncanny how often the card would mirror the messages exactly.

My Facebook groups grew and the lives doubled, then tripled, in size. This then led to many regular consultations, and I made many new friends. Some were true friends, and others just wanted to be friends to get information. At first, I couldn't tell the difference. And, although I treated everyone the same, sadly they didn't treat me the same and they were soon plucked from my garden by my Team. Thank goodness for that!

My true friends remain to this day and have been absolute rocks during my time on the road and since my return to Victor Harbor. My true friends know exactly who they are, and I have acknowledged them at the front of this book and tell them personally every time I speak with them or think of them.

True friends taught me how to accept Unconditional Love as a human (I was very good at giving it) and trust (which I was very bad at, as I trusted everyone). What kind of a Psychic couldn't see who was using them? But that's what us 6s do, right? We trust everyone the same. Well, there's the lesson in itself, right?

This book is dedicated to those who loved me when I didn't know how to Love myself.

I am blessed.

Most people who book a personal consultation with me seem to have similar issues:

- They feel lost, yet more connected than ever.
- They are experiencing their own Dark Night of the Soul following the loss of loved family members, partners, jobs or finances.

- Many of them feel called to go Home.
- They are experiencing a huge increase in coincidences that they interpret as Signs that are always perfect for them. They are answers to their prayers, if you like, but they are unsure of their meaning and how to apply them to their life. All this information and experience is doing 'their head in' as their mind struggles to come to terms with information meant only for the Soul.
- They have become Empaths and are feeling overwhelmed as they become more and more aware of everyone around them. Their situations, their feelings and their emotions have become all-consuming.
- Their dramas, stresses and traumas are present and recurring as they try to make sense of their lives, yet they can't and 'normal' counselling hasn't helped.

My role has since changed to that of a counsellor for the Soul – a Soul Clinician, if you like. While normal psychological counselling has its place, it is unable to reach down into the depths of your Soul to where life REALLY counts.

I pride myself on being able to see you at these depths and show you to YOU! I see the Soul Contracts and who is who in your zoo.

Over time, my work in mediumship has reduced. My Team showed me that, more often than not, many people go Home with Spiritual awareness. Nowadays, when I sit with family members of Loved Ones passing away, I always encourage them to discuss the Signs that their Loved One will show them once they've returned Home and are ready to reconnect.

My Team told me that this life, right here and now, is the life that counts and that many people are so far off their path and making really bad choices. They needed Soul work to rescue them from themselves. I tried to talk my Team out of my new role by asking how I could help people when I wasn't a 'trained by the book' counsellor. They reminded me that it wasn't a counsellor that these people needed, and that I had already had life experience accumulated during many incarnations and helped thousands of people through Readings or just conversations and interactions without even realising it. I had already adopted and was working in my Soul purpose.

I would like to help you also!

Earth Angels are beginning to dominate our living world. They too are Soul Clinicians and their consulting rooms are the café's, hairdressers and classrooms they work in. They are everywhere. Earth Angels just like Marie:

Marie's story

You may identify with Marie. She was your typically unaware Earth Angel – a weirdo who is actually Wired! She was connected and delivering messages to humans through her place of work without realising it!

Marie was quite distraught by the time she came to see me for a session. After settling her with a cuppa, hot water bottle and blankie, I asked Marie where she would like to start. The following is an excerpt of our session with her permission, though names have been changed.

Marie told me, 'Marion, you have to help me. I'm going to lose my job!' I asked her why, and she responded, 'I keep making customers cry. It's weird. I don't know why, and my boss doesn't like it. She is scared that I'm pushing the customers away.'

As Marie was explaining this to me, I asked Opa to show me what was going on with Marie's work situation. Opa told me:

Opa: Marie works in a café, the one near the beach. (Opa showed me what it looked like with its distinct features, and I recognised it). Marie often finds that when she is clearing people's tables, customers just open up to her, telling her their life problems and stories. Marie is an Earth Angel and always seems to find herself in exactly the right place offering messages of comfort, peace, love and insight that she channels – albeit without realising it.

I told Marie what Opa had told me.

Marie: Yes, that's where I work – I wait tables. I need the money. People do always tell me their stories, and I try to help them. I don't know where the words come from, but they tell me they're always perfect and just what they needed to hear that day … then they leave. When this happens, only the person who needs to hear what I say is present – all the other patrons have gone.

I gave her Opa's message.

Opa: Marie, you are an Earth Angel. In our human life, we have heart, lung and eye specialists, and they all have their own clinical rooms to consult out of! You are a Soul Specialist, and the café is your consulting room. People think they are coming in for a coffee! Aren't they in for a surprise – coffee AND a Soul session is more like it! Please tell your manager what's happening. We see that she will understand and support you!

I'm pleased to say that Marie still works in her café all these years later – yes, with the same totally supportive boss – and business is thriving.

Tori Mc – show her the pearl necklace

Tori is a very gifted young lady who lives in the USA. Tori frequented my 'live' Facebook sessions on a Thursday night. The time difference between Australia and the USA worked well for her as she was a really bad sleeper! I had been particularly drawn to Tori's amazing energy from the very first time she commented. I knew there was something very special about her. While she was a stranger to me, I could see and cared about her Soul.

I always gave Tori and any of the other visitors from overseas Angel cards and messages when I saw their names. I did this for a few years. Sometimes Tori would message me to tell me how appropriate her card and message were that evening. I asked her about her Gift, and Tori shared it with me. She also shared her struggles with me. Tori is a gifted 6 and is unknowingly surrounded by 5s in her life. We have worked through these struggles together.

I hadn't heard from Tori in a while when she messaged me letting me know that she was in hospital. She had been very sad for a long time. I sent her a few voice messages of positivity and friendship. No, we didn't know each other and no, we've never met. However, when you live and work on a Soul level, you don't need to travel such long distances to meet each other. Souls can do it easily, and ours did! Tori's grandfather came to me as I was leaving a voice message for her. He said, 'Please ask Tori to tell her mum where the pearl necklace that I gave her is, and ask her to bring it in. When her mum brings it in, I ask that she holds it, and I will be there right with her!'

I gave Tori this message through a voice message so she could hear the love in my voice from her grandfather.

Tori replied to my voice messages with her own. She explained that she had totally forgotten about the pearl necklace and would certainly tell her mum where it was so that she could bring it in. Tori was very grateful for her special message.

Slowly, slowly, Tori regained her strength! I stopped doing the 'live' sessions, and life went on for both of us on opposite sides of the world. That was until I received a message from Tori that her 18-year-old brother had taken his life, and she wanted me to contact him. I was absolutely gutted for her. This kind of grief is so hard for anyone at any time, anywhere. Again, we started communicating to help her move through the early days of grief when it was all-consuming.

Every now and again, we message each other, knowing that we are kindred Spirits that just 'get' each other. Soul friendship is the most special friendship there is! There is no time and there is no distance when you have a Soul connection. It's the 'Wired-in' energy that connects us every single time.

I feel so very blessed to know Tori and her mum.

Elyse is a GEM

I am going to try really hard to express what these two Readings were like for me, but it's going to be very hard to find the words.

It was in May 2017 that I first met Elyse and her incredible dad, George. I have never met a Soul like George before and never will again! Lucky for me, he still pops in from time to time whenever Elyse is near me. He is always with her. The power of George's Love is incredible.

I had been invited to speak at the Psychic Body and Soul Expo in Adelaide. I also had a stall that we decorated in the colours of my new book *Caught Between Two Worlds*. I had a good friend helping me on the day – thank goodness, as my Team of Guides had people backed up trying to have a session. There was one woman though that wouldn't come in!

Every time Elyse walked past my stall, her dad George (in Spirit) would say to me, 'That's my daughter! Why doesn't she come in here? You can hear me.' I would always look up or stand up. I knew exactly who George was looking at as I could see their resemblance.

My friend, S, was acting as hostess for me that day, which was a fantastic help. She would bring through each person and introduce us. I would then invite them to sit down, and we would commence their session.

Elyse walked past about three times that afternoon. She was there with a friend. Each time, George pointed her out to me! George really wanted to talk to his daughter, but I couldn't help him.

I continued with my Readings and tried to work through the line of people as quickly and efficiently as possible once S escorted them to my table. I know better than to interrupt Spirits when they come through with messages. Consequently, I ended up running an hour and a half behind! It was getting quite late.

Then the next person that S brought to me was Elyse! George was over the moon. I swear she must have heard him through me. He was SO loud and SO excited! This is how the next bit went:

George: She came, that's Elyse. She's my daughter and she's wearing my ring on her thumb! Go on, grab it, hold it for me. Don't let go of her thumb or her hand, because it's me holding her thumb and her hand … Oh that's my daughter! She came in! I'm so glad.

I could see tears on George's face. I could also see the pure Unconditional Love of a father – a gentle-man!

I reached out and took Elyse's thumb and held it, pointing out her dad's ring.

Me: Oh Elyse, your dad, George, has been here all afternoon waiting for you. Each time you walked past, he would interrupt me and show you to me. He even made me stand up during Readings to point you out to me. He really wanted you to come in – I could hear him. I had to leave it up to you to come in, now here you are! He loves you so much, Elyse! Please sit down.

I didn't let go of her hand, nor did her dad. By now, Elyse was in tears and so was I.

And that, my friends, was the whole Reading. Well, the bit in words, anyway! Elyse and I sat at the table, howling like long-lost family friends, together with her dad. I was oblivious to what the people in the line thought about what was happening at the little round table in my booth. But we didn't care. George was reunited with Elyse, and that was all that mattered.

I was so very blessed to be able to transmit George's abundance of love to his daughter.

Elyse: Yes, George is my dad. Yes, this is my dad's ring! I walked past here several times this afternoon and really felt drawn to you. I kept walking around to see if I was drawn to anywhere else to have a Reading. But it was you! Now I know why! Thank you so much Marion, thank you!

As it was getting late, George and I had to say goodbye to Elyse. I was in shock, and it took me a while to get back on track and finish reading for the others waiting in the line! I felt so very blessed to have been able to reunite father and daughter.

Elyse's second Reading

I used to do Readings at my home right on the beach front at Victor Harbor. I found that by positioning my table in front of the big picture window, I was mesmerised by the waves coming into the beach, and this really helped me tune into my Team and Readings. When people came for a Reading, they would ring or send me a text requesting an appointment. I only ever took their first name and their phone number and gave them an appointment time and my address in return.

During this time, I was caring for both of my parents. My Team encouraged me to keep doing Readings because they said that by helping others I would end up helping myself! They were right – it took the focus off my sadness, which became unbearable later in the year!

I opened the front door, and the first thing I was greeted by was George's ring! Wait! What? I looked up at the beautiful face of Elyse standing at my door.

Me: Hi, it's you! This is your dad's ring – he's here with us now. Come in, come in. Weren't the messages you got at the expo enough?

Elyse: Hi Marion! Yes, they were! They were perfect. I couldn't believe it. I thought I would come back and see if there was anything else for me!

George: Oh, she's back – my Leesee is back. Please tell her how much I love her! I LOVE HER so very much. She is a beautiful daughter!

Me: Elyse, your dad wants you to know how beautiful you are to him and how much he Loves you!

As became the norm for when Elyse and I get together, there were happy tears.

Elyse: Thank you, Marion. Tell him I love him too!

Me: He hears you, Elyse. He knows.

Elyse: Is there anyone else with Dad?

George: Marion, I would like you to meet Pearl and Ruby! While they are both 'gems', my daughter is my real GEM!

Me: Elyse, your dad is showing me two ladies, one named Pearl and one named Ruby. He said that pearls and rubies are both gems, but that you are his gem. Does this make sense to you?

Before I had even finished, Elyse was in tears again!

Elyse: Oh, yes! Yes, it makes sense. Pearl was my auntie. This is very special to me. Thank you. Marion, please look out the window and look at the number plate on my car!

I did, and when I looked at the number plate on her car, it had the word 'GEM' on it! You could have knocked me over with a feather! How incredible. Elyse said that she got the special number plate to always remember her dad.

The rest of the day was spent oohing and aahing over the information that had again come through her dad that afternoon.

Elyse is certainly a very blessed Soul, I'm sure you will agree … and it just continues! While sitting in the Proserpine Library writing this book, I kept getting the name 'Leesee' every time I typed the word 'Elyse!' As I had been messaging Elyse during the day, I sent off a quick message asking who used to call her 'Leesee'. Dorothy, 'Dot', came through and told me she did. I immediately replied to Elyse, telling her I already knew the answer to the question.

I quickly explained to Elyse how Dorothy had shown herself to me as a 'wind-up doll with Eveready long-lasting batteries', along with some other personal attributes. Elyse confirmed everything I said and told me that was exactly how she remembered her favourite aunty.

I have known Elyse and her dad for seven years now, and I simply cannot imagine my life without her in it. It's people like Elyse that make our world a much more beautiful place just by being in it.

My experience of Elyse's Readings

How can I possibly find the words to share how I feel about Elyse's journey through our sessions together? Words like 'magical' and 'miraculous' are good, but they don't capture the 'feeling' or 'energy' associated with Elyse's reunion with her dad. It's always amazing when someone comes through during the first Reading I do for a person. My Gift constantly surprises me. I certainly feel very blessed to have been involved in a reunion like theirs. Even though a person comes to see me for a Reading, it's not just about them – it's about anyone who chooses to come through for them too. The healing occurs on both sides of the veil, and it's their shared Unconditional Love that makes it possible.

'Expect the unexpected' is what I always say!

Kim and her John Travolta-lookalike brother

The morning Kim came to see me, Opa told me that our session would be very special and memorable. He does this sometimes, and he is always right. So, I looked forward to it. However, when Kim walked in looking extremely fragile, I was concerned that I had misinterpreted Opa's message to me. That was until I saw who was walking behind her – her brother, dressed in a long trench coat and with wings that rose above his head and down to the floor! He was incredible. He took my breath away. Kim didn't notice though. She was buried in grief and sadness, a true shadow of her former self.

L: I've brought Kim to you, please help her know that I am here and that she can stop being a sooky la la. I am her Guide now, by her side to help her, and will never leave!

L was gorgeous with long, dark tousled hair and teeth whiter than his wings! It's interesting when Loved Ones show themselves to me. I always wonder whether this is what they really looked like when they were alive. L told me he was 42 when he died and said Kim knows only too well how he died.

I was excited to reunite Kim with her brother and almost couldn't wait the appropriate amount of time before asking her to sit down.

Before she could even speak, I/we said:

Me: Kim, your brother has come with you today. He told me that he is always with you. Did you know that?

Kim: Really? What does he look like?

Me: Oh Kim, he's so beautiful. He has long, dark, wavy hair and wings! You should see them! He told me that he died at 42 but can't remember how. He said it doesn't matter anyway, because now you have your very own Angel by your side, day and night.

I continued on, looking from Kim to L and back again. L was perched on the back of the lounge next to Kim, encouraging me to keep talking.

Me: Kim, your brother is very special. He was an Earth Angel in the lifetime he just left. Everybody loved him. He is giving me the impression of a modern-day priest. He's showing me that he helped so many people by being in the right place at the right time saying the words a person needed to hear. He was loved by everyone. He had a very special energy that only belongs to Angels, and people felt that about him. Actually, you know who he reminds me of? He reminds me of John Travolta in the movie *Michael*! Have you seen it? Does this make sense to you?

L put his hand over his heart and bowed his head, acknowledging my description of him to his sister. Kim needed a few minutes to have a good cry.

L waited. So did I.

Kim: Oh Maz! How perfect that you see him too. I don't see him … I do feel him though, all the time. Maz, he died such an awful death, did he tell you about it?

Me: No, he said he couldn't remember how he'd died this time!
Kim: He was working on roadworks and was run over by a steamroller and killed (here she started sobbing).

L: Marion, please tell her that I'm fine. It was always going to happen. It was a complete accident, and I was to blame for not watching where I was going. But I know that they have become more cautious prior to rolling now. I was their karma – they had to learn! Please tell Kim how good I look now. I'm all in one piece and don't look like I've been ironed!

Me: (After telling her what her brother had said) Kim, your brother is sitting on the back of the sofa right behind you!

Kim: I can feel him! I always do.

Kim then showed me a photo of her other brothers and asked me to describe what was going on with each of them. So I did, starting by pointing at one of the men in the photo.

Me: Kim, L is telling me that this brother is not coping at all and that he has never talked about the incident with anyone. He's never talked about his feelings about losing his big brother. I'm really worried about him and don't know how to help him. Do you think he would come and talk to me?

Kim: That's G, and he's exactly as L describes him. He has isolated himself from his family and is only in this photo because it was taken at the funeral. Since then, he hasn't spoken to his other brothers or family. We all worry about him. I can only ask G if he talks to me again, but I doubt he will. We fear he'll take his own life. He is very secretive about his grief. I feel like I've lost two brothers, even though I feel L around me all the time. I feel safe when he is around, and I know he helps me!

L: Tell Kim that I am always with her – she is absolutely right. I'm glad she believes! Tell her that if G were to take his life, then I will look after him until what would have been the time of his natural death.

I relayed this to Kim.

Kim: That's so good to hear. I never thought about L being able to do that. I miss him as a physical brother but knowing that he could do this for our other brother is amazing. I am glad. Please tell him!

Me: You just did! Your brother L has his arm and wing around you, Kim.

Kim: This has just been so amazing, Marion. I am so glad that I came. I wanted to tell you that I felt my brother around me, but I also wanted to see if you saw him before I did so I could truly believe that it's real!

Me: Oh Kim, this is as real as it could ever get! You have your very own Angel. He was a good man to so many when he was alive. People looked up to him, confided in him and considered him a counsellor in their lives. He loved that they felt this way. He knew his role in the life that he has just left and accepted it. Such a beautiful Soul. Thank you so much for bringing him in to meet me today.

Kim left shortly after, looking much taller, younger and more peaceful than when she walked in.

My experience of Kim's Reading

Time stands still during Readings like this, and nothing outside of the three of us existed during those couple of hours. L was what I would call the 'perfect Earth Angel!' He knew his role and played it. He was so much like John Travolta in the movie *Michael*. At one point, L actually said that that movie was made about him and not John Travolta at all!

Personally, I am very grateful I met Kim's brother that day and have been grateful every day since. Kim sometimes comes into my human workplace, and L is always with her. I always greet them both, not just because I see him, but because I want Kim to know that he is still there. Some people want to ask if I see them but feel it's respectful not to ask. Kim is one of these beautiful respectful people, so I tell her. Sometimes L interrupts us and then apologises. He's a character, that's for sure.

I absolutely love helping people and Angels this way!

I died in that shed, Mummy

The Goolwa Ghost & Historical Tour hosted by the local radio station has been running for many years. For five years, I hosted the tour on behalf of the station as a volunteer Psychic. I had grown up in the area, and it was a privilege to be able to share my experiences, history and memories.

I'll never forget the first time I met Lyn. Lyn took me for my first ghost walk, albeit in the daytime, to highlight the areas to talk about in and around the local radio station.

Goolwa is a beautiful historic town where the Murray River flows out into the sea. It was the first river port in Australia, and paddle-steamers frequently shipped their wool, wheat and other cargo through its very busy port. If you ever come to the Fleurieu Peninsula in South Australia, be sure to come and visit the Goolwa region – the local radio station would be only too happy to provide you with ghost tour information.

Lyn took me to the first maternity hospital in the area on Goyder Street in Goolwa. It was situated on a corner block. Lyn was bringing me to meet the lovely couple who owned it now – the husband had actually been born within its walls.

The maternity hospital had a very colourful history.

As we wandered through the old hospital quarters, we were given an insight into the workings of the old maternity hospital and its subsequent life as an accommodation house.

It wasn't until I was wandering in the garden that I felt and saw a young girl in Spirit form. Telepathically, I reached out to her. She told me she had been born there and that her brother's remains were buried in the garden, then she was gone. I saw her again later during an actual tour. We were standing inside the remains of a lean-to shed, where apparently the original owner had hanged himself. I felt someone put their hand in mine – it was the beautiful young girl. Our photographer on that tour saw her as well and took a photo of us as she put her hand in mine. The photographer was able to see the girl in the photo initially, then she faded out of the picture altogether! Nonetheless, it was undeniable that she was there with us that evening and with her brother.

The owners of the maternity hospital play recordings of guests' experiences whenever we come to visit. There is a particularly poignant one that I will share with you now.

One day, Margaret and her seven-year-old son Adam were walking past the maternity hospital. Neither had ever mentioned anything about the hospital before. On this particular occasion, however, Adam motioned to his mum and said, 'Mum, see that shed? I died in that shed!' Mum didn't know what to say, so apparently she didn't say anything. This had happened about 35 years earlier.

Margaret was curious though and went to visit the owners of the property. She explained what Adam had told her and asked if there was anything that they could tell her about what he had said.

The owners confirmed that the original owner of the property, before it became a maternity hospital, did in fact hang himself in that shed long ago. There was no way Adam could have known that information, which had been substantiated through the homestead's records.

In 2020, I used to frequent a local hairdresser. On one occasion, I was telling her about my upcoming ghost tour, and she mentioned she would like to do it. I told her that we visit the maternity hospital and about Adam's experience there. She was shocked. She sat down next to me, then said, 'Oh Marion, it really is real. Adam's mum is a good friend of mine and I remember when this happened for Adam and his mum. I can absolutely substantiate his story. It's the truth.'

I was completely floored. I asked my hairdresser if Adam might like to talk to me about his experiences now that he had grown up. She said she would ask, but I never heard anything.

It makes me wonder what life is like for people when they have past-life memories like this come up. Personally, I never get past-life memories and I'm not sure how I would process them, to be honest. Maybe you get glimpses of your past lives. I know many of you do because you tell me about them in your Readings with me.

Fascinating! Adam's story was the highlight of our Ghost Tour.

A scary vision that had me screaming

We had taken the kids out for the day to a well-known place in Perth. I screamed like a woman possessed at the sideshow ride, but I was on the ground!

My vision showed me that the seat my daughter was sitting in had a broken protection chain at the front. I saw the ride flinging her out midway, and it terrified me. How was I going to deal with this standing next to my husband, who didn't believe in my Gift at all?

The ride attendant went along and checked that everyone had strapped themselves in correctly. He was satisfied everything was in order and proceeded to start the ride in motion

I was shitting myself!

What do I do? Say something, yell something or be quiet to make my partner feel comfortable? As the ride started, I realised I didn't give a rat's arse what anyone thought. I started running, screaming at the attendant, 'Stop the ride, stop the ride!'. He did, then came over to see what was making this hysterical woman make all this noise!

I told him, 'The chain on my daughter's chair is broken! I want her out!'

Both kids were teenagers and were quietly wishing that the ground would open up and swallow me whole. They were completely embarrassed. However, they both got off the ride. The attendant checked the chain and locking mechanisms and found that he couldn't lock it! My daughter would have flown out!

He put an 'out of order' sign on the seat and recommenced the ride.

My partner said nothing!

We walked past that ride a few times that day. The 'out of order' sign remained on that particular chair. I wonder what the ride attendant thought? Interesting!

Once I calmed down and regained composure, I was able to enjoy the rest of our stay at the theme park. That vision has never left me though!

My notes to this experience

You know what? If you get a gut feeling that something is wrong, it probably is. If you get a gut feeling that something is right, it probably is! Either way, your intuition is for your benefit. This particular vision disturbed me to the point where I consulted my human mind for clarity, wasting precious time because I was more worried about what people would think of my behaviour than my daughter flying out of the fast ride and appearing on the 6:00 pm news on television that night. How crazy is that?

I didn't know anyone there that day except my family. If I hadn't intervened, and the vision came to fruition, what would I have said then? 'Oh! I saw that happening!' Nope, not an option. I didn't give a rat's arse what people thought – my daughter was getting off that ride with my help!

Parents, trust yourselves!

Living with Spirit and the voice of your Soul

How connected are you really?

We are all energy. Dead or alive, it makes no difference. The only difference between us and those who have gone Home is that we still have a human body.

That's it.

That's the illusion right there.

Life itself is the illusion.

Our Soul IS us, not our physical body.

We all think that the physical components – heart, brain, lungs, eyes, flesh and blood and so on – are who we are, but that would be like saying that we are our car! Our car only works when we drive it, and so does our body!

Spirituality comes with lifetimes lived. It is not a sense that awakens from reading books. It comes through lifetimes and living through your Dark Night of the Soul.

Being Spiritual and being Psychic are two very different things. They don't always go hand in hand in a lifetime.

Being Spiritual is about having learnt and continuing to be aware of and learning your lessons from the 'Big List' and living with pure Unconditional Love and awareness in your Soul.

Being Psychic is really about your 6th sense and knowing things before they happen or knowing the outcome to a future event or question if asked.

As a 6, you will be able to 'feel' someone's genuine level of Spirituality: their authenticity.

Some people are barely in their Soul, and others live fully in their Soul. In your final lifetime, you are aiming to be in your Soul 100% of the time on a Spiritual, ego-free level.

I have met two people in my lifetime I was unable to read because they just ARE – there was no benefit to them having a Reading. They had already reached Nirvana. Personally, I like the Buddhist definition of Nirvana (from Google): 'a transcendent state in which there is neither suffering, desire, nor sense of self, ego and the subject is released from the effects of karma and the cycle of death and rebirth. It represents the final goal of Buddhism/Spirituality.'

These two are Michelle and Terry. They are both fully enlightened and in their last incarnation. They live every day in a state of pure bliss and joy as they continue to live their human incarnation for the last time.

These people have a quiet, spectacular energy that expands out of their physical body, touching you in a way you didn't know you needed, often without saying anything at all. They are pure energy, fully accepting of their Soul selves. They are ready to step into their next role as a Guide back Home.

Many people say, 'I'm not coming back again!' They normally say this as the human has found the stress and drama too much and would rather walk away from the lesson than learning it. If that's the case, then I say that when a lesson is presented to you, do your Soul a favour and learn it while it's small!

People think that if they turn their back on a lesson that's presenting as a conflict or issue, it will go away. Maybe it will in this lifetime, but it won't be removed from your Soul Contract. All you're doing is deferring it. You may as well learn it and benefit from it, but people often think they know better. This is how you know they are still a 'young' Soul.

Most of us know that if we don't learn a lesson when it's presented to us, it will come back bigger. Worse though is that there will also be a greater price to pay.

Many people feel that they are insignificant and treat themselves this way, so others treat them the same. Ultimately, we teach others how we want to be treated. <u>Read that again</u>. This is why the universe brings us opportunities, disguised as people, to help us find our own voice and our own way. Some call them our 'mirror', reflecting ourselves back to us. This is about being assertive, not aggressive – a big lesson for many.

My dear friend Michelle has given me two very valuable pieces of advice. I go to her for guidance when I am unable to understand 'human' behaviour! Whenever I sought counsel from Michelle, she would say one of two things. The first was, 'Marion, what would Love do?' The second, my favourite, is, 'F*CK 'EM!' One was Spiritual advice and the other was good old Michelle advice. I love them both, and her.

Feel free to follow Michelle's Spiritual advice – you will find solutions and your own Soul voice. For many, me included, finding and listening to our own voice takes too long. For me, part of the reason is that I have always been the way I am. I always thought I was thinking or listening to my human mind … until I learnt the difference. It was confusing for many years … conflicting, even. I always felt caught between two worlds! If you feel the same way, I hope the experiences I've shared in this book will help you 'hear and listen' for yourself.

For years, I struggled to listen to hear my Soul voice asking for what it really wanted. Why? Because I always put more value in the human voice of others. I believed that others knew what was better for me and were making decisions for me that best served my interests.

I believed them.

But, of course, I shouldn't have, because they didn't! They couldn't! How could they? They were external to me! They didn't know ME.

THEY weren't *my* Soul.

I am.

My Soul speaks a language that only I can hear and understand.

Many of you ask what it is like to 'hear' Opa or my Team. It's hard to put into words. When I think, I think in my voice inside my head. When my Team talk to me, it is in their voice, a male's voice, inside my head. Hearing them is not just about 'hearing' them. They bring an incredible feeling of Unconditional Love with them. If I receive messages that are not accompanied by this 'feeling', then I generally don't listen to the guidance. If the feeling does come with the messages, then I know I have to trust them. Opa's voice has always sounded the same. I am used to it. This way I am also able to distinguish it from any other. Nonetheless, it's a voice and it's inside of my head. I hear it with my inner ears and trust it with my Soul.

I finally accepted that voice around eight years ago, about the time I released *Caught Between Two Worlds*. It had always been there – I just started listening to it and believing it. There were many people in my life that had let me down with their suggestions and advice as to what I should and shouldn't do in my life. I decided not to listen to others anymore as they didn't know what was best for me, only what suited them.

This is when I stopped 'humaning', as I call it. I don't 'people'. Peopleing is overrated, I say. I only 'human' at work and the rest of the time I am guided by my Soul. After all, my brain is only as old as my body and my Soul is as old as all my lifetimes, so of course I'm going to listen to and be guided by it. It knows what's best for me.

That was when I truly started to listen to my Soul's voice. All the other 'voices in my head' belonging to my parents, my kids, my husband, colleagues and people who thought they knew me were evicted once and for all – banned from ever entering my head or heart space again.

I finally felt free.

It all happened one night in 2018 while travelling in my caravan. It was 3:03 am and a crystal-clear night. I had cried day and night for four months until that moment when Opa woke me and told me no one was coming to rescue me and that I needed to rescue myself.

That was the turning point and the exact time Marion left me and Maz came back into my life. Maz was a name I had been called when I was a kid but, as an adult, I used the name my parents gave me. Now, when I use the name 'Marion', I feel I am referring to the 'me' that died along with all the sadness, trauma and grief prior to February 2018. Maz was the one who stepped up and started listening to her Soul voice from that point. I've never looked back or listened to anyone other than the united voice of my Team since then.

I have found it now, and I am blessed. I don't take it for granted, and my Team give me a hard time if I even try to!

It also taught me that learning a lesson will also involve teaching a lesson. I/We will try and explain the best we can.

So, a person – in this case, me – was presented with many, many opportunities throughout my life to love and believe in myself. However, I had always sought validation and acceptance through the opinions of others. This was largely because of my upbringing and experiences with my ex-fiancé as detailed in my first book.

If I had learnt to believe in, accept and love myself by listening to my Soul voice, I may still be married. But, because I didn't, I paid an enormous price. In paying that price, I learnt my lesson. Remember what we said earlier? You can choose to ignore a lesson but, by doing so, you are merely dismissing it from this lifetime. Next time, the price to pay will be bigger. Learning to use my Soul voice, which is always kind, quiet and knowing – as opposed to my human voice which, at times, was very loud, argumentative and wanted the last word (recognise the ego here?) – would have saved me relationships and jobs.

One of the hardest situations I have had to live with, navigate and understand in my life is living while seeing that life is an illusion when no one else seems to see it the same way.

But really, the hardest lesson of my life has been listening to and trusting my Soul voice – believing in MY voice and loving me.

I wish to thank each and every person who has walked my journey with me in my life and given me opportunities to grow, learn, share and teach. Some have stayed with me throughout my whole lifetime while others have come and gone, playing their part then moving on.

They taught me to share the lesson of Unconditional Love. When I look back at the 'humans' that played this role in my life, I can clearly see that they are/were 6s and members of my Soul Family. To them, I will be forever grateful.

'Believers' who don't walk the walk

I don't know how to address this issue, so I'll just have a go.

I have been to many meditation groups in my life. I was very disappointed many years ago in Perth when I went to a big Spiritualist centre only to find it was full of ego and hierarchy. I'm pretty sure that I didn't even finish the first night's session.

During the evening, there had been constant talk about 'Spirits' this and 'Spirits' that! It gave me the impression that they didn't even believe there were Spirits in the room at all, because if they did believe, they wouldn't have treated them as if they weren't there! It was like they spoke that way in case the Spirits *were* real.

Did they realise that Spirits are just us 'dead'? They're not us dying then waking up holy. Well, these groups tend to talk about Spirits as if they can't hear what these people are saying.

I cringe, honestly.

I also cringe when so-called mediums call in these Spirits, often introducing them to the group and trying to link them to someone. They would say things like, 'I have an elderly lady here with grey hair and pink lipstick who smells like lavender!' Really? Whatever happened to the names they had when they were alive? I always give the names as a connection.

My experience is that if a Loved One genuinely comes through, the Gatekeeper will take their name and pass it to me, leaving out any guesswork as to who Molly, Frank, George or Enid belong to.

It shouldn't be a circus, but I have seen this circus act many times. However, it might not all be a complete waste of time, as Opa reminded me once.

I had been to a show with my parents. It was put on by a Psychic at a local theatre. Afterwards, I said, 'Opa, what on earth was that performance tonight? I can't even call it an act – it was so pathetic! I felt really sorry for the people who believed it as there was no one upstairs wanting to speak to their Loved Ones. I knew it was all an act!'

Opa responded:

> Lieve meisje, to those receiving the messages from the person on the stage, they were everything. They *were* a connection to the Loved One they had been missing. It was very healing for them. Their Loved Ones may not have actually been present at the time, but this has given those still living something to believe in, and we all need that. You never know, but maybe those people will now continue to talk to their Loved Ones themselves in private, and their Loved Ones may respond as they would rather talk to them directly rather than through someone standing on a stage!
>
> You see ... everyone is at a different Soul level. They have different levels of understanding and awakening. These 'basic' messages, as you call them, were heard exactly as they

were meant to be by these people. It helped them realise there really IS more to life after death, and that's what's important. The names aren't important at all. Sure, they make a connection in the way you are given them and you pass them on, but what *is* important is the message itself. Many Loved Ones who have gone Home are only given one or two chances to show themselves to a Loved One or give a message to them. Quite often, they've even forgotten the name from their lifetime anyway! It's the content, Marion! It's the feeling of Unconditional Love that brings healing with it. That's what counts.

God, I love Opa! I love the way he takes the time to explain things to me so that I can understand. He never judges me. In fact, he gives me the message at the level I can hear it or know it to be true.

Just like the Psychic I was watching on the stage. We all get messages differently, after all.

Beautiful. Poignant. Thanks, Opa!

Empathy explained

Do you ever suddenly feel happy, scared, angry, sad or emotional for no reason? Welcome to your life as an Empath!

I have had people come to me for sessions who look completely exhausted. I feel for them – these people are Empaths and may not even realise it! When they sit down, I say, 'Where would you like to start today?' That's when they usually release a huge sigh, and their eyes fill with tears! Their stories are generally very similar. 'Oh Maz, I'm exhausted. You see, I'm an Empath … you understand what it's like!'

I usually just nod and encourage them to talk.

'Maz, no matter where I go, I know and feel everything that's going on with everyone around me. It's such a burden to know and see what is happening in their lives. I see the lies, addictions, deceit, mind games and emotional blackmail. I can deal with feeling the happiness in people, but there seems to be less and less of that these days. Am I supposed to be helping all of these people? Do you help everyone you "feel", Maz? It's an impossible job isn't it?'

'Breathe,' I say. 'Just breathe and I will share some insight that my Team shared with me. I'm sure it will help.'

Then they relax and I let my Team take over and explain to them what's going on in their zoo! My Team explain about 5s and 6s then explain Empaths.

The following is an excerpt shared with a client in my Team's voice:

> You, our lovely Soul, are doing it all wrong! The true purpose of an Empath is to observe. Just observe. Every person you come into contact with is a teaching opportunity for you ...
>
> It's around the 5 ½ mark that a Soul begins to feel true empathy and compassion for those in their lives, regardless of whether they know them or not. This can come as an unpleasant surprise. But it's around this time that a Soul's 6th sense begins to awaken and that the universe starts to teach you how to 'read' other Souls. This is so that, when you are a true 6, you will feel comfortable seeing, hearing and interpreting Spirit, Guides and Loved Ones that have passed over.
>
> It's NOT about you solving the problems in the physical world, one Soul at a time. It's about you just observing and watching Soul Contracts unfold. You generally aren't involved in their Soul Contracts. You are just there to see, sense and learn what you do, then watch it unfold and see if you are accurate with your Readings of the Souls you have read.

It's important that you keep all human emotion and judgement out of these experiences and just watch life unfold in front of and around you.

I remind them that not everyone is involved in your Soul Contract … crikey, imagine if they were! We would be getting advice from everyone and everywhere, and we would end up as a much more mixed-up bunch of humans then we are now! The same goes for you – you are not involved in everyone's contract. Our Soul Family is just NOT that big!

Spirit and our Guides teach us how to be empathic, to truly sense Spirit and energy. This is so that when you have finally evolved into an Old Soul and become a 6, you WILL know how to deal with Spirit and their energy when they talk to you, show themselves to you and guide you down the path of your Soul purpose. This is your training, because they have groomed you to listen to their energy through the humans around you.

It's a big responsibility to feel people's energies as an Empath! It's even harder as the beautiful human that you are to resist getting involved with the Souls around you, but this is your only lesson.

If, however, you are part of their Soul Contract, it will feel that an even bigger responsibility has been bestowed on you by Spirit to do their work for them as an Earth Angel when you are a 6. You have to know what each vision means, and how to interpret and deliver messages when they are channelled through to you. It's not just hearing the words of Spirit and your own Team of Guides; it's translating the visions into messages for someone with or near you in a way that can be heard by their inner ears.

Messages are given to us Soul Clinicians and Earth Angels as visions to help guide people around us. They must be delivered with integrity, sincerity and Unconditional Love.

So, instead of getting bogged down in the dirt of other people's lives, start in your own life and relish the opportunity to observe and learn what Spirits want you to see and hear. Get excited knowing that you don't have to do ANYTHING at all.

See it all as training and learning tools for your own spiritual toolbox and growth. Then leave it alone and stop overthinking and analysing it, because you are doing so with your human brain. Your brain is NOT capable of thinking about this stuff! It'll drive you nuts!

Remember what I said earlier: You don't see monks running around helping people, do you? No! They know their place, and their place is just to observe while the Soul/human tries to work through their Soul Contracts and lessons.

No one gets a shortcut, so don't give any either. No one learns anything by cheating on their tests. They just end up cheating themselves!

Just observe, and life will fall back into its own natural balance and rhythm.

Are you a worrier or a warrior?

If you chose worrier, ask yourself this: what were the benefits to all the worrying you've done? There are none, weirdo!

Just like you, I have also spent years filled with worry. When I look back, I can see that the worrying has not benefitted me in any way at all. At times, the worrying destroyed my life. It's debilitating. It's self-inflicted and as damaging as cutting yourself physically, except you are doing it mentally and emotionally to yourself. It's crazy.

But that's the power of the mind. Meanwhile, your Soul waits for you to tap into it as it knows it can help you through anything.

Anxiety levels are escalating as people wake up and start to realise that life is an illusion, which scares them. People feel completely overwhelmed now that they have come out of the Covid lockdowns. Life has changed so much for everyone, and a lot of people feel like they are on shaky ground. Suicide rates are higher than they have ever been as people struggle with life and the changes they see in the world!

But it doesn't have to be this way.

Trauma, grief and fear can change who we are forever if we don't rein them in.

When my 25 years of marriage ended and I lost both my parents very close together, I felt like the grief was insurmountable and that my life would never be the same again. I cried every day for four months. I was miserable. Attempting suicide didn't change anything for me, nor did counselling, so I ran away and took my cocoon with me.

Was I glad that I persevered? I am now because I'm in the middle of doing another 12 month caravan trip, and this time I haven't cried. Last time had been my Dark Night of my Soul. I learnt so much about grief, trauma, PTSD, heartache and worrying.

On the journey in 2018, my Opa woke me at 3am. He told me, 'No one is coming to rescue you – no one! You have to rescue yourself!' He had my attention, that was for certain.

I replied:

> Okay Opa, I hear you, but it's not that easy! What am I supposed to do with my worrying and all the thoughts that go round and round in my head all day and night, every day and night? It's killing me!

Opa said to me, 'Lieve meisje, look back over the past 12 months … has all that worry paid off?' I said, 'No, but…' Then he asked if I would listen to his idea, and of course I said yes.

He said:

> You have so many, too many, thoughts going round and round in your head, all going nowhere. They are all fighting for your attention and time. The best thing you can do is address each thought individually with an appointment of their own.

Pick a pressing thought and book an appointment with it. Tell it you will give it 30 minutes of your time and 100% of your attention without any other thoughts intruding. Tell the thought what time you will sit down with it, say 10:15am, and that it will have your undivided attention till 10:45am. Then at 10:15am, armed with pen and paper at the ready, address your worry and only that worry. Turn it inside out, look at all the options surrounding it, solve it if you can. At the end of the 30 minutes, get up and tell the worry that it's had its time with you and that you are now going to get on with the other things you have to do in your life.

When you have so many, too many, thoughts running around in your head, none of them get any quality time and none of them get sorted or solved. By making individual appointments, you can address one worry at a time and give it your undivided attention.

It sounded like a great idea to me. But which thought did I need to tackle first? I felt they were all screaming for attention inside of my head.

It soon became apparent which thought I needed to deal with, and I spoke to it just like I would a client or friend. I gave it an appointment time and heeded it. Over the next few days, I was able to get to the bottom of the worry. I sorted through what was rational and what was irrational. I looked at what was in my control and what wasn't. I looked at what was a potential part of a Soul Contract, or not. Sometimes the first session would work with a particular worry and sometimes it wouldn't. Nonetheless, I persisted.

In the first week, I dedicated myself to wading through the rubbish tip that was my mind. Every day I kept busy with appointments with each of my thoughts. Initially, I gave each of them 30 minutes. Some thoughts needed to be addressed two or three times a day, every day. Then slowly, I found that I was able to cut the time down to 15 minutes a session, then down to once a day, to once every couple of days, to once a week, then once a fortnight and suddenly, as if by magic, my diary was empty. The thoughts had stopped running rampant in my mind and I could breathe again.

Working through each thought methodically like this was incredible. It was the best therapy I have ever had, and I urge you to try it for yourself. It may work for you too, and it can't do any harm. No counsellor had ever given me such a great tool. It came from my Opa, and I am truly grateful.

Dealing with each thought like this gives each thought respect and way more quality one-on-one time than being left to run rampant with all the others. When none of them get any attention, they all scream louder and louder each day to get your attention. This kind of rampant overthinking, ruminating and worrying is slow suicide.

Opa's idea was brilliant, and I still use it today. I've also recommended it during many sessions. People have told me they love it, and it's been much better for them than any traditional form of therapy. While that often took weeks and months for any noticeable improvement at all, Opa's method worked within a week or two.

I/we also recommend that, as you start to heal, you replace the appointments with quality Soul, meditation and quiet time, where your mind can be still.

Basically, you are 'defragging' your brain. Do you remember when we had to do that with our computers? This is the same.

Please try it and let me know how you go. It's a little piece of Angel magic, I promise.

These days I am a warrior, no longer a worrier.

Visualising my time

The second thing Opa taught me that I would like to share is this pie chart. As 6s and Empaths, we like to give and GIVE, but you only have 100% to give at any one time, and you cannot give 100% to everything. We often give 100% to others and expect 100% in return. When we don't get it, we feel disappointed and disillusioned. However, it's actually unfair to place these expectations on others.

So, draw your own pie chart, cut it into pieces and allocate your priorities through percentages. Then REALLY feel it. Feel how much you can give to each part of your life or relationships and how much you can expect in return.

1. Time to BE with my Soul
2. Time for my relationship
3. Time for my kids
4. Time for my work/job
5. Time for friends
6. Time for exercise
7. Time for creativity
8. Time for meditation/relaxing
9. Time for chores
10. Time for nothing

Note: If everyone made one of these pie charts, you would be able to see how much time others allocate to YOU. You are not THEIR world. They should be their own world!

My pie may not be your pie. You may prefer to give yourself the whole 100% and that's fine, or you might like to break it into quarters and have different labels. It is YOUR pie to have your way.

Gut feelings and spidey senses

Your 'gut' plays a very important role in your intuition and may, at times, even be a Sign that shows up right when you need it without even asking for it!

That's when you really need to pay attention!

We don't always need to ask for Signs from our Guides. Our intuition plays a very strong role in our lives, particularly if we are a 5 ½ and above.

I'm sure that most of you reading this book have experienced your own gut feelings, spidey senses and knowings. All of these are your higher self helping you navigate this life and lay the foundation for your true 6yness!

As an aside, please pay attention to your daydreams and dreams at night. This is another way your Guides will communicate with you. Most of us accept that our dreams carry messages for us sometimes, especially our lucid dreams. I'm sure many readers are nodding their heads as they recall the dreams they can't shake. Did you heed the information that came through, or did you dismiss it as just a 'dream'?

During the day, sometimes you may find yourself absent in your life. Some call this daydreaming. To me, it's when the Psychic postie arrives and I sift through the messages. You may be being shown visions/images during the day, particularly if your Guides have a real message they want to impress on you. I recommend that you carry a small notebook with you all the time now and note down anything that you know is not connected to your thinking! By writing down these experiences, you will end up with a story that will contain messages just for you and guide you in your life.

Please remember that your Soul knows way more than your mind!

You are a very unique and special Soul having a human experience. It takes time to adjust!

REGRETS and the role of the 'F' word

The 'F' word = Forgiveness

Do you know who the most important person you need to forgive is?

YOU!

All my life, I have found it hard enough to like myself, let alone to forgive myself, for all I've put myself through – all those bad thoughts and bad decisions along with the too many regrets we all have! Forgiveness has been my biggest lesson in this life. Not only of other people, but also myself.

Now, I frequently wrap my arms around myself in the biggest hug full of Unconditional Love, understanding, empathy, compassion and forgiveness. I've thanked myself for bringing me through to the age of 61, and for trying, trying and trying again. I've thanked me for looking after myself even when it's hurt others, mostly due to their unrealistic expectations. I've come from a place where I was bulimic for two years, depressed for too many more and pulled from a lake after cutting my wrists! I've driven myself from Perth to Adelaide and another 30,000 kilometres towing my 22 foot caravan trying to find a place where I fit in and where my Soul could finally be at peace. I've pushed myself through nervous 'breakthroughs' and many nasty friendships and work relationships.

I am proud of me and happy to hug me the way I want to be hugged. The loveliest thing about hugging yourself, once you are ready to do so, is that you actually 'receive it!'

Do you know how you like to be hugged?

Did you know that it's best to hug left to left? That way, hearts meet! Let's start a 'hug left to left movement!' My dear friend Michelle T taught me this. I thought it was weird at first, but now I hug the Souls dearest to me left to left, and everyone else gets a token right to right!

Try it – you will like it!

But hugging yourself AND meaning it is the best, especially once you have forgiven yourself! YOU are the most important person to forgive! Accept your own forgiveness and apology. You have just tried to get yourself through each day the best you could. Tell yourself that you LOVE you!

Then, and only then, can your life truly begin.

It's a big word, isn't it? 'Forgiveness' – it's massive! It conjures up so much pain for so many. It's an 'f'ing hard thing to actually do but, once it's done, it's one of the best lessons to have learnt! It's also one of the biggest lessons we have to learn and/or teach as a Soul. I am so proud of having done both.

During our lives, we have all experienced times when someone has really hurt us, and we really dislike them for what they've done to us. Hate is a big word, but sometimes it's the only 'f'ing word that fits.

People often ask me about forgiveness during a session, and I help them by explaining how Opa taught me to forgive. I hope this helps you too. It goes like this:

'Lieve meisje, it's time you forgive him.'

I replied, 'But Opa, I can't! Forgiving him would be condoning what happened, what he did, and I will never ever do that! I know I should, but I won't … I can't.'

Opa replied:

> Do it this way. In your heart, thank him 'for~giving' you the opportunity to learn about Unconditional Love. That's what he's actually done. He gave you an opportunity to learn, through tolerance, how to love without condition. You can do that, can't you? You can even tell him, say the words that he needs to hear. Everyone has a different idea of what 'for~giving' is. This is what 'for~giving' is to you. It's also very healing. You can even say it to him in person and it will help him let go of this life so he can go Home in peace. Please promise me that you will try.

I promised him, then I said the words to my dad. It was incredibly healing. I hope this helps you too!

Trust

Don't 'try' – it won't work. Trust is one of the biggest of all our Spiritual lessons in this life. In order to feel trust, you need to get outside of your human self and lay aside all your preconceived ideas and human expectations.

It's a bit like knowing that when you hit the light switch, the light will go on. Like how you know that even though the propeller on a plane looks like it's not turning, it is and it can lift you off the ground. It's knowing that night follows day and day follows night.

It's about knowing and accepting that your human mind cannot comprehend trusting the unseen or unknown, but your Soul does. This is trust, and the only way to achieve it is to learn it.

By growing through what you are going through,

you can turn hindsight into foresight!

The 'H' word – a lesson in Honesty!

One of the biggest lessons in Spirituality is honesty, honestly! Many of us are good at giving honest advice, but not many of us are good at taking it. We don't really listen to it. We think, 'What would they know about my situation?', yet we expect them to listen to us.

Who do we think we are? Before you give advice to someone, please check that you are not interfering in their Soul Contract. Keep your advice to yourself! Often, fools rush in to help, and the receiver ends up feeling worse than they already were. They thought they were doing well and starting to get somewhere in their lives, and then along comes you with unsolicited advice.

Look at it like this: you are a hairdresser, and you carry a pair of scissors in your bag. One day, you're walking through the mall when you spot a guy in dire need of a haircut. You walk up to him and say, 'G'day, mate, I'm a hairdresser. Can I just fix your fringe for you?' What do you think his response will be? Maybe something like, 'I've just paid $120 for this haircut – go away!'

You don't have to give someone advice just because you have it. Maybe it's in your Soul Contract to keep your advice to yourself or, better still, see if the advice is actually for you instead.

This is where honesty comes into it.

Honesty is our benchmark, our truth, our foundation.

We are all individuals living life together, but some choose to live with the lies they are telling themselves.

The universe knows your truth, my truth, everyone's truth.

It seems to me/us that the world has been built on lies and deception. That's the human way, not the Spiritual way. If you want to pursue a Spiritual life, face your own truth and live it – it's much easier to live with truth than lies!

Sometimes I resort to a little white lie to get me out of things, but karma comes and quickly bites me on the bum, so I gain absolutely nothing. I gave up lying to myself years ago. Not only do I hate the way it feels to live with a lie, but my Team are always watching me. They remind me constantly that I cannot do their work if I don't live it!

They are, as always, correct.

The importance of spending time on your couch!

It's now post-Covid, and the world feels like it's spinning out of control … spinning itself right out of this universe. Fortunately, that's not what's happening. Before Covid, the lives of the unawakened were spinning out of control. Constant striving for material possessions and owning anything and everything at any price depleted our world of Unconditional Love.

Covid was a huge, worldwide wake-up call to attention. The 'Awakening', as I/we called it, was the new pandemic! It was a Spiritual pandemic this time. The universe, in her wisdom, pressed 'pause'. She got our attention good and proper.

Fear crept in to the human lives of many 5s. How would they get money if they couldn't get to work? 6s, however, welcomed the isolation, as they could finally get off the non-magical roundabout of life and reconnect with themselves and their Loved Ones. We learnt to sit still. We learnt to reconnect with the stillness within us, and it wasn't scary at all. It was delicious, and we revelled in it.

We learnt to 'BE!'

We spent time on our couch just sitting, contemplating our lives, talking to our family members under the same roof or through the internet. Reading, journalling, playing board games, practicing mindfulness and watching movies, hours turned into days, days turned into weeks, and weeks turned into months.

The couch was our cocoon. It was where we transformed from the crawling caterpillar going through its paces, ticking all the boxes we thought we had to tick and buying what we thought we needed to buy just to pass the time.

Some of us bought new couches so that we could spend even more time on them. It was comfortable there – all those soft pillows and warm throw rugs! So many ideas were born on that couch, and probably many babies too! The couch had become the most important member of the family.

On the couch, we realised exactly what and who was important to us. We found who we were without the influence of people. Then, slowly, we began to venture outside again, returning with new awareness about what we wanted for ourselves and our lives.

Many have not returned to the jobs they held before Covid as they are not those people anymore. Their alarm clocks have woken them from a deep sleep – they've unfurled their wings and are now able to fly like never before. Souls are being listened to. Hearts have started to fill with joy as people started to follow their dreams.

Many years ago, I couldn't think of anything worse than spending time alone with myself. I lived with bulimia for two years, and my weight plummeted to 45 kilograms. I knew I was killing myself slowly, deliberately, one kilogram at a time because I didn't like myself, or life, for that matter. These days, I'm very guarded of my private time and miss myself when I don't get enough.

Now, I'm a lot heavier and a lot happier. Some people get 'older and wiser'. Me? I just get 'older and wider!' – and I'm okay with it!

It's after my solo caravan journey in 2018/2019 of 22,000 kms in 14 months, living alone for eight years now and experiencing Covid isolation alone, that I am finally at peace with myself. I'm great company. I hold great parties, hold my own hand in sad movies, dry my own tears, take baths in the middle of the day and night and laugh at myself for stuffing up on the odd occasion that I do. Oh, and I love driving my own TV remote control!

The time alone was very necessary, and I now feel fully aligned with my Soul. I trust and have faith in it and my Team of Guides. Everything before Covid prepared me for this time. I want to inspire you with my story. I want you to know that YES, everything WILL work out. I promise you.

My caravan trip has also been about meeting many new people and transmitting the Spiritual word. I feel I have a calling to be a nun and that's why the Universe is constantly keeping me topped up with energy, so I can do their work. Nuns wear clothing called 'habits' but I'd rather have bad habits than wear a habit!

I'm fully 'awake' now. I probably have been for years, if I'm honest. It was my human side hiding the real 'me' from the world. This was mostly because I never knew anyone like me and always thought there was something wrong with me.

However, after Covid, I am thrilled to say I know lots of former weirdos who are now Wired into their Soul and universe after hiding themselves away for fear of being burnt at the stake, figuratively speaking.

Social media is full of Spiritual groups of all shapes and sizes, and one is sure to fit you! If you can't find one, start one. My Opa encouraged me to start the 'Soul Clinic' Facebook group – a place where awakened Souls like us could feel normal, understood, supported, connected, healed and Wired to Source. The group is capped at 400 Gifted Souls, and Souls learning from these Gifted Souls, through healing and wisdom. I pretty much know each one of them. This is a different online social group to my public profile page. It's special. Each Soul is handpicked to enter. Some stay a while, some longer than others, and some leave because they've learnt what they needed or shared what they needed to, which makes room for new Souls. We help bodies that are sick and provide these bodies and minds with comforting Soul food.

The Group is a place where those on their true Spiritual journey feel supported and understood. I could never ever have imagined having a group of likeminded Souls like this. Thank you Opa, they mean the world to me. We support each other as we navigate our human life. For many of us 6s, it is our last lifetime, and it is filled with trauma, dramas, sadness and grief of extreme proportions. We are learning our final lessons together. Many of us in our Soul Group are related as Soul sisters and brothers, supporting each other through Unconditional Love.

This group and many others like it support those of us who are awake to help those who are slowly waking up into this new fifth dimension. I also have a public Facebook/Insta page 'Marion Weatherburn Soul Clinician and Psychic' where I support likeminded Souls and those seeking Spiritual insight and enlightenment through (often perfectly timed) posts.

It seems that I have been waiting for this time my whole life. I felt it coming. It's needed. Now here it is. This is why we incarnated into this lifetime at this time – to help so many others realise and learn too. I am/we are no longer alone, no longer weird. We are connected. WE ARE WIRED!

The role of detachment in your life

'Bloody hell! What's going on?'

Can you relate to this? I bet you can.

However, I'm not writing to dwell on the shit that's happened to all of us – it needs to be flushed away.

What I WILL focus on is how magically the universe works.

You see, you are not brave enough to move the negative people out of your life because you are a people pleaser! Admit it! You are not brave enough to take yourself out of jobs, relationships or friendships that no longer work for you because you worry about what people think. You would like to believe that there is a force much greater than you that you can rely on and that has your back, don't you? I do!

Aren't we all lucky that this force IS REAL, and we *can* rely on it to have our back? What it also has is the world's biggest broom to sweep out the rubbish in your life so that you can, eventually, live in light, love and peace.

The universe knows what's best for you, always. This is your lesson in trust. Putting your faith in the unknown and the unseen creates faith.

My/our advice to you is to detach. Let me explain how I did it.

We all know when we've had enough … when we just can't take anymore and when we are beyond broken. Yes! there comes a point.

After years of relentless S H * T, Opa taught me about detachment. Initially, I was worried that it meant I couldn't love the people involved in the turmoil anymore. Turns out that I was wrong – I could, in fact, love them more. You see, detaching is really a way of stepping aside, not away, and taking off the rescuer hat that you wear and laying it to one side.

For me, I had been running to rescue my children on the other side of the country over and over again. Each time, I berated myself as their mother for not being able to do more. Every time things went bad, and I mean incomprehensibly bad, I blamed myself. I would then completely stop my life to help, or rather rescue, them.

They were adults, but this was my life and it was killing me.

As parents, we feel every emotion when our kids are in trouble. It's a cruel situation for everyone involved. However, the rescuing and advice I had been giving over the years wasn't being heeded. I couldn't understand why.

Over the past couple of years, those who are close to me know the heartbreaking, wrenching traumas I have experienced. After one of those experiences, I found myself sitting on a plane back to Adelaide after supporting my family in Perth through indescribable trauma. I was sobbing. I felt like I was turning my back on them even though I had done more than enough for them. At 35,000 feet, I felt closer to my Team than ever.

I looked up higher, hoping to see them materialise. I screamed in my heart and mind, begging for guidance on how we would ever get over the traumas of the previous weeks and, in fact, my life. I felt so close that it took all my might not to open the door and jump out, hoping to float up to heaven – as a skydiver, I knew I would end up freefalling down and not up!

Then I felt them – here's what they said:

> Close your eyes and rest, lieve meisje. We will bring you through this, just like we always have. We do this together with you. We have never let you down, and you have never let us down. The best way forward for you now is to detach from the traumas and focus on your and our Unconditional Love and share that Love with others. You see, lieve meisje, in helping others you will help yourself – just like us, your Team, we help others and it helps us evolve too. You are safe and very loved. Your work as an Earth Angel is vital to many, and you can only truly experience what others go through by going through it yourself. That's where true insight, empathy, understanding and Unconditional Love reside. You feel it, we

know you do, and it's that that you need to share. We will bring many more Souls that need the insight, clarification, direction, confirmation and guidance to you so you can share it with them.

Your family have chosen their Soul Contracts and lessons with those in their lives. Your role is one of emotional support, stability and financial support. You have got this, and we have got you! We cannot begin to imagine what it has been like for you and your family to go through all that they have; however, we experienced the horrors of World War II, and your loss feels familiar to us. Back then, we didn't know that we had Guides that could help us through such significant life experiences and losses. We do now, and we will support you as you continue to travel on your Soul journey. You are NEVER alone. Your work on our behalf is profound on so many levels and, for that alone, we are here to support you. We are here for you and have been through every incarnation. We are You. You, lieve meisje, are part of OUR Team.

When we landed in Adelaide, my recovery and the way forward for me was very clear.

I told my children that I had 'detached' from them. Initially, one of them was horrified. 'How can you abandon me like this?'

Opa! please give me the words:

'I'm not abandoning you – I'm loving you *even* more. I see the role that I play in your Soul Contract very clearly now, and it's not one of rescuing you. I had to rescue myself in my dark times, and I did. In your Soul Contract, it is my role to be your foundation, your soft place to fall, to love you unconditionally.'

'But what does that mean for me?'

'It means that, before today, I loved you the best I could. For me, it never felt enough. I never felt enough. As your mum,

I should have been able to make everything better for you. I see that this is the journey you chose, the life lessons you chose. While I'll ask myself every day why on earth you chose such a difficult contract, only you and the universe know why. There is something great waiting for you at the end of this. You will get through this, regardless of my input, in your own time and in your own way. By detaching, it means I am no longer turning myself inside out trying to fix your situation. I am no longer taking your situation personally. I am your foundation. I agreed to support you without conditions in this lifetime so that you can undertake this massive contract. I agreed to always be there for you through every single situation that has nearly taken your life away from me. I agreed to love YOU, no matter what you go through.'

And I do.

I took my human role as their mother out of the equation entirely. I could not understand their lives through my human eyes but, through the eyes of my Soul and theirs, I understood us perfectly.

So, if you are going through shit, take a step back and check to see what role you are contracted to play in the individual's life. Are you a teacher or the student?

If you, like me, see that you are there to be a foundation and provider of Unconditional Love, then be sure your love really does have no strings attached – you can't put conditions on it like, 'I love you if you do "xyz"' or 'I won't love you if you do "abc".'

The universe provides everyone with an abundance of Unconditional Love. One day, the world will run out of fossil fuels and oxygen, but it will never run out of Unconditional Love. So, get 'Wired' in and get connected to your Source. Plug in to your life and detach from the lives of others so that you can offer much more to everyone, including yourself!

And that my friends, is how you avoid the mess when S H * T hits the fan – detach!

Tools for your spiritual toolbox

You can also call it window shopping! As your Soul starts to progress through its incarnations and lessons, it will start to look for teachers and tools for your spiritual toolbox.

This starts to happen around the 5 ¼ Soul level, or after you have lived a few incarnations. You become curious and feel drawn to the tools listed in this section, any of which will help you get to know your Guides and your Soul Self.

What I am going to share with you now are my personal experiences of each and how they have or haven't worked for me. You will find your own way. Regardless, I ask that you treat these activities with the respect they deserve. They are not games.

We are not our human body

- 'Enjoy your ride,' the universe said as you were born into this life.
- We will navigate your path for you.
- All fares are paid, and we bring all passengers, troublesome as well as friendly.
- Look after your human body – it's your only real possession for this incarnation.
- Have the ride of your life, and we will welcome you Home again when the time comes.

The problem with the world is that people forget why they are actually here (mostly because they refuse to stop hitting snooze) or think it's all about accumulating material wealth and pandering to their ego.

That's the illusion that is this life.

This lifetime is actually about accumulating Love – real, Unconditional Love (not sex and the number of partners you had) – and also learning lessons so that your Soul may continue on its own beautiful journey.

Choosing the human experience is the best way for your Soul to learn.

Asking for a Gatekeeper

Before you do any work with Spirit at all, please ask for a Gatekeeper to be assigned to you. You can ask for this either out loud or telepathically. You 'should' be able to 'feel' their protection. Once you feel safe, go ahead and work with your tools.

Get used to how their energy feels so that you know when something changes or someone who does not have your highest good in mind comes through. That is when you need to stop. If you ever become concerned, please just message me – I'm here to help at any level.

Listening to and hearing your Guides

If you are feeling nudged to work with Spirit, whether for yourself or in your Soul's purpose, it might be time to start filling your spiritual toolbox.

While you may be begging your Guides to show themselves to you, the truth is that the last thing they want to do is come back in a physical form. Our physical forms are just so heavy for our Soul to get around in. However, your Guides are very happy to work with you, mostly because it's in their best interest to guide you and in your best interest to listen.

One of the first things I recommend is to have a session with me where I can teach you the 85/15 principle (although your percentage split may be different, as every Soul is coming from a different incarnation Soul level). By learning the difference between a thought and a message, you will know for sure what you need to listen to and what you don't! This skill is a necessity in your spiritual toolbox and will take all the guesswork out of it for you.

For some of you the percentages will be different, dependent upon where you are in your Soul journey. Some people may process 50% as thoughts and 50% as messages. Everyone is completely different. The tool is the same for everyone. If you would like to find out more, please visit my website and book a session. You will be glad you did.

Learning this skill will save you a lot of time and confusion and allow you to start using other tools.

Ouija boards

Once you have established the difference between a thought and a message, you can start to establish a relationship with your Team of Guides. They'll be thrilled to work with you.

The first thing to do is to create the right environment for you to be comfortable in. Choose a time, day or night. If you choose to work at night, candlelight provides the perfect ambience, as does soft music. I don't play music during my Team chats as it tends to distract me. It's up to you.

When I was growing up, whenever my parents felt like they would like to spend some time making 'long-distance calls' to their families via a ouija board, they would sit quietly and let their families know that, that afternoon or evening, they would like to connect. Mum and Dad always treated their visit as if our Team, their dads, were visiting in person. They would clean the whole house, pick fresh flowers from their gardens, meditate to raise their energy vibration, talk about things they loved, including each other, then light candles and sometimes play very soft background music. They would then get ready with pen, paper and their board.

Be honest, that's the kind of environment you would like to visit in, right? Well, our Team loved this time, and so did my parents. They always created a really warm, inviting environment and, once the family came in, the energy was incredible. I always found it funny that no one ever telephoned or popped in to see us when we were having these sessions. I guess Opa B's job as a Gatekeeper worked in these situations too.

Whenever I do Readings, regardless of the type of session – in person, video, phone, in my consulting rooms or home visits – I always clean my whole house and sit quietly prior to, listening to relaxing music and working on releasing all negativity from my energy fields. I need a completely clean head, heart and Soul space to do this sacred work. 'Sacred' is the key word for me here, and it was a sacred space I/we created. We respected the family, their messages and their ability to come through to us. Your session may be 60 to 90 minutes long, but please know that I have prepared for hours prior to your arrival. A lot more goes into a Reading then the actual appointment time itself.

While you don't need to go to this length, I/we do believe you have to take this relationship with your Guides seriously, and that you should treat them and yourself with complete respect.

If you are not at the stage of being able to 'hear' your Guides yet, then a ouija board is the perfect tool. Our Guides are all energy, and part of their learning is how to use that energy.

It's important that you let your Guides know what time you would like to meet with them. I know you may feel weird talking out loud to an empty room. If this is the case, do it telepathically. Invite them, like you would your friends, to be with you. Let them know that you are very interested in developing a relationship with them. Let them know that you would like to develop spiritually and will have questions ready for them. Initially, it's important to ask closed questions (questions that can be answered with a yes or no). As you begin to understand and interpret each other's way of communicating, you will be able to understand their replies. They may come in the form of words on the board. If so, it's important that someone scribes the messages. They may also send the answers through visions that you need to interpret.

When your Guides send you answers via images, it's important to write down what you feel is the theme of their vision and how it correlates to your question/s. If you feel that the answer is confused, revert back to yes/no questions until you get used to their way of communicating.

Communicating in the human world is hard enough already, never mind learning to communicate with Spirit Guides. But persevere – it's very worth it.

Also, automatic writing comes through like verbal diarrhoea, so get ready!

You need to train your Guides, not the other way around. They already know how to do what they do. You will potentially process their information at a tenth of the speed they send it out. My advice is to start slow. While I can fill an exercise book in one sitting, and have done, I have also been doing it for over 40 years. Initially, all my very early communications were stilted, mostly requiring yes/no answers.

Even that, I found amazing. Slowly but surely, as my curiosity and experience with them increased, I realised I/we had tapped into an incredible library of Spiritual and universal information. It was absolutely fascinating, and I would love to teach anyone how to do it for themselves so that they get their own experiences rather than reading about mine.

'I want to do it too!' I hear your cry!

I say, 'Be patient'. When you're learning, Soul language can be open to misinterpretation, which won't help you or your Team. So, baby steps. Just like primary school, where you learn the sound of each letter of the alphabet, you now need to learn the sound of your Team's voice. It takes practice, practice, practice.

Journalling – thoughts and knowing

Some people like to try journalling and automatic writing with their non-dominant hand. Spirits don't care which hand you use, as long as the message gets through.

I recommend you try something like this, just in your own words:

> Hi Guides, I would really like to develop a relationship with you. You know me, and now I would like to get to know you. Today at 6pm, I will create an environment that I would like to invite you into. During this time, I would love it if you would teach me how to hear or know you. I will begin by asking questions that require a yes or no answer only. Once I get to know you better, I will explore further. Thank you so much.

Then, at the time you chose, get ready. Still your mind. This would be a good time to rule up your notebook like this:

85% = THOUGHTS	15% = KNOWING
Your answer	*Spirit answer*

You can either write all your answers in the columns, or you can draw these columns under each question to record the answer separately. By the time you have really learnt to 'hear and/or feel' the way your Guides communicate, you won't need to do this anymore.

Examples:

You: Is there a Guide with me today?
Then you can write down your answer.

85% = THOUGHTS	15% = KNOWING
Your answer	*Spot on row*

You: Will you please impress my brain with your name over the next two days? This can be in the form of repetitive names in my head or repetitive outside influences/Signs, such as street names, number plates etc.

85% = THOUGHTS	15% = KNOWING
Your answer	*Spot on row*

I like to make sure that each of my answers comes complete with the 'feeling' that I am used to. Then I know it's definitely my Team that I am communicating with.

Then you can move on. Remember earlier in the book when I talked about how, after finding a breast lump, Shirley told herself that she needed to go visit Dr Roberts? The name Roberts was significant in Shirley's signs. Seeing the name Rob three times was enough for her to take notice. You can ask the same of your Guides when asking them for their names. Ask them to show you signs that really jump out to you, much like Robertson Road, Robbie the car number plate and Rob at the checkout did for Shirley.

If you receive Signs like this in relation to the question you asked, you could write this in your journal:

You: Is my Guide's name Robert?

85% = THOUGHTS	15% = KNOWING
Your answer	*Spirit answer*

Then you will get your answer. From there, the Spirit world is your oyster. Be prepared to not sleep for days! I never used to, as I would get very excited at getting answers to some of the deep, probing questions I had been asking for years!

If you are like me and still have doubt, the next section on pendulums can assist you further. Pendulums are the way I used to 'check' the answers I was receiving.

Pendulums

My mum taught me how to use a pendulum to ask questions. She also showed me the power of our mind and how we could make the pendulum move. Mum still had her dad's (my Opa D's) pendulum. I now have it. Mum preferred using her wedding ring and a piece of cotton to make a pendulum whenever she wanted to ask a question that she wasn't getting a 'direct' answer to. She said this was because it already had her energy in it. My dad had a pendulum too.

Mum used to love predicting the sex of babies being carried by expecting mothers. She would use their wedding ring, tying it to a piece of cotton then asking it to show her the sex. Mum had a certain swing for a baby boy and a different swing for a baby girl. Many thought it was a bit of a laugh – Mum did too, especially when they told her she was right! In those days, we had to wait until the birth before we knew whether Mum was right or not, but she always was.

I used to watch Mum all the time. While she was still holding the pendulum over the future mum's belly, I would ask Opa to tell me the sex of the baby too. Opa always told me the same as Mum's ring. Sometimes, the pendulum would tell other stories too. Mum would use a ring and cotton to tell a woman if she was going to have any more children by telling them how many she'd had (and sometimes lost) and how many more were yet to come.

I've seen heartache in expectant mums when they were positive they were carrying a boy, for example, and had prepared the nursery for one, but the pendulum told them it was a girl. Those times were hard and made me decide it wasn't a path I wanted to pursue. Also, I never really understood why mums would want to know the sex before a baby was born!

To use a pendulum, the first thing to do is to find one and put your energy into it. You can put it in your pocket (or your bra, if you wear one!). You may also prefer to do what my mum did and use your wedding ring and a piece of cotton. Either works.

Just like automatic writing, you and your pendulum need to get to know each other. Try and put it out under a full moon and ask for it to be cleansed and re-energised. After this, you can put your energy into it by finding a time to sit with it quietly and hold it. You may have one hand that gravitates more naturally to the pendulum. It doesn't matter, but what I'm about to say does:

You CAN make the pendulum move yourself with the power of your brain!

Once you try this, you will find it aMAZing! It's also a very important process to follow so you know when you are using your mind and when you are not. It's when you aren't using your mind that you will know that the pendulum is giving you the correct answers and not the answers that you are hoping to receive and/or expect.

You're interested now, aren't you? Let's get you started. I'll tell you how I do it, then you can adopt it for yourself:

How to use your pendulum

I sit very still and talk to my Team. I may say something like: 'I am asking for clarity through my pendulum around the following question that I am currently struggling with.'

My left hand is my healing hand and is the hand all energy flows into and out of. The heat is tangible. My right hand is just my right hand, nothing special about it!

I sit at a table and prop both elbows on it. I lay the pendulum on my left palm. Holding the thread in my right hand, I slowly, very slowly, lift it up until it's about three centimetres off the centre of my palm. I keep my mind totally empty (that part is easy for me!).

I then ask the pendulum to make the following moves in no particular order and visualise each move in my head as follows:

- Pendulum, move side to side
- Pendulum, stop
- Pendulum, move in clockwise circles
- Pendulum, stop
- Pendulum, move in anticlockwise circles
- Pendulum, stop
- Pendulum, move up and down
- Pendulum, stop
- Pendulum, stay still
- Pendulum, stay still
- Pendulum, stop
- Pendulum, go in all directions at once
- Pendulum, stop.

You will only ever need to do this once. It's REALLY important that you know, without a doubt, that it's YOU moving the pendulum each time. It's incredible, isn't it?

If you would like to see me doing this exercise, watch my video on YouTube on using pendulums.

Now you have that out of the way, you are ready to start asking your pendulum questions. But be warned – this practice is addictive, and you will feel flooded with questions.

The first requests to make of your pendulum are:

1. Please show me a YES:

Place the pendulum in the palm of your hand, whichever hand, then pick up the string and ensure that you do NOT start it swinging. Make sure your mind is completely blank, remembering that you can influence its motion. Make sure it's completely still before asking, 'Please show me a yes.' The pendulum will then do something … let's say it goes side to side. Thank the pendulum, then close it into your palm. Write down the word 'yes' and, next to it, write the direction the pendulum chose.

Between each question, clear your mind completely of thought. Do this each time you get your answer after asking a question. Then make the next request.

2. Please show me a NO:

Repeat the steps from above, this time asking to be shown a 'no'. Write down the direction the pendulum moves in.

Ask your pendulum to show you a 'yes' then a 'no' each time you start a new session. Never assume that it will do what it did last time. It will keep you on your toes, let me tell you!

Now you are ready for the pendulum to show you its magic! Make sure you keep your mind empty of a preferred outcome so that you don't influence it.

Start by asking a couple of obviously dumb questions like 'Did I park my car in the lounge room?' or 'Did I have cornflakes for breakfast?' regardless of whether you did or didn't. Then let the pendulum answer you.

Do you think you are ready now?

With a fresh, empty page in your journal, write your first question that requires a yes or no answer. Then, with a completely empty mind, free of any expected outcomes, ask the pendulum to show you the answer. The answer you get will determine your next question. Be prepared for the truth, and date each question-and-answer session so you can track the messages going forward.

As you gain more confidence, the universe becomes your oyster. Make sure that you ask very specific questions that require yes/no answers. If your pendulum does not move, it either doesn't know the answer, the question you asked is too difficult for it to answer, or you've overworked it that day! Put it aside and pick it up another day.

I personally use a pendulum to confirm messages that came to me through automatic writing. This was how I eventually got used to feeling when my Team were with me. It took a few years, but eventually I stopped using the pendulum.

These days, I use automatic writing when I know the answers might be a heavy truth that I need to know and work through, or one where the information flows really fast.

Automatic writing

Automatic writing tends to flow really fast and looks unlike your own handwriting. Mine tends to have no punctuation or capital letters and can look like one long sentence from beginning to end, pages upon pages upon pages. I never read the message until my Team are finished dictating it and I have put down my pen.

When my husband asked for a divorce, I was livid. But, before I could react, Opa asked me to get a notebook and a pen, lock myself in the bathroom and to start writing what they wanted to say to me. I sat there for four hours and almost filled an entire exercise book.

I had wanted to call my husband every name under the sun. I was hurt and shocked by his request. Then I read the Reading. I dissolved into tears. I had been given a huge wake-up call and kick up the bum by my Team. They listed everything my husband was doing right in our relationship, and everything I was doing wrong. I was so embarrassed.

They were right.

This was not the outcome I had expected. After all, I thought they were on my side!

I swallowed my pride, cut myself a huge slice of humble pie and went out to ask my husband if we could talk.

We stayed together another ten years. The end was always inevitable, but it was certainly easier for a while, particularly after the lecture I'd received. I could have just switched off the communication between my Team and me, gone out as my arrogant self and played the victim. But I couldn't because the proof was in the writing, and my Team were 100% right.

You can also start a session with your Guides by setting up a time to talk with them, as you learnt earlier. Write the question at the top of the page, then ask them to write the answer through you. They will drive the discussion, so be prepared to hear what they have to say. Writing may come through as a word, a sentence, a phrase or a shitload of writing, so turn your phone off, get a drink and go to the loo before you start, because you just never know whether you will be in for a four-hour session like I was.

Once the writing starts to flow, do not stop it, do not question it and do not read it. Just let it flow. Once it stops, put the pen down and you will know you have reached the end. You will no longer be able to feel your Team near you energetically. They will have gone to rest and to let you absorb what has come through.

On my YouTube channel, you will find a video about automatic writing. I hope it helps.

Telepathy – the original form of social media

Ah! The old telepathy phone! I LOVE telepathy and have so much fun with it … probably way too much fun, to be honest! After all, life IS about having fun.

Opa introduced me to telepathy when my kids were young and impossible to discipline. I've got your attention now, right? I'd had a lot of practice at being a good nagging daughter, wife and mother, but what good did it do me? None!

Well, let me share a secret with you: if you want something done, use your mind to transfer your requests and/or ideas into the mind of another. They will think it's their idea – you can praise them for it, and they'll do it because they'll think they thought of it! But that's where they're wrong!

I feel naughty sharing this secret with you. There's certainly some events that have occurred as a result of powerful telepathy that I haven't always used for the highest good. I will never, ever share them with anyone as it's bad enough that Opa has seen it! Telepathy is a weapon, it really is, and it must be respected and handled with care. I've used telepathy for a variety of reasons without the other person even knowing. I've started conversations telepathically when there were awkward silences by repeating one word over and over in my mind. I would try to pick who would 'hear' it and start talking about it! Ah! Such glee!

I've spent a lot of time in shopping centres waiting, usually for someone to come back from the bathroom. While waiting, I would focus on someone with their back to me and say to them telepathically, 'Turn around, turn around!' I would wait and, sure enough, they would turn and look around to see who had been calling them. Of course, they could never find anyone because it was me all along!

I remember one experiment with telepathy. I was 17 at the time and had taken myself down to the beach on a fresh autumn day. The tide was a long way out. I had positioned myself in the sandhills, just relaxing. I saw a cute guy walking by the water's edge and yep, you guessed it! I called to him – not out loud, just telepathically! Poor bugger, it was funny because there was no one on the beach at all. He looked around and around. As he started walking, I said, 'Up here in the sandhills, come up and say hi!' He obviously heard the message as clear as day because up he came and introduced himself! He was gorgeous.

You see, youth of today! You are NOT the first one to use instant messaging! But I digress. The point of this message is that if you have been really trying to get through to someone, whether in your family, a colleague or a friend, try telepathy.

Clear your mind. Start with repeating one word over and over. For example, if you want your child to do the dishes but they seem to be suffering from domestic deafness, speak to their inner ears! 'Dishes, dishes, dishes.' The key here is that, once you engage in telepathy, you cannot use your spoken words for any further instruction.

I used this method for years. Even now, I use it in varying forms. My kids will only find out I did this if they read this book.

Telepathy is a very powerful tool and should never be abused. Always remember that the universe may have your back, but she is always watching too!

You may remember earlier in this book where I shared a story about Y and her grandchild singing 'Row, Row, Row your Boat'. That's another really good way to practice telepathy –start singing in your head and watch how infectious it is. If you do this in an elevator, you will soon find people whistling or humming it as they walk out the door.

Such fun!

Crystals

I never grew up with crystals, and my parents never owned any. To me, they were always decorative – strategically placed and colour-coded to my interior décor. I used to use them as paperweights!

I know that there are many of you that have a crystal collection. You know their names, their properties and their healing powers. While it's not something I use, I have respect for people who do. I listen to all their amazing stories about their crystals and can't help but wonder about these incredibly coloured stones.

I would like to share a story about crystals that was shared with me a few years ago by a lovely friend of mine – let's call her Arlynn. Arlynn's 56-year-old dad had been rushed to hospital as his body was racked with sudden internal pain. The doctors rushed him in for exploratory surgery but were unable to locate the problem. They told Arlynn's dad that he needed to get his affairs in order and called his family in for what they were told would be their last opportunity to visit him. The doctors believed he was dying.

Arlynn didn't believe this at all.

On the third day, Arlynn brought some crystals in and slipped them into her dad's bed. Neither her mum nor her dad knew they were there. Arlynn prayed to the crystals and her Angels. At this stage, her dad was in a coma and his organs were barely functioning. The doctors had still not been able to determine what was wrong.

On day five, Arlynn's dad woke from the coma. Although the bed had been remade, Arlynn was pleased to see that the crystals had been placed at the bottom of the bed again. Arlynn then snuck one into his pillowcase.

On day six, when Arlynn arrived, her dad was sitting up in bed drinking a cup of tea. She noted how well he looked. Arlynn checked for the crystals and found they were still in place.

On day seven, the doctors told Arlynn and her mum that as her dad had been pain free for three days, was eating and drinking, and his vital signs had returned to normal, they felt confident they would be able to discharge him the next day.

On day eight, Arlynn's dad went home and hasn't had a day sick since! That was six years ago now.

The cause and the recovery remain a mystery.

Arlynn calls it her miracle!

Oracle or Angel Cards

Aren't they beautiful? There are so many to choose from. I'm actually making my own set, which I hope will be ready soon. They have all been created using the amazing photos I took with my crystal ball.

Back in the 1980s, I had a really special pack of Angel cards. Every day, I would spread them out, face down, in a heart shape. I would then connect with my Team and ask them to connect me with the right card for me that day. I used my left hand, which is the hand I feel energy through, and it would always know just which card to stop on. The cards and their extended messages in the handbook were always what I didn't realise I needed to hear.

Back in 2018, my beautiful friend in Sydney, EG, talked me into holding 'live' sessions on Facebook using cards. I told EG that I would rather just give my messages to those watching, but she said that I should do both as people would really love it and relate to it. I trusted her, and so started my Thursday night 'live' sessions.

It was incredible. Every time I saw a name on the screen, I felt a message come through and gave it to them. The amazing thing was that the card would always complement the message perfectly. There were some amazing times. One Reading in particular still stands out today and it was for Dezirae, who lives in the USA.

If you haven't treated yourself to a pack of Oracle or Angel cards yet, they can be purchased at any big chain stores, New Age stores or online.

The trick to buying a pack is to let them pick YOU! That may sound weird, but it's not. You won't be able to explain why you bought that particular pack, but it's the beginning of a really beautiful relationship.

You will spend many hours laying out the cards in various formations, asking them many questions then considering the outcome. Sometimes the message may not be right for that moment, but give it time and you will see. If you want just one card with a message for the day, shuffle the pack and ask for the card that you need to see to jump out. It invariably does!

If you feel so inclined, you may also like to research tarot cards. My good friend LL said that she first fell in love with her tarot pack when they picked her a few years ago. LL has spent countless hours getting to know her pack, testing them and using them in Readings. LL's use of the tarot is incredible.

Using tarot cards goes hand in hand with the previous section on honesty. You can't deny the truth in the cards. But, while I find them interesting, I'm not drawn to them. I do, however, have many packs of Angel cards.

Dezirae's shock revelation and proof!

'I am NOT dead!' was the message that came through for Dezirae, loud and clear! Dezirae was another regular on my weekly 'live' sessions – the times worked for her even though she lived in the USA. Dezirae is another living Earth Angel. In fact, I even said to her once or twice, 'I could learn from you, Dezirae!' She had such an incredible and beautiful energy! I could feel her from the other side of the world. We would message each other and help each other. I liked that about her.

One day, Dezirae messaged me.

Dezirae: Marion, I have booked a session with you. I would like to send you some photos. I would like you to read each of them for me. I'm sending photos of people who have died.

Me: Sure, no problem. I can do that.

I received the photos of 'dead' people shortly thereafter. I sat with each of them, then video called her.

Me: Dezirae, you said you were going to send me photos of people who have died. You must have made a mistake, because one of them is certainly still alive!

Dezirae: Which one are you referring to?

I explained that the guy who looked to be in his late 20s was still alive and asked if she wanted to replace his photo with another photo for me to read.

Dezirae: Marion, do you really 'feel' that the guy in that photo, my brother, is STILL alive? Are you sure?

Me: Yes. why, what's happened?'

Dezirae: I believe he's alive too, but he went into hiding after winning a lot of money! I don't want to send you another photo as you've given me exactly what I needed to know. I meant to put that photo of my brother in there. My other brother and I do not believe that he is actually 'dead', even though we went to his funeral! His funeral was honoured with guards all around him as he was in the Forces. None of us identified the body, and his coffin was closed. We believe he faked his own death after winning a lot of money that he wanted to keep to himself! We can't say anything to our parents because they were at the funeral and believe he's dead. My brother and I don't – our own intuition tells us that he's not dead! Do you know where he is? Can you ask your Team?

Me: Wow! What can I say! That's incredible. I have asked my Team, and they are silent. I have never experienced anything like this before! I can't explain how, but my Team have shown me that he's not dead and is very much alive. I'll work on it with them and see if they can find out more. If they do, I'll reach out to you again.

Dezirae: That sounds perfect! Thank you!

The following week, I did another 'live' card session. I was using three decks and, for the first time ever, merged them into one great big deck of 166 cards. I went through my usual routine of choosing people's names, offering them a message then allowing the deck of cards to choose a card for them. It's funny how they always seem to offer the right card for the right person as confirmation of my message! It has always fascinated me. I saw Dezirae's name in the comments and said that I was about to pull a card for her.

Me: Dezirae, remember that person you and I have been talking about in our sessions recently? Well, I would like you to focus on them right now as I ask for clarification through the cards.

Dezirae: Thank you, I will.

I began shuffling the cards and they took on a mind of their own! Suddenly, one flew out. Out of 166 cards, this one, saying 'I am not dead', came out. I could barely speak. A few people asked what had happened. I apologised to the viewers and said I would have to leave the 'live' session there so that I could ring Dezirae. She picked up immediately.

Dezirae: Marion, that's incredible! Out of all those cards, that was the one that came out! I saw it with my own eyes! He HAS to be alive! I know it. My brother and I both know it. What do we do now? Where do you think he is?

Me: I've worked on your situation over the past few days, and Opa simply can't give me any information. We know for sure that he doesn't want to be found. It's even hard for us to uncover what the Soul Contract or lesson is here for him and your family. If anything changes, we will let you know, okay?

Dezirae: Marion, thank you so much. I can't express the comfort that you've given to me. My brother and I are grateful. I know that you and I will keep in touch. Thank you again for everything!

Since then, Dezirae and I have randomly connected with each other, even though no new information has come forth. This may have to remain one of life's mysteries unless something significant changes. Watch this space!

Here is the link to the recording of the 'live' session. Fast forward to one hour and six minutes in, and see Dezirae's comment on the post! https://www.facebook.com/marionweatherburnpsychic/videos/3922457991135947

Meditation and mindfulness

Enough cannot be said, written or shared about meditation and/or mindfulness. It would be nice, wouldn't it, if we could all meditate the way it's shown in movies or on the internet! Alas, it's not like that for me … or you, I expect.

I believe that meditation can play an important role in our lives. If, however, you're like me and your past and future are fighting to be in your present whenever you sit still, it just doesn't work.

In saying that, I believe you can take a step *before* meditation to make appointments with all your thoughts, like I/we explained in the section on worrying. There's no point trying to meditate while you are overthinking and over worrying. Do yourself a favour and make those appointments – during them, nothing else matters ... the worries are your priority!

Spirit and our Teams do not expect us to jump straight off the treadmill to sit around with our legs crossed, mind switched off, trying to meditate and reach Nirvana. So many people have tried and failed. Good on those who don't do their shopping or to-do lists during this time, because I do. I can't meditate to save my life!

Mindfulness worked for me, for a while. I used to sit then ask myself, 'What are three things I can hear? What are three things I can see? What are three things I can feel?' and so on.

Then I would drift away again.

To be honest, I've stopped trying.

What we're trying to achieve by meditation or mindfulness is really a state of peace and feeling of oneness/connectedness with the universe. How you get to this place (without the use of substances!) is irrelevant. All that matters is that you get there.

I often just sit and take in my surroundings. I prefer to call it my sacred time of peace. I have learnt not to think. How? As Opa taught me, I make appointments with all my pressing thoughts. Once I have acknowledged the thoughts and given them my 100% focus, they go away. It's when you try to meditate without acknowledging your thoughts first that you get into trouble.

I can sit quietly for hours, and have done, regardless of where I am. I watch day turn to night and night to day. My eyes follow the birds, wondering if they know where they are going. I feel gratitude until it softens my heart, mind and Soul. I sit until I truly feel blessed, because I know I am.

I prefer to do this on the water when I sail. Water is so healing for me. I don't need to be in it, just near or on it. And yes, I can concentrate on sailing at the same time. It's all part of the ritual for me.

So, maybe I do meditate – after all, there is no such thing as the meditation police. You need to do what suits you, when it suits you, for however long it suits you. Be your own Guide and follow your own lead. Find what works for you and enjoy the peace. It is very healing and important to you and your Soul ... both of YOU!

Manifesting

So many people come to me for Readings and ask about manifesting. They want to know if it is real or not! If you are going to ask me that question, you are going to get the truth – yes, it's real!

I could give you enough specifics to fill a whole other book. However, that would be all about *my* experience! I would rather share how to do it so you can share *your* experiences.

To start, you need to either be open minded or believe in a force greater than yourself, even though manifesting starts with you!

In my twenties, I broke up with my then-fiancé. You may remember me writing about him in my first book. At this time, my dad gave me the best piece of advice he ever gave me!

'Marion,' he said. 'What are two things you REALLY want to do?'

I had a think about it, then told him I wanted to skydive *and* get paid to travel.

He said, 'Write it down. Believe in what you have written. Think about it as if it has already happened. Think about it every day, and you will attract it to you! I have no doubt that you can create your own future with your own mind ... that's how powerful your mind is!'

I believed him.

Dad was right.

I can look back on my life and see that everything I ever wanted to have or experience, that was for my higher good, has come about through Dad's teachings about manifesting. I clearly see that everything I want to have or to experience can be mine.

My own life experience gives me undeniable confidence in the power of thought. I want you to try this for yourself. The power of your own thought for your own life makes my heart sing!

These days, I am very, very careful as to the thoughts I think or words I say. There have been times when I've forgotten how quickly the universe delivers after letting the words come out of my mouth. Regret has been immediate.

If you are just starting out on your own Spiritual journey, journalling is one of the best Spiritual tools that you can use to help you manifest.

Sit with a pen and paper. Connect to your Team, if you can. Speak to the void if you don't feel that anyone is with you. While you may not feel your Team's presence, they will be listening.

Always ask for what is for your highest good. Starting small, add items that you want to have or experiences that you want to happen to your list. As you write each item, really *feel* each request. Specify a time that you want to experience it by. Believe that it will happen, then wait. When it happens, it may just feel like an ordinary transaction, but afterwards the wow factor kicks in.

Manifesting could also be seen as looking into your future or destiny. Things, experiences or situations that are meant to be part of your life will show themselves to you, and you will go 'Yeah, that's a good idea. I would like to try XYZ.' Then, when they happen, they will feel transactional and obvious. That's manifesting at work.

If I look more closely at how I actually do it, it's hard to explain. Whenever I visualise what I would like to happen, I read my 'book.' Not literally, but it's like reading a book, complete with pictures. I clearly see the scenarios, timelines and outcomes. I pick the ones that resonate and are available to me and tick their box (so to speak).

If you are computer savvy, I could explain it like putting something into a search engine, selecting images, then choosing the image that fits what I want to do. Sometimes, on a computer, 'things' are greyed out and can't be selected, so these aren't an option for me. I choose from the ones that are not greyed out, add them to my list then wait for the right time and the right place. I've never been let down.

I manifested the 2018/2019 trip together with my parents and Team. We also manifested the 2023/2024 trip and pretty much everything in-between, including my house. Obviously, these things are meant to be in my life for my highest good, and I am grateful.

Once your manifestations start to occur, please ensure that you thank your Guides for bringing them through for you. This part of the process is as important as the initial manifesting.

Opa asked me to share the following scenario, which will help you to manifest:

> We all go through the drive-through at our favourite takeaway store at times, right? Imagine if you pulled up at the speaker and said something like, 'Hi, I would like a burger, fries and a drink,' then drove to the window to get your food.
>
> But would you get what you wanted?
>
> Let's say that you wanted a chicken burger (not red meat), medium fries (not large or small) and a cola (not a lemonade). If you aren't specific, the teenagers running around inside the store will try to fill your order. But, when you get to the window, they will have nothing there for you. How frustrating would that be for everyone? You and your hungry belly would be extremely disappointed! Well, your Team are the same. They are more than happy to manifest

with you, as long as you specify exactly what you want and when you want it.

I hope this makes sense now.

Smudge sticks and incense

These are for *your* benefit, not Spirit's! Back in the 1990s, when I first started giving Readings from home, I would go to my local markets and/or New Age shop, searching for the best incense for the best environment for Spirits to come into. I would then come home and excitedly set up the room and light the incense, only to have Opa tell me, 'Get rid of it straight away! I didn't like it when I was alive, and I certainly don't like it now!' So, of course, I did. Opa told me that the use of incense and smudge sticks is for the human in us, not for Spirits.

I was glad, because I didn't like the smell of it either.

During a Reading one time, my client asked my opinion about the use of smudge sticks. I had never used one, so I asked Opa what he thought of them. 'Lieve meisje,' he replied, 'if a person broke into your home through your front door, would you attack them with a smudge stick? No, of course you wouldn't. They would laugh at you and dodge every sweep in their direction. It wouldn't change the outcome.'

Opa is right. The use of smudge sticks is more for you, the human, to make the room smell better and potentially 'feel' better by ridding yourself of negative energy. 'If it makes you feel better, use it,' Opa says, 'just know that, to us in the Spirit world, it makes no difference and it certainly doesn't make a bad Spirit leave your place of energy, if that's what you're hoping. The only way that can happen is by talking to the Spirit itself and helping it!'

I write about house clearing in my first book *Caught Between Two Worlds* in the chapter entitled 'Fright Night.'

Guides

We all have them. Comforting, isn't it? Please remember that Guides are just us, dead. At the end of each incarnation, we go Home. During this time, we are given the option to return in human form to keep learning so we may become better Guides in the future or to stay for an incarnation or two as a trainee Guide.

Our Guides also have Old Souls that they learn from. There are many layers to the Spirit world before we get to the Omniscient Force itself. Many humans have had glimpses of life back at Home, and it makes them long for it. They may see these visions in their dreams. These types of dreams are incredible to experience because of the feeling that comes with them and the fact that we remember them forever.

You are probably receiving daily messages from your Guides but don't realise. If you haven't heard your Guides yet, please book a session with me and I will teach you how to hear and get to know your Guides for yourself.

An interview with my Team

I find it fascinating and also normal to chat with my Team. I can talk to them for hours about anything and everything. They share their insight and wisdom with me, which helps me make sense of my life. I would like to share some of our dialogue with you:

Me: Opa, what is it like where you are?

Opa: It just IS.

Me: What does that mean?

Opa: It means that it just IS.

Me: Do you think where you are?

Opa: I know what I need to know.

Me: Come on, you know what I'm asking.

Opa: (*laughing*) Yes, I do know. However, it is very hard to describe Spiritual life to a human brain, especially yours! Let me send you the feeling of what it is like here.

Suddenly, I am filled with a feeling of complete Unconditional Love, warmth, safety and security. It's a feeling I feel every time I talk to Opa and my Team. It feels like Home!

Opa: You felt that didn't you?

Me: Yes!

Opa: Right, now describe it to me.

Me: I can't.

Opa: That's right, and that's exactly what it's like for me too. Home feels like a feeling, and it feels like you don't need your other 5 senses here! You know that 6th sense you have? Well, it's that sense that prepares you for being back Home. It's the only sense you need here – all the other senses stop the minute you leave your human body.

Me: Oh Opa ... I don't know what to say, that feels so beautiful!

Opa: That's right, don't say anything ... Just feel!

***

Me: Opa, what frustrates you and the Team about working with us humans?

Opa: We don't get frustrated when our role is to teach you the lesson of patience, which we have already learnt and mastered! But I understand your question – I find it more comical than frustrating to work with humans again. Nothing has really changed from when your Team and I were alive – people still do exactly as they please according to their brain. We know from experience that they need to have lived many incarnations before they 'wake up.' We know that they wake up when they're ready and not before, so our patience helps us wait.

Me: Opa and Team, do you mind that sometimes I exercise my human 'right' to be 'wrong?'

Opa: Yes, of course we understand, we were human once too, you know! But we don't understand why you would when it costs you $456 because of a speeding fine to be 'wrongfully right'. Maybe next time you will listen!

Me: Yes, I know! Stupid me! I've got the help, yet I don't listen. That's the plague of being human!

Opa: The thing is, it's not up to us to make you listen. You know well enough when we are talking to you, and when your mind is. You made the choice to ignore us, and you paid the price.

Me: Why didn't you just tell me that I would get a fine if I went the other way?

Opa: Why didn't you just listen? We nagged you more than we should have to!

Me: *Undecipherable swearing*

Opa: Don't swear!

***

Me: Opa, sometimes during a Reading with a client, they ask me if I can tell them who their Guides are. I always feel like I let them down when I can't. Can you please explain why this is.

Opa: Sure. We have been Guides for many incarnations. We are Old Guides. Just like you have young Souls and Old Souls, we have young Guides and Old Guides. Our young Guides are like apprentices. They come fresh from their human existence and last incarnation into their first incarnation as a young Guide. Young Guides are assigned many humans during their first few incarnations as a Guide. This means that they are transient. If you were to identify and present a client with their Guide's name, there's a good chance that if they went to begin a relationship with them, that Guide would be uncontactable, having moved on and been replaced by another. They would feel like they 'couldn't do it', and that would be disheartening for them. Also, their Old Guides, as in Soul Family members that are also Guides, may be helping other Soul Family members when you're asking for information. Instead of giving them the names of their Guides, talk to them about how they can find out who their Soul Family Guides are through the 85/15 method we shared with you. And, if somebody told you the names of your Guides, you wouldn't believe them, would you? You would still have doubt until you saw them yourself. Remember when you found out about us, then Mark and Staven. Remember how excited you were because you found out for yourself? No one told you. Everyone needs to have this experience. Do you understand this message?

Me: I understand, thank you.

***

Me: Will everyone get to know their Guides in this lifetime like I do?

Opa: Lieve meisje, many do hear but don't realise. They think it's their thoughts talking to them. Some people don't want to hear their Guides, some want to believe their Guides are real and still have doubt, and others just don't believe and therefore don't want to hear.

Me: How do they learn their lessons if they're unaware?

Opa: The Soul learns the same way as you humans do in school, by reincarnating over and over again, aiming to level up each time, as they have agreed to new lessons and Soul Contracts each time. Then, one day, their internal alarm clock goes off and they start to remember what they've forgotten. This is marvellous to witness. Everyone starts off as a young Soul and finishes as an Old Soul. No exceptions. It's just the way it is and not for you to worry about. We will, however, bring people to you who you are able to help.

Me: Opa, how can I teach others to accept that they are Wired not Weird so they too can benefit from working with their own Team of Guides in this life?

Opa: We will share everything they need to know in this book.

Key messages

I'd like to take the opportunity now upon reading *Wired not Weird* for myself to summarise the key messages.

We've now passed through the year 2024, and what a year it was for all of us!

The universe, it seems, knows exactly what She is doing through our current Awakening.

What is this Awakening, you may ask?

It's time to wake up and *really* realise that we are Spiritual beings choosing to incarnate in this lifetime as a human. This condition, being human, is a complete illusion.

The Soul, however, knows what to do. Trust it with your human life.

Humans are WEIRD.
Souls are WIRED.
There is *nothing* more real than your SOUL.

We chose to incarnate as Humans in this incarnation as it is one of the most important lifetimes to be alive.

You see, the universe, frustrated at how off-track we were Spiritually, has made available all our Soul's lessons in this incarnation. Normally, we would get only one or two lessons per incarnation. It seems that the universe thought that our Spiritual growth was taking way too long and has now provided us with the Wired-in connection we all need to really 'wake up' in this lifetime.

Living within the illusion known as the human condition, we were destroying our Souls by not listening to them.

We were not listening to our Soul because we could no longer hear it —we were too busy being Weird when all we need to do was plug in and get Wired in to the universe.

Connected.

BOOM!

The universe had our attention.

Over the past few incarnations, as Souls we have chosen to either learn or teach lessons as individuals within the collective consciousness for everyone's benefit.

However, this wasn't working.

We became materialistic and EGO got in the way.

We forgot how to love each other *and* ourselves.

We stopped loving Souls and started loving things.

We were given the chance to 'level up' and we blew it. Now we have no choice but to face all of our lessons and traumas in this lifetime.

The process has now been accelerated so that we, the entire collective consciousness, could awaken together. Why? So our Souls could all benefit from living an awakened Spiritual life truly connected to Source.

To Love.

We are actually part of something much, much bigger. We are a link in the chain called the universe and we need to ensure that we are part of the whole chain and not just a link. Those on their Spiritual path know this. Those new to the Spiritual path are quickly learning the difference.

BOOM! There it is again ... the universe stepping in.

During this period of Awakening, we have seen the truth that is our Soul and the universe. You now have the very valuable opportunity of becoming 'Wired' into the Soul *of* the universe – to plug back in and reconnect.

Our Soul did and always will know way more than the mind. As humans, we thought we knew better.

We were wrong.

Almost anyone you talk to will agree that the world as we knew it has changed ... and not for the better!

Not yet! But it's coming.

Your snooze button no longer works. All unlearnt lessons must now be learnt. Your Soul has awoken into a world where courage gives us the confidence to continue the fight.

Our Souls have a responsibility to the collective consciousness to accept our role in this incarnation, and the only way we can do that is by facing our traumas and subsequent lessons head on. You are NOT alone in going through this.

Everyone from 5s (young Souls) to 6s (Old Souls) must now go through this Awakening process. Human behaviour has changed so much since the beginning of the Awakening. Humans are showing their painful lessons and traumas so they can be learnt once and for all.

I struggle on a human level to understand human behaviour. Friends know this about me. It's not because I judge humans – I don't judge anyone. It's because I see the Soul behind the human mask.

Once you awaken and remember that you are a true Spiritual being, you will no longer need to go to a Psychic or a Medium for a Reading. Why? Because as a Spiritual being you can access your Guides and Loved Ones back home for yourself. *Wired not Weird* teaches you how to do it for yourself.

I can help you fill in the gaps.

As you struggle to find your way on your Spiritual journey, take heart that you are not alone. We are all walking each other home.

It is vital that you take time out of your human life for your Soul's benefit and growth. Rest and sleep when your body and Soul tell you it's important. You will feel new levels of exhaustion and fatigue as you 'level up'. Levelling up means to match the universe's energy of Love. Here there is no judgement or hate. No selfishness or greed. No regrets or hostility.

It is completely normal to feel like you want to cut yourself off from those in the world that push your buttons. Consider first whether there is a Soul Contract in place before you isolate yourself, then do it. Your Soul will truly love you for giving it the opportunity to rest and get plugged into the universe.

Many of you will get sick as toxicity rises in your physical body. This is the Soul's way of making room for L O V E.

Your Soul is L O V E.

Anything else is of the human condition.

The universe gives you permission now to rest. This is when the best healing and work gets done.

Take the time to come back to LOVE.

It was always there … you just need to get Wired in.

Michelle's advice

I would like to leave you on this closing note. If you take nothing else away from this book, please feel free to use my dear friend Michelle's advice anytime you are dealing with the 5s in your lives: 'f*ck 'em' or 'ask yourself, what would Love do?'

Bless her, hey? That's true Spiritual wisdom right there!

Let's start a heart-to-heart left hug movement

About the author

Marion Weatherburn is a 4th generation family Psychic and Soul Clinician.

She specialises in working on a deep level, helping guide you to being the BEST YOU in this lifetime in accordance with your Soul Contracts and Soul Journey.

Marion has given almost 7000 readings to date and has worked on a variety of levels including: relationships with both children and adults, personal guidance, court cases, life planning and spiritual teachings. If you are on your own spiritual journey, Marion is available for readings and her delightful books have been written in easy, everyday language from the heart of a gifted and warm soul.

In 2016, Marion published her first book, *Caught Between Two Worlds*, which includes over 30 real-life readings. Each story is a true account of these readings, complimented by the testimonial given by the person she read for and also the spiritual meaning uncovered, each one different. These stories were chosen for the heartfelt and inspirational message within. Messages of hope, closure, guidance, clarification, direction, inspiration, humour, understanding, enlightenment and love.

These books are available direct from Marion's website or from your favourite bookshop (if not in stock, ask them to order your personal copy). To enquire about Marion's publications or to book a private reading, please visit:

Website: www.marionweatherburn.com.au
Facebook: Marion Weatherburn Soul Clinician and Psychic

If you've enjoyed reading this book, please consider writing an online review or sharing with Marion the positive effects on your life. Thank you for supporting an independent Australian author.

www.ingramcontent.com/pod-product-compliance
Lightning Source LLC
Chambersburg PA
CBHW071229070526
44583CB00017B/2101